BALLET IN ENGLAND: A BIBLIOGRAPHY AND SURVEY

c. 1700 – June 1966

by
F. S. FORRESTER

With a foreword by
IVOR GUEST

THE LIBRARY ASSOCIATION
1968

© F. S. Forrester, 1968
SBN: 85365 230 9

Library Association Bibliographies, No. 9

Z
7514
D2
F6

Published by The Library Association
7 Ridgmount Street, Store Street,
London, W.C.1, 1968

Set in 11 on 12 point 'Monotype' Bembo (Series 270)
Printed and bound by
STAPLES PRINTERS LIMITED
at their Rochester, Kent, establishment

CONTENTS

PLATES

FOREWORD

ANYONE who has ever undertaken research must have blessed those studious compilers of bibliographies whose careful lists stand on the reference shelves of libraries to guide them in their search for material. This book is such a guide, and it comes to fill a much needed gap, for with English ballet now occupying an important place in our cultural life, the volume of source material, in the shape of books, essays and articles, will continually increase and the student of dance will be faced with an ever growing mass of material to sift. He will now have this excellent compilation of Miss Forrester's at his elbow, as reliable and readable as a Baedeker, to draw his attention to things which he might otherwise overlook.

An important section of this bibliography reminds the reader that English ballet has a long history, reaching through the heyday of the Romantic ballet in the early years of Queen Victoria's reign, when London became one of the important centres although its ballet was mainly a foreign importation; back in time, more than a century earlier, to the productions of John Weaver who foreshadowed a generation earlier the ballet d'actions of Noverre; and further back still to the masques which were the English counterpart of the court ballets of Bourbon France. Of more immediate significance is the emergence in England within living memory of a truly national ballet which today takes its place alongside the time-hallowed companies of Russia, France and Denmark. The course of the art of ballet in this country is a fascinating story, which one can foresee will become more and more widely known as the acceptance of ballet as an academic subject for the General Certificate of Education bears fruit. So will the usefulness of this book grow, both for teachers and for students.

This bibliography was compiled as a thesis for the Fellowship of the Library Association. In choosing her subject, Miss Forrester was guided by a long held enthusiasm for the ballet which shines through her pages. She has succeeded in conveying something of the pleasure of browsing alone and at one's leisure in a library. Students of the dance will all be in her debt.

IVOR GUEST

PREFACE

THIS Bibliography was originally prepared to be offered as a thesis for the Fellowship of the Library Association. It was submitted in April 1966 and accepted by the Association, which agreed to publish it if certain changes were made. These have now been carried out. The main alteration was in the arrangement of the entries. Previously they had been arranged either alphabetically or chronologically; the arrangement is now almost entirely chronological by date of publication or by subject. A more detailed account of the arrangement is given below. Another change was in the index. Previously it had been a name index only, but now subject entries relating to the introductions to chapters have been added. Other minor alterations have been made.

For the thesis, the time limit of December 1964 was set, but the more important books and periodical articles which appeared in 1965 were included. For this publication, the time limit has been further extended to include items issued up to June 1966.

I have interpreted 'English ballet' fairly widely. Ballet like all the arts is international, and aspects of it, for example, technique and aesthetics, have a universal application. A translation of Noverre's *Lettres sur la Danse* . . . or Vaganova's work on the training for classical ballet should have an interest for any student of the ballet regardless of national considerations.

Inclusions and exclusions. Books.

Many sources were searched for likely titles – the bibliographies named in Chapter I, the catalogues and indexes of sources described in Appendix B, book reviews in periodicals, book-lists and of course more general and comprehensive sources such as The British Museum *Subject Index*, *The British National Bibliography*, Besterman's *A World Bibliography of Bibliographies*, Chamberlin's *Guide to Art Reference Books*, *The Library of Congress Catalog. Books: subjects*, the London Library catalogues and *The Times Literary Supplement*.

I stated originally that I intended to include material published in England only, but I have, in fact, enlarged the scope slightly. I hvae included a few books which were published in Scotland, but more important, I have included some American books which can be obtained in this country. In some cases the American publications deal with subjects not covered by English books. I have excluded books on ballet in general which have only one or two pages on English ballet.

I have not attempted complete coverage for children's books. I hope that I have included all the more worthwhile and well-known titles, but do not pretend to have searched for every junior book with a ballet background. Children's books are indicated with a capital C placed after the item number in the left-hand margin.

Inclusions and exclusions. Periodical and newspaper articles

Periodicals concerned chiefly or exclusively with ballet are dealt with in Chapter XIV. For ballet material in other periodicals the following indexes were consulted – Poole's *Index to Periodical Literature* (1802–81) and its five Supplements (1882–1907), The Library Association's *Subject Index to Periodicals* (1915–22, 1926–61) and *British Humanities Index* (1962–), *Art Index* (H. W. Wilson, 1929–), *Biography Index* (H. W. Wilson, 1946–), *Bibliographic Index* (H. W. Wilson, 1937–). Possible references were followed up. Not all periodicals were indexed consistently for every year in the above indexes. E.g. *The Subject Index to Periodicals* did not index *The Listener* for the years 1947–53. In such cases I have searched through the periodicals for the years not covered, where I considered that the periodical might reasonably yield articles on English ballet. I have also searched through complete runs of some periodicals not indexed.

I set certain limits to the periodicals' articles included. I have not included any articles from popular magazines, nor articles in periodicals published abroad concerning the tours of English companies in foreign countries. Opinions from these countries have been given space to a certain extent in English dance periodicals. All articles included are 500 words or over. Other points have been taken into consideration – whether the article adds useful information; whether the more general article has any material for the reader who is interested in English ballet; the standing of the author; whether the article includes bibliographical material.

Complete coverage is not claimed. This would have meant searching through periodicals of general interest. A choice has been made from periodicals devoted to subjects allied to ballet, e.g. *The Studio* for articles on design for the ballet. Articles have been included from the following periodicals, some American – *About the House; The Adelphi; All the Year Round; Aspect; Belgravia; Britain To-day; British Book News; British Journal of Aesthetics; The*

Connoisseur; Contrast; Country Life; The Criterion; Film Monthly Annual; Foyer; Horizon; The Idler; Journal of the English Folk Dance and Song Society; Journal of the Royal Society of Arts; Life and Letters Today; The Listener; The London Mercury; The Magazine of Art; Monthly Musical Record; The Music Review; The Musical Quarterly; The Musical Standard; The Musical Times; The National and English Review; The New English Review Magazine; New English Weekly; The New Statesman and Nation; Opera Ballet Music-Hall . . . Penguin New Writing; Philological Quarterly; Physiotherapy: Journal of the Chartered Society of Physiotherapy; The Print Collector's Quarterly; Proceedings of the Musical Association; The Sackbut; Scotland's SMT Magazine; Scrutiny; Sight and Sound; Studies in Philology; The Studio; Theatre Notebook; Theatre World; Time; The Times Literary Supplement; The Universal Review; World Theatre.

Reviews of performances have been excluded except where they have an historical interest, e.g. reviews of the Camargo Society productions. In effect some books are collections of reviews (C. W. Beaumont's *Dancers under my Lens* is a case in point). In Chapter XIV, the chief newspapers which carry reviews have been indicated.

I started with the intention of including newspaper articles, but this proved too difficult. There appears to be no reasonable means of tracing articles in any paper but *The Times*, which is indexed, and a few articles in *The Guardian*. I wrote to the following newspapers – *The Sunday Times; The Observer; The Sunday Telegraph; The Guardian; The Daily Telegraph; The Financial Times* – to enquire whether they maintained a press cuttings file including ballet as a subject, and if so, whether I might be allowed to use it. I was unsuccessful in every case. I also wrote to press cutting agencies to see if they could help, but I was unsuccessful here, too. Therefore the inclusion of newspaper articles is erratic.

All items have been examined with the exception of a very few, which I have indicated by placing the item number in square brackets.

Arrangement within each chapter.

Arrangement is chronological throughout either by date of publication or subject matter except in parts of Chapters VI, VII, VIII, X and XI. In these chapters there are books and/or articles on individual ballets, choreographers, dancers, designers and composers. Where this is the case, arrangement is alphabetical by dancer, ballet and so on. Where there is more than one item under any one name, arrangement is chronological.

Bibliographical details: Entry

Author entries have followed the Cataloguing Rules . . . compiled by the Library Association and the American Library Association, in the main. The best known form of the author's name has been followed. Dancers and other specialists in the ballet world tend to use professional names, and would not be recognized under their own names. It seems pointless to enter Ninette de Valois under the name of Edris Stannus or even to make a reference from Stannus to de Valois. I have traced the forenames of authors who have used initials on the title-page, either in the British Museum catalogue or the *British National Bibliography*. I have been unsuccessful in a few cases, and in one have deliberately not included them. Philip J. S. Richardson was well-known in the world of ballet, and as far as I know was usually referred to in this style. I have omitted the use of square brackets in an author entry to indicate that an author's forename is not set out fully on the title-page.

Title

Information concerning editor, translator, writer of introduction, preface or foreword has been removed from the title, and included in the annotation. This information has, in any case, only been supplied where the length of the introduction, preface or foreword, or the standing of the person who wrote it or who edited or translated it, warranted inclusion.

Imprint

Place of publication has been given only where it is not London.

Collation

The order laid down by the cataloguing rules compiled by the Library Association and the American Library Association has not been followed exactly. Descriptions of illustrations have for the most part been placed at the end of the annotation. Portraits have not been indicated. Practically every book on ballet includes a portrait of someone. Pagination in square brackets indicates either that the pages of the book are completely un-numbered or that the last page of the text is un-numbered.

Price

Prices have been recorded for books published after 1900 wherever pos-sible, from information in the *British National Bibliography* and H. W. Wilson's *Cumulative Book Index*. It is possible that some prices have altered; some items may now be out of print.

Acknowledgements

I would particularly like to thank Mrs. J. Walford, who supervised my work and who has done a great deal towards this revision, and Dr. A. J. Walford for advice and for glancing through this bibliography and correcting many errors. I am grateful to Dr. and Mrs. Walford for giving their time. A. M. C. Kahn's *Theatre Collections* . . . Library Association, Reference and Special Libraries Section (S.E. Group), 1955, was a useful guide to resources, and Miss Kahn herself kindly arranged an introduction to Mr. Ivor Guest. I would like to record my thanks to him for looking over the notes for the introduction to each chapter, and for the advice he gave on several points. Mr. Guest was also kind enough to write a foreword to this work and to suggest some corrections. I would like to thank Mr. A. V. Coton, too, who took the trouble to give me details concerning the periodical *Dance Chronicle*, which he edited. Thanks are also due to the Editor of *The Dancing Times* for her kind interest and assistance in providing the illustration facing page 81, and to the Librarian of the Institute of Choreology for her advice and help; also to the representatives of the libraries, institutions and societies listed in Appendix B, who read over the relevant sections in that Appendix and made comments on the descriptions I wrote. I have made use of the facilities offered by the following libraries, and would like to thank them for help received – Bodleian Library; British Drama League Library; British Museum Library; British Theatre Museum Library; Finsbury Borough Library; Hendon Borough Library; Oxford City Library; Oxfordshire County Library; Reading Public Library; Royal Academy of Dancing Library; Vic-Wells Association Library; Victoria and Albert Museum: (a) The Gabrielle Enthoven Theatre Collection, (b) The Library; Westminster City Libraries: (a) Pavlova Memorial Library, (b) The Central Music Library.

The following bodies were tried as possible sources of information but contained little material on English ballet – London Museum; Royal Opera House, Covent Garden, Archives; Society for Theatre Research Library.

The following bodies were approached but access to their collections was not possible at the time – London Archives of the Dance; Raymond Mander and Joe Mitchenson Theatre Collection.

I have not examined special collections in private hands. One fine library of books on the dance I have been able to consult; that of the late P. J. S. Richardson. It was bequeathed to the Royal Academy of Dancing. I was allowed to look at these books in the Library of the R.A.D.

February 1967. F. S. FORRESTER

I. PUBLISHING AND BIBLIOGRAPHY

THE number of books on ballet published in the United Kingdom from 1928 to 1939 inclusive was on average only about six a year.[1] This is understandable, for before the Second World War, the art reached a comparatively small audience, which was concentrated in London. There were few companies which toured regularly. During and immediately after the war, however, the picture changed. Cyril Swinson, a former director of publishers Adam and Charles Black, pointed out that ballet was one of the entertainments which offered an escape from the monotony of war and its aftermath, and that this was a major reason for the growth of the audience.[2] The demand for books grew, and was satisfied by too many titles, some of a not particularly high standard. As restrictions were lifted and there was a wider choice of goods on which to spend one's money, the demand died down. Mr. Swinson estimated that the mid nineteen-fifties were the turning-point, and that from this time sales of books on ballet fell. This estimate is borne out if one studies the titles on ballet listed under 792.8, 793.3 and 927.92[3] in the annual cumulations of the *British National Bibliography*, taking into account a time-lag of a year or two between the drop in demand and the drop in the number of books published. From 1952 to 1958 the figures were 29, 23, 20, 23, 28, 20 and 29 respectively, but in 1959 they had dropped to 13. In 1960 there was a rise to 22, but in 1961 the figure was 10, in 1962, 19 (six of the titles were ephemeral and priced at half-crown) and in 1963, 13. It seems that the trend will continue. The publishing of fewer titles may prove to be advantageous in that the average quality in writing and production may improve, but it will not encourage publishers to try out new writers, nor will the potential 'new generation' be encouraged to try. Few new names have appeared recently among those authors who have been writing on ballet for years.

Although during the twenty years since the end of the war, the historical studies of Cyril Beaumont and Ivor Guest, the criticism and other writing of

[1] Based on a straight count of the titles with English prices, including new editions and reprints, listed in the *Cumulative Book Index*, New York, H. W. Wilson, 1928–39.
[2] *Why so few new ballet books?*, by Cyril Swinson. In *The Dancing Times*, December 1961 pp. 146–7.
[3] 792.8 Ballet; 793.3 Dance; 927.92 Biography, Theatre.

James Monahan, Peter Brinson and Cyril Swinson, the photographs of
'Baron', Roger Wood and John Hart, to mention a few names only, have
set a standard to be emulated, a number of books of poor quality have been
produced. They give an impression of hasty writing, second-hand opinions,
a personal view emphasized to the point of unfairness, over-stressed enthusiasm for a particular dancer or type of ballet. Some collections of photographs
have been arranged without care for balance in the content, giving undue
prominence to 'human appeal' portrayal. The format and make-up of books
have not always been good either; poor paper, narrow margins, small and
imprecise illustrations making an unattractive whole, although to be fair,
poor quality and inadequate supplies of material during and immediately
after the war were inevitable.

Two houses which developed something of a specialist interest in ballet
were the Beaumont Press and Adam and Charles Black. The former, a
private press owned by Cyril Beaumont, came into being in 1917. For the
first ten years or so his list contained books of literary interest only,[4] but in
1930 he published three works on ballet written or translated by himself,
indeed all the works on ballet issued by this press originated from the owner.[5]
From 1931 to 1936 twelve titles were published under the Beaumont imprint; there was a pause until 1942, then in this year *Supplement to the Complete book of ballets* came out. The last title on ballet was issued in 1952.

Adam and Charles Black is an old-established firm, founded in 1807. It was
not until 1936 that *Balletomane's scrapbook*, by A. L. Haskell was published.
Cyril Swinson was responsible for introducing this first ballet title,[6] and it
was followed by a second in 1939. From 1942 there has been a steady annual
flow of four or five titles (some reprints and new editions) of worthwhile
books from this house. The continuity of interest may have stemmed from
the fact that Cyril Swinson remained a director of the firm until his death in
1963. One wonders whether it will continue, especially as the *Ballet Annual*
was dropped from the list in 1964.

Two other notable publishers of ballet material are *The Dancing Times* and
the Society for Theatre Research. Since its formation in 1948 the Society has
provided a regular output of volumes, for its subscribers at first, and from

---

[4] *The First Score: an account of the foundation and development of the Beaumont Press and its first
twenty publications*, by C. W. Beaumont.   The Author, 1927.
[5] For an account of the literary work of Cyril Beaumont, *see* 'Forty years' writing on the
ballet', by C. W. Beaumont. In *Ballet Annual 1952*, 6th issue, pp. 69–78.
[6] Obituary of Cyril Swinson. In *The Dancing Times*, February 1963, p. 307.

1959 for non-members, who may order through booksellers, and who are charged double prices. These volumes, on various aspects of the theatre, appear every two or three years. The majority do not have a bearing on the subject of this bibliography but two are relevant. These are the volumes for 1952–4 *The Italian opera and contemporary ballet in London 1789–1820 . . . ,* by William C. Smith, and for 1959–60 *The Empire ballet,* by Ivor Guest. Future research may yield other volumes on some facet of ballet. The Society also publishes Occasional Pamphlets, of which nine titles have appeared. The *Dancing Times* has published titles for many years, e.g. Beaumont's *Bibliography of dancing,* 1929 and *La Fille mal gardée,* edited by Ivor Guest, 1960.

There is no comprehensive bibliography on ballet, in the English language, to display this material conveniently for the interested reader. Ivor Guest has provided the most useful list, in the catalogue he compiled for the exhibition on ballet sponsored by the National Book League in 1957 (*see* no. 7). This is included in the following items which comprise bibliographies and reading lists on ballet and the dance.

BIBLIOGRAPHY

Arrangement. 1. Bibliographies published separately. 2. Bibliographies appended to books on the dance. 3. Bibliographies printed in periodicals and other serial publications. 4. Indexes to periodicals. 5. General sources. Within each category the arrangement is chronological by date of latest edition, or latest volume of serial.

BIBLIOGRAPHIES PUBLISHED SEPARATELY

1   BEAUMONT, CYRIL WILLIAM, *comp.*   A bibliography of dancing.   New York, Rolland Press, Benjamin Blom, 1963.   xi, 228 pp.   63s.

   Reprint of the 1929 edition published by *The Dancing Times.* '. . . primarily intended as a work of reference for . . . dancers, teachers of dancing, producers and all those workers in the several arts of the theatre who from time to time require to know where information relating to particular dances may be obtained.' Confined to books on dancing in the British Museum Library (B.M. references are given). Most items are annotated, and arrangement is alphabetical by author, with a subject index appended.
   422 items – 67 on English ballet.

2   MAGRIEL, PAUL DAVID, *comp.*   A bibliography of dancing: a list of

books and articles on the dance and related subjects.   New York,
H. W. Wilson, 1936.   229 pp.   front., illus. $4.75.
— —Fourth cumulated supplement, 1936–40. New York, H. W.
Wilson, 1941.   104 pp. $0.85.

> Part 5, 'Ballet' includes Section B, 'England'. Aimed at including in a
> 'single volume a comprehensive list of reference works on the dance in all of
> its phases and of the arts definitely related to dancing'. (Author's Preface.)
> Other parts are 'General Works'; 'History and Criticism of the Dance';
> 'Folk, National, Regional and Ethnological Dances'; 'The Art of Dancing';
> 'Mime and Pantomime'; 'Masques'; 'Accessories' (décor, costume, music).
> There are mainly brief annotations to about one-third of the entries. Appen-
> ded is an author, subject and analytical index. The 17 illustrations are fac-
> similes of title-pages of books important in the development of dancing. The
> Supplement follows the above arrangement, but there are no illustrations.
> Locations are given for rare and out-of-print books.
> 665 items – 24 on English ballet.
> Supplement 359 items – 38 on English ballet.

[3] EVANS, BERNARD C.   Ballet and dancing.   National Book Council,
1940.   2 pp.

> National Book Council Book List, no. 173.

4 HASKELL, ARNOLD LIONEL.   Ballet: a reader's guide.   Cambridge
University Press for The National Book League, 1947.   12 pp.   1s.

> An annotated reading list compiled by W. A. Munford in consultation
> with A. L. Haskell, who wrote the introduction. Alphabetical arrangement
> under the headings 'Introductory Books' and 'A Mixed Batch of Reading'.
> No index.
> 51 items – 30 on English ballet.

5 THE LIBRARY ASSOCIATION.   County Libraries Section.   Readers'
guide to ballet.   L.A. County Libraries Section, [1948].   16 pp.
(Readers' Guide.   New series no. 1.)   4d.

> Information on some of the books was given by C. W. Beaumont. ' . . .
> compiled to provide the general reader with a practical guide', it includes
> American and foreign publications. Arranged under the following headings –
> 'Aesthetics, Appreciation and Criticism'; 'Modern Ballet, Twentieth Cen-
> tury'; 'Stories and Descriptions . . .'; 'History'; 'Biography and Memoirs';
> 'Photography'; 'Décor and Art'; 'Technique'; 'Miscellany'; 'Periodicals'.
> There are a very few brief annotations, but no index.
> 180 items – 90 on English ballet.

6 FLETCHER, IFAN KYRLE. Bibliographical description of forty rare books relating to the art of dancing in the collection of P. J. S. Richardson, O.B.E. *The Dancing Times*, 1954. 20 pp. front., illus. Private circulation.

> The author wished 'to place on record accurate descriptions of a number of important books relating to the Dance, which have been brought together over many years' . . . Some . . . are not to be found in the British Museum; of others no bibliographical descriptions are available, and of a few (and these include some of the most famous) the records in the usual reference books are vague or misleading'. Among the authors listed are Lewis Theobald, John Thurmond and John Weaver.

7 NATIONAL BOOK LEAGUE. Ballet: an exhibition of books, MSS., play-bills, prints, etc. illustrating the development of the art from its origins until modern times. N.B.L., 1957. 70 pp. 2s. 6d.
— — Ballet: supplementary catalogue of pictures, journals, MSS., costumes and current books (in print November 1957). N.B.L., 1957. v, 4 pp. 1s.

> The exhibition (7th November, 1957 to 4th January, 1958) was organized and the catalogue written by Ivor Guest. 'The cosmopolitan character of ballet . . . (was) stressed. . . . The other aspect . . . emphasized . . . (was) its history and tradition.' Annotated entries are grouped in 16 sections covering 'General Historical Studies'; 'Ballet before 1830'; 'Romantic Ballet'; 'Post-Romantic Ballet in Paris'; 'The Imperial Russian Ballet'; 'The Diaghilev Ballet and its Successors'; 'Contemporary Ballet and its National Traditions'; 'Technical Manuals'; 'Design'; 'Criticism'; 'Aesthetics and Belles Lettres'; 'Reference Books'; 'Photography'; 'Humour'; 'Dance Notation'; 'Period-ical Literature'; 'Manuscripts'. Within each section the items are arranged chronologically by subject.
> 319 items – 100 on English ballet.
> Supplement – 100 items.

8 NILES, DORIS, *and* LESLIE, SERGE. A bibliography of the dance collection of Doris Niles & Serge Leslie . . . Part 1, A–K. Beaumont, [*The Dancing Times*, distributor] 1966. vii, 279 p.p. 63s.

> The annotations are by Serge Leslie and the work has been edited by Cyril Beaumont. The collection was started by the American dancer Serge Leslie in 1929. He later married Doris Niles, also a dancer, and they built up this collection during their travels. The entries are arranged alphabetically by the name of the author.
> 1,083 items – 180 on English ballet.

BIBLIOGRAPHIES APPENDED TO BOOKS

9 CHUJOY, ANATOLE, *ed*. The dance encyclopedia. New York, Barnes, 1949. xv, [4], 546 pp. bibliog. $7.50.

Section B, 'Ballet'. The bibliography is based on Magriel's *A Bibliography of dancing* . . . and the fourth cumulation (*see* no. 2), with the addition of English and American publications issued since 1940. *Books* in English only have been included. The Editor consulted publishers and booksellers in America and England concerning new books and the availability of older publications. Other sections are A, 'General Works'; C, 'Modern Dance'; D, 'Dance in Education'; E, 'Folk Dance'; F, 'Ballroom'. There are occasional brief annotations. (*See also* no. 32.)
154 items – 65 on English ballet.

10 NOBLE, PETER, *ed*. British ballet. Skelton Robinson, [c. 1950]. 358 pp. 48 pl., illus., bibliog. 21s.

'A selected list of books dealing with, or containing sections on British ballet.' Primary arrangement is alphabetical by author's name, then chronological. The entries are un-annotated and include analytical entries for *Ballet Annual*, *Ballet Rambert*, edited by Walter Gore, *Covent Garden book*, 1947, *Footnotes to the ballet*, edited by Caryl Brahms and the work which contains this bibliography. It is not well set out nor easy to refer to. (*See also* nos. 55 and 93.)
100 items.

11 CLARKE, MARY. The Sadler's Wells ballet: a history and an appreciation. Black, 1955. xv, 336 pp. front., 30 pl., bibliog. 21s.

The bibliography is arranged alphabetically by author. Periodicals are listed separately. (*See also* no. 278.)
70 items.

12 SWINSON, CYRIL WILLIAM. Guidebook to the ballet. English Universities Press, 1960. 192 pp. 24 pl., illus., bibliog. (Teach Yourself Series.) 7s. 6d.

'History' section includes a division for England. Other sections are 'General and Reference'; 'Aesthetics and Criticism'; 'Music'; 'Choreography'; 'Design and Costume'; 'Dancing – technical'; 'Biographies and Memoirs'; 'Pictorial Biographies'; 'Illustrated Books'; 'Ballet Periodicals'. A brief annotation is given in a few cases. The system of arrangement within each section appears to be chronological, although date of publication is not given. (*See also* no. 118.)
80 items – 58 on English ballet.

13 GUEST, IVOR. The dancer's heritage: a short history of ballet. Rev.
ed. Harmondsworth, Penguin Books, 1962. [171] pp. front.,
24 pl., bibliog. 6s.

> Appended is 'Suggestions for Further Reading'. Un-annotated items in
> English are listed under the following headings – 'General Historical Studies';
> 'Ballet before 1830'; 'The Romantic Ballet'; 'Ballet in the West before
> Diaghilev'; 'The Imperial Russian Ballet'; 'The Diaghilev Ballet'; 'Pavlova';
> 'Contemporary Ballet'; 'Ballet Design'; 'Ballet Music'; 'Reference Books'.
> (*See also* no. 215.)
> 65 items – 28 on English ballet.

14 VAN PRAAGH, PEGGY, *and* BRINSON, PETER. The choreographic art: an
outline of its principles and craft. Black, 1963. xxiv, 387 pp.
39 pl., illus., diagrs., bibliog. 60s.

> The books listed in Appendix II, 'Suggestions for Further Reading' 'have
> contributed in one way or another to our own study of choreography'
> (authors' note). Arrangement is alphabetical by author's name, without
> annotation. (*See also* no. 405.)
> 129 items – 35 on English ballet.

15 LAWSON, JOAN. A history of ballet and its makers. Pitman, 1964.
xiii, 202 pp. 32 pl., bibliog. 50s.

> A List for Further Reading, which sometimes ranges outside the limits of
> ballet, is appended to each chapter. These titles are cumulated into a biblio-
> graphy at the end of the book. Arrangement is alphabetical by author's
> name. (*See also* no. 406.)
> 175 items.

BIBLIOGRAPHIES IN SERIALS

16 BEAUMONT, CYRIL WILLIAM. 'The literature of the ballet: a select
bibliography, 1830–1948.' *In: British Book News* 1949, pp. 14–17
(Cumulated volume). 4 pl.

> 59 items – 30 on English ballet.

17 SWINSON, CYRIL WILLIAM. Books about the ballet: (a bibliography of
books published in England, 1st January, 1938 to 31st October,
1949). *In: Ballet Annual 1950*, 4th issue, pp. 140–2, 145–6.

> Includes new editions and reprints issued after 1938, of books originally

produced before 1938; also books published in Australia, but does not claim to be exhaustive. The primary arrangement is alphabetical by author's name; the titles of prolific authors being listed chronologically by original date of publication. There are occasional brief annotations.
130 items – 90 on English ballet.

18 GUMMER, DOROTHY. 'Ballet and the dance: British publications of the last ten years. I.' *In: British Book News*, no. 219, November 1958, pp. 701–5.

67 items – 36 on English ballet.

19 GUMMER, DOROTHY. 'Ballet and the dance: British publications of the last ten years. II. Aesthetics and technique.' *In: British Book News*, no. 220, December 1958, pp. 771–5.

Folk and Modern Dance included.
62 items – 47 on English ballet.

20 The Ballet Annual.   Black, 1947–63.

Book lists were provided in the 5th (1951) to 12th (1958) issues inclusive, the number of titles ranging between 13 and 23. The majority were annotated and the arrangement was alphabetical by author's name. Cyril Swinson was the chief reviewer; others included Cyril Beaumont and Ivor Guest. After the 12th issue these book lists lapsed until the 18th (1963), when a more ambitious scheme was started. About 65 annotated items were arranged under country of publication, i.e. Great Britain, France, Germany and Austria, U.S.A. and U.S.S.R., then alphabetically by author. The reviewer was anonymous. After this issue *Ballet Annual* ceased publication. (*See also* no. 45.)

INDEXES TO PERIODICALS

21 The music index: the key to current music periodical literature. Detroit, Michigan, Information Service, 1949–.

Indexes under ballet companies and dancers, and gives references from ballets to composers. There are headings under English companies, dancers and ballets. 'Complete indexing . . . is the general rule for all music periodicals. Publications with coverage broader than the music field are indexed only for material pertinent to music' (Preface, 1949). At the start about 50 periodicals were being indexed: this rose to about 220 for *Music index 1962* (published 1965). The majority of periodicals indexed are American.

22   Guide to dance periodicals: an analytical index of articles. . . . Volumes
         1.1950–.   Cormpiled by S. Yancey Belknap.
       V. 1: 1931–5.   Gainesville, University of Florida Press, 1959. $7.50.
       V. 2: 1936–40.   New York, Dance and Music Archives, 1950. $6.
       V. 3: 1941–5.   Asheville, North Carolina, The Stephens Press, 1948.
       $6.
       V. 4: 1946–50.   New York, Dance and Music Archives, 1951. $10.
       V. 5: 1951–2.   Gainesville, University of Florida Press, 1955. $7.50.
       V. 6: 1953–4.   Gainesville, University of Florida Press, 1956. $7.50.
       V. 7: 1955–6.   Gainseville, University of Florida Press, 1958. $7.50.
       V. 8: 1957–8.   New York, Scarecrow Press, 1960. $10.
       V. 9: 1959–60.   New York, Scarecrow Press, 1962. $10.

       Provides a subject and selected author index. English periodicals indexed
   are *Ballet* (in v. 2, 4, 5), *Ballet Today* (from v. 4), *Dance and Dancers* (from v. 4)
   and *Dancing Times*. Other periodicals indexed wholly or partially up to and
   including v. 4 are *The American Dancer, Dance, Dance Index, Dance Magazine,
   Dance News, Dance Observer, Educational Dance* and *Theatre Arts*. From v. 5
   the scope was enlarged. In all, 19 periodicals were indexed; those with a
   wider range, in respect of articles pertinent to ballet only. This volume also
   included, for the first time, a separate illustration index, which became a
   regular feature. 'The Explanation' in v. 6 states that 'Since it is hoped to
   include in a separate series music and theatre, such periodicals as *Theatre Arts,
   Music and Musicians, Opera News* and *Theatre Notebook* are not found in this
   volume'. 'No praise is high enough for the patience and thoroughness of the
   compiler. Speaking only for *The Dancing Times* and *The Ballroom Dancing
   Times* . . . the references to these two publications are more comprehensive
   than the running index we keep in our own office.' (Review of v. 9 in *The
   Dancing Times*, August 1962, p. 713.)

23   Guide to the musical arts: an analytical index of articles and illustrations
         1953–6.   New York, Scarecrow Press, 1957.

       Compiled by S. Yancey Belknap . . . 'indexes some 15,000 articles and
   6,000 illustrations in the world's leading journals dealing with music, opera
   and the dance and the theatre, including *Theatre Arts, Music and Musicians,
   Opera News,* and *Theatre Notebook*. In general it includes articles and illustrations published from 1953 through 1956, but in a few cases articles as far
   back as 1949 have been included.' Part 1 indexes articles and Part 2 illustrations by author and major subject.

24   Guide to the performing arts.   New York, Scarecrow Press, 1960–.

       Published as a supplement to no. 23; covers 1957. The index is divided into 2 parts – the main section and a television arts section. Under each heading article references are entered first followed by illustration references. There have been 7 annual indexes to date. It is 'highly recommended for theatre, music and dance' by the *Library Journal* (15th December, 1964, p. 4892).

GENERAL SOURCES

Apart from these specialized bibliographies, it is worth consulting other more general sources.

25   BRITISH DRAMA LEAGUE.   The player's library: the catalogue of the library of the British Drama League.   2nd ed.   Faber, 1950.

First published 1930, with a supplement published 1934. 3 supplements to the 2nd edition were published in 1951, 1954 and 1956. Each volume contains sections on ballet and dance under the class number 600 in the British Drama League scheme in 'Books on the Theatre'. The secondary arrangement is alphabetical by name of author.

26   BAKER, BLANCH MERRIT, *comp.*   Theatre and allied arts: a guide to books dealing with the history, criticism, and technic of the drama and theatre and related arts and crafts.   New York, H. W. Wilson, 1952.

27   Based on *Dramatic bibliography* . . . (New York, H. W. Wilson, 1933), which had no separate section on ballet. The compiler has re-written her earlier work, and brought it up to date. She claims that 'about six thousand volumes have been examined and selected for their usefulness as reference aids and working guides'. The material is limited to books written in or translated into English between 1885 and 1948, with the exception of some foreign works in the section on costume and some pre-1885 publications which have become standard works, or where books of a later date do not exist; also a few important books published in 1949 and 1950. The material is divided as follows – Part 1, 'Drama, Theatre and Actors'; Part 2, 'Stage-craft and Allied Arts of the Theatre'; Part 3, 'Miscellaneous Reference Material'. There are separate subject and author indexes. Section 7 'Dance' of Part 2 covers 44 pages. The two main headings in this section are 'History, Theory and Criticism' and 'Technics of the Dance'. The latter includes a sub-heading for ballet, and the former contains references for the reader interested in English ballet too. It is as well to look under both headings when searching for a particular book because one finds the occasional un-expected title listed under 'Technics of the Dance', e.g. *Ballet then and now*, by Deryck Lynham.

28 WESTMINSTER PUBLIC LIBRARIES. Classified catalogue of non-fiction books. . . . Westminster Public Libraries, 1957–65.

Includes additions to the Pavlova Memorial Library, a special collection devoted to the dance. These catalogues cover the period 1952 to 1964, arranged according to the Dewey classification scheme in which the number for ballet is 792.8. There are annual and five-yearly cumulations and separate name and subject indexes. A separate catalogue of the Pavlova Memorial Library, comprising several hundred items, may be printed in the future and will include microfilms of rare books on the dance which formerly belonged to the late P. J. S. Richardson, now in possession of the Royal Academy of Dancing. This proposed catalogue will be printed from a sheaf catalogue which, at the moment, is stored in the Reference Librarian's room, and may be consulted on application.

29 Enciclopedia dello Spettacolo. Rome, Maschere, 1954–66.

9 vv., with supplements (*see also* no. 38). Furnishes a bibliography of books and periodical articles appended to the entry on ballet (balletto) in v. 1, columns 1377–9. (About 150 items of which about 30 have a bearing on English ballet.) There are other references under related headings, e.g. 'Fonteyn, Margot' (14 references – books and articles). The arrangement under the main entry is – Bibliographical Works; General Histories; National Histories; Individual Ballets; Popular Works; Guides to Ballets; Dictionaries and Encyclopaedias.

Ifan Kyrle Fletcher, the antiquarian bookseller, who specializes in theatre material, has issued over 200 catalogues publicizing books, designs, autograph letters, playbills, music and all aspects of the
30   theatre including ballet, e.g. Catalogue 209. History of entertainment (1963), lists 'a substantial portion of the archives of the Arts Theatre Club. . . . Three ballet companies performed there, the Arts Theatre Ballet, the London Ballet and the Ballet Rambert'.

II. ENCYCLOPAEDIAS, DICTIONARIES AND YEAR-BOOKS

THE dance is reasonably well supplied with reference works in English, for the period after the Second World War, but there are few published prior to 1939. For the latter it is necessary to consult material with a wider scope.

The reference books under (b) 'General' sub-divisions are not described in detail either bibliographically or in the annotations; nor is it claimed that coverage is complete. The aim has been to indicate where an historical outline, a resumé of a season's work or factual information may be found, if a more specialized work is not available.

BIBLIOGRAPHY

Arrangement. 1. Encyclopaedias and dictionaries. 2. Year-Books. 3. Biographical sources. Each section is sub-divided into (a) Specific to Ballet; (b) General; and each sub-division arranged chronologically.

ENCYCLOPAEDIAS AND DICTIONARIES

(a) Specific to Ballet

31 D'ALBERT, CHARLES. The encyclopaedia of dancing. Rev. ed. T. M. Middleton, [1920]. 157 pp. front., 9 pl., bibliog.

First published 1914–15. Dances and technical terms of social dancing and ballet are explained, but proper names are not included; about one-third of the entries are concerned with ballet. Possibly of more interest to the ballroom dancer. The main text is preceded by a glossary, and the bibliography contains 150 items. 2 plates reproduce Blasis' 5 positions, the remainder are reproductions of photographs of ballet and ballroom dancers.

BEAUMONT, CYRIL WILLIAM, *comp.* A French-English dictionary of technical terms used in classical ballet. 1939.

See no. 512.

32 CHUJOY, ANATOLE, *ed.* The dance encyclopedia. New York, Barnes, 1949. xv, [4], 546 pp. bibliog. $7.50.

28

The author, a naturalized American writer and critic of the dance, founded and edited *Dance Magazine*, 1937–41 and *Dance News* from 1942. This very useful reference work includes entries under dancers, choreographers, composers, technical terms, periodicals, etc. There are 87 longer articles, many signed, for which there is a contents list. The majority cover from less than one to five pages, but 8 cover up to 10 pages; the latter being printed in single column while the main body of text is printed in double columns. Special articles include 'Sadler's Wells Ballet'; 'Antony Tudor'; 'John Weaver' (George Chaffee); also 'Dance Notation' (Ann Hutchinson); '*Giselle*'; 'Iconography of the Dance' (George Chaffee); 'Music for Dance'; 'Opera Ballet' (Boris Romanoff); 'Romantic Ballet'. There is also a bibliography (*see* no. 9) and a discography of about 300 items, compiled by Manning Solon. P. J. S. Richardson considered that though this volume 'is far from perfect' the author 'has laid the foundations of what could, if properly handled grow in its subsequent editions, into an invaluable publication' (*The Dancing Times*, July 1949, p. 570).

33 GADAN, FRANCIS, *and* MAILLARD, ROBERT, *eds.*   A dictionary of modern ballet. . . .   Methuen, 1959.   [8], [360] pp.   illus.   36s.

Originally published by Fernand Hazan as *Dictionnaire du ballet moderne* (Paris, 1957).
The English edition, supervised by Mary Clarke and Ronald Crichton, contains new articles, and differs from the original, but details are not given. Articles tend to describe and reflect opinion. There are about 650 entries under companies, ballets, dancers, musicians and designers, but no explanation of technical terms. About 95 entries deal specifically with English ballet. There is also nineteenth-century material relevant to contemporary ballet. The 373 illustrations are small, but excellently chosen and reproduced, including reproductions of photographs and sketches of dancers and ballets, and designs for costume and scenery, many in colour.

34 WILSON, GEORGE BUCKLEY LAIRD. . . .   A dictionary of ballet.   Rev. ed.   Cassell, 1961.   xvii, [313] pp.   16 pl., illus., diagrs.   (Belle Sauvage Library).   18s.

Originally published in 1957 by Penguin Books, this edition is brought up to date to October 1960.
Of the dictionaries of ballet listed here, this work gives most information about English ballet. About 900 entries give information on companies, ballets in the contemporary repertoire and of historic or special interest, and dancers; also those composers and designers who have made a special contribution to ballet, ' . . . a very few' writers and 'hardly any teachers'. Technical terms of the *danse d'école* are illustrated with drawings by Peter Revitt. Other entries are under the titles of general headings, e.g. 'photographers', 'salaries' . . . about one-quarter have a direct bearing on English

ballet. The 31 illustrations on the plates are uninteresting and somewhat blurred. '. . . the most remarkable mixture of scholarly research and sheer balletomania; of academic impartiality and obvious predilection . . . not one major or vital omission.' (A.H.F. writing of the first edition in *The Dancing Times*, Christmas 1957, p. 129.)

35 CROSLAND, MARGARET. Ballet lover's dictionary. Arco, 1962. [183] pp. 16 pl., illus., bibliog. 18s.

The entries are so short and simple, that it might be difficult for a 'new-comer to the ballet' to gain a background to the subject, which is claimed in the introduction. Choice of entry seems a little arbitrary, but some are up to date and unusual, e.g. Irish National Ballet; Nureyev, Rudolf; *Turned out proud*. The 24 reproductions of photographs on the plates are unusual too. Drawings are by Freda Daventry.

(b) General

36 DOWNS, HAROLD, *ed.* Theatre and stage: an encyclopaedic guide to the performance of all amateur, dramatic, operatic and theatrical work. Pitman, 1951.

2 vv. Deals with ballet from a more practical angle. V. 1 contains 'Ballet Dancing', by A. L. Haskell (p. 179–215), with an introduction by Marie Rambert. Main headings are 'The Dancer', 'The Choreographer', which contains a section on 'British Choreography' and 'Practical Points in Ballet Production'. There is also an article by P. J. S. Richardson on 'Stage Dancing' (p. 216–32). There are 39 illustrations in the text appertaining to ballet. The index to both volumes is appended to v. 2.

37 GRANVILLE, WILFRED. A dictionary of theatre terms. Deutsch, 1952.

Contains about 35 common technical terms used in ballet, out of a total of about 2,150.

38 Enciclopedia dello spettacolo. Rome, Maschere, 1954–62.

Published in 9 vv., with 3 supplements as follows – *Le Grandi voci, dizionario critico- bibliografico dei cantanti con discografia operistica; Appendice di Aggiornamento – Cinema* (1963); *Aggiornamento 1955–65* (1966). The most valuable work of reference on the theatre.

There are 9 sub-headings under the main heading '*Balletto*' (columns 1,355–1,379) in v. 1. These cover – Origins; Court Ballet; Comedie-ballet and Opera-ballet; Growth of Professionalism; *Ballet d'action*; Dramatic Ballet; The Romantic Ballet; from Blasis to Petipa; The Diaghilev Revolution; Birth of Modern Ballet. A Bibliography is appended (*see* no. 29). There are separate articles for such subjects as '*Ballet Blanc*', '*Ballet d'Action*' and '*Ballet Sinfonico*'. The following English companies are accorded separate articles – Ballet Guild, Ballet Rambert, International Ballet, London's Festival

Ballet, Metropolitan Ballet and the Royal Ballet – with chronological list of first productions or repertory appended. There are also articles under the names of choreographers, dancers, directors of companies and writers. There is no entry under 'Balletto' in the *Aggiornamento 1955–65*, but there are articles on younger dancers such as Lynn Seymour and Merle Park. For the more important names chronological lists of ballets are provided, or roles created, or books written; also references in books and periodicals on the subject of articles are given. There are a generous number of illustrations. Ivor Guest has been adviser on ballet since 1958.

39 GROVE, SIR GEORGE, *ed.*   Grove's dictionary of music and musicians. 5th ed.   Macmillan, 1954.

In 9 vv., with a supplementary volume 1961. The 5th edition was edited by Eric Blom. It contains a fairly substantial resumé of ballet history (p. 378–92). It reaches as far back as Greek dance and Roman pantomime and forward to the development of ballet in England and America. There is a section on 'First Character Ballets in England' which plots John Weaver's contribution to the *ballet d'action*, and another on 'The British Ballet'. There is also a section on choreography. The first part of the article up to but not including Diaghilev's later phase was written by D. L. Murray and J. F. Stainer, while the later parts are by Dyneley Hussey. The bibliography contains 21 items in English, French and German.

40 HARTNOLL, PHYLLIS, *ed.*   The Oxford companion to the theatre.   2nd ed.   Oxford University Press, 1957.

The article on ballet (pp. 47–54) provides material on origins, development and history, with 3 columns under England, which also takes in the de Basil and Blum companies. ' . . . a few librettists have short notes, as have some ballet dancers and choreographers', but the choice is selective for there are entries under 'de Valois' and 'Rambert', but nothing under 'Fonteyn'.

41 SANDVED, K. B., *comp.*   The world of music: a treasury for listener and viewer.   2nd ed.   The Waverley Book Company, 1957.

Provides a few paragraphs on British ballet (column 126–8) under the heading 'Ballet: the marriage of music and movement'. The article is divided into the usual historical periods. Appended is a glossary of ballet terms, and 'Ballet Music by Great Composers'. There are separate entries under the titles of some famous ballets. There are 18 illustrations in the text.

42 Chamber's encyclopaedia.   3rd ed.   Newnes, 1959.

In 15 vv. Contains a reasonably full article on ballet (pp. 76–9), but it is not

---

[1] The article article on ballet in 3rd ed. (1967), signed by I. Guest has been expanded by some 2 pages.

so detailed as that in the *Encyclopaedia Britannica*. 'Early History' is sub-divided under Western Europe and Russia, and 'Later Developments' under 'England' and 'Other Countries'. There is 1 plate with 4 photographs, and a bibliography which contains 24 items. This includes nothing published after 1946 apart from *The Ballet Annual*.

43   SCHOLES, PERCY A.   The Oxford companion to music. 9th ed. Oxford University Press, 1960.

The article on ballet (pp. 76–80) deals with general development of the art, with sections on 'Ballet in Opera' and 'Loans from Ballet to Concert Repertory and Vice-Versa', but there is little about English ballet as such.

44   The Encyclopaedia Britannica. 16th ed. London, Chicago.... Benton, 1964.

In 24 vv., with an index. Contains an article on ballet written by Lillian Moore (pp. 24–35). The main part, 'Development of the Art' includes 'Ballet in England'. Other divisions are as follows – 'Court Ballet'; 'Ballet under Louis XIV'; 'Rise of the Virtuoso'; 'Dramatic Ballet'; 'The *Ballet d'Action* of Noverre and Angiolini'; 'The Romantic Ballet'; 'The Italian School'; 'Ballet in Russia before 1900'; 'The Diaghilev Ballet'; 'Pavlova'; 'Ballet in America 1735–1932'; 'France after 1929'; 'Ballet in Denmark'; 'Soviet Union'; 'Ballet in America after 1932'; 'Trends'. The second main division is 'Ballet Technique and Terms'. There are 4 plates with 26 illustrations on them; also sketches by Arline K. Thomson to illustrate points of technique. The bibliography contains 87 items and follows the sub-divisions listed above fairly closely, with the addition of 'Collected Biography' and 'Collections of Ballet Stories'. The 6 items listed for English ballet include Mary Clarke's *The Sadler's Wells Ballet*, published 1955, but not her *Dancers of Mercury*, published 1962. The articles in the 11th edition (the last English ed.) published 1910, and in v. 2 of the 3 supplementary volumes published 1921–2, which added to 11th edition are designated as 12th edition, have historical interest. Each contains paragraphs on English ballet, which give the point of view of the period.

YEAR-BOOKS

(a) Specific to Ballet

45   The Ballet Annual: a record and year-book of the ballet. 1st–18th issue. Black, 1947–63. front., illus. 21s.–30s. (18th issue 18s.).

Edited by A. L. Haskell. From the 2nd issue (1948) the following became Assistant or Associate Editors – Ivor Guest, Cyril Swinson and G. B. L.

Wilson. Mary Clarke, who had joined the editorial staff from the 7th issue (1953), appears on the title-page as joint Editor from the 15th–18th issues.

Permanent features are – 'Outstanding Events of the Year' (in which important balletic events, and performances by English companies and foreign companies visiting the British Isles for the current year, are reviewed), checklists of ballets and companies showing in London, and from the 14th issue, foreign centres, and obituaries. There are articles of more general interest on British and foreign companies, dancers and choreographers, reports on the year's work by correspondents from ballet centres in Europe and America, the history of the dance, and 'fringe' interests, e.g. pantomime, programmes. From the 5th–12th issues, book lists were provided (*see* no. 20) and this practice was continued in the 18th issue, on a more detailed scale. Provision of an index was erratic; one being included for the 8th–14th issues, but not for the others. *The Ballet Annual* was discontinued after 1963.

46   *Ballet decade*, Black, 1956, is made up of a selection of articles chosen by A. L. Haskell from the first 10 issues of *The Ballet Annual*. The period covered is 1946–55. 'Diary of Events' is given for each year. A 'Short Index' is supplied and there are 4 colour plates.

47   MELVIN, DUNCAN, *ed.* Souvenirs de ballet: a book for lovers of ballet . . . no. 1, 1949. Mayfair Publications, 1949. 95 pp. illus.

Intended to be an annual publication, but the first number was the only one to appear. Peter Williams was Assistant Editor. It is slighter in content than *The Ballet Annual*, with less factual information. It includes articles on foreign as well as native companies and dancers. There is no index.

This publication and no. 45 contain many photographs to reinforce the text, as well as drawings. *The Ballet Annual* made a feature of enlisting artist(s) to supply sketches for one issue, e.g. Milein Cosman, Bernard Daydé and June Ryan in the 6th issue (1952). *Souvenirs de Ballet* has a greater proportion of illustrations to text, but these are not as clearly defined as those in *The Ballet Annual*.

Relevant articles from both publications are listed separately under the appropriate chapters.

(b) General

48   'The Stage' year-book, 1908–. Carson & Comerford, 1908–. Annual.

Since 1949, has included an article on ballet by Eric John, in which he discusses the balletic events of the previous year, in the United Kingdom. Another feature is 'Ballets of the Year' which includes productions of visiting foreign companies as well as English companies. The arrangement is alphabetical by the name of the ballet. Information given is the name of the choreographer, composer, company performing, the theatre and date of performance, sometimes the designer, with an occasional cast list. There is a list of current English companies for each year, and a list of publications on the theatre for the previous year. This includes items on the ballet.

49 Britannica book of the year.   Benton, 1938–9, 1949–.   Annual.

The year's events in ballet are found either under 'Ballet' or 'Dance'; the *Britannica Book of the Year 1966* has the entry under 'Dance' (pp. 233–6). Up to 1964 coverage was mainly for activities in the United Kingdom. The scope was wider in the 1964 *Book of the Year* and included the year's work in other countries. This policy has been continued. The contributors were as follows – 1938: Hubert Fitchew, musical contributor to *The Sunday Times*, 1939: Cyril Beaumont, 1950–64: A. L. Haskell, 1965–6: Lillian Moore.

50 Hinrichsen's musical year-book.   Hinrichsen, 1944–58.

The first volumes devoted a few pages to reviews of the ballet in London. The Year Book for 1944 contained 'The Ballet in 1942–3', by Edwin Evans, who ranged approximately over the period September 1942–1st July, 1943. Appended is 'Ballet Repertoire September 1942 to August 1943' for the Sadler's Wells Ballet and the International Ballet. Under each company the arrangement is by choreographer (there is also a group heading for classical ballets). The Year Book for 1945–6 contains a similar review – 'The Ballet in 1944', also by Edwin Evans. In the following year 'The Ballet in 1945 and 1946' was written by P. W. Manchester. This was the last to appear. Vv. 4–5 (1947–8) and 6 (1949–50) carried bibliographies of books and periodical articles on music. Both are divided into Part 1, 'Subject List', in which there is a sub-division for ballet, and Part 2, 'Personal List', which is arranged alphabetically by the name of the person written about. The bibliography for vv. 4–5 was compiled by Alfred Loewenberg, that in v. 6 by Jack Werner.

51 Penguin music magazine 1–8.   Harmondsworth, Penguin Books, 1946–9.

Although not strictly a year book, Penguin Music Magazine carried regular articles on 'Ballet in London', by A. L. Haskell. He reviewed ballet activities in the capital, and sometimes touched on more general topics. These articles were illustrated by a varying number of plates.

52 Year's work in the theatre.   Longmans, Green, for the British Council, 1949–51.

There were 3 issues covering the periods 1948–9, 1949–50 and 1950–1. Each had an article entitled 'The Year in Ballet', the first two of which were written by Philip Hope-Wallace, the last by Cyril Beaumont. Both authors described performances in London, with some criticism. These articles were illustrated with clear plates, some in colour.

53   Theatre world annual (London): a pictorial review of West End pro-
     ductions . . . 1–.   Rockliff, 1950–.   Annual.

> The period of time dealt with in each number follows the annual theatre
> season, e.g. the first number covers productions from 1st June, 1949 to
> 31st May, 1950. *Theatre World Annual* gives only a little information on
> ballet. From the second number it has included a section 'Ballet and Opera'
> placed at the end of the book. About 2 pages of reproductions of photographs
> indicate the editor's choice of one or two outstanding new productions of
> the year, giving the usual information for each ballet. A written 'Review of
> the Year' precedes the photographic record, in which ballet receives a
> passing mention.

BIOGRAPHICAL SOURCES

(a) Specific to Ballet

54   HASKELL, ARNOLD LIONEL, *and* RICHARDSON, PHILIP J. S., *eds*.   Who's
     who in dancing 1932.   *The Dancing Times*, 1932.   140 pp.   7s. 6d.

> ' . . . Compiled by the publishers' (title-page). The main part is devoted
> to 'Biographies' which lists executants and teachers of all types of dancing
> alphabetically by name, giving concise information on careers. Great Britain
> is dealt with 'as fully as possible' although some people written to did not
> reply. Of about 740 entries about 60 are concerned with English ballet.
> Included are lists of 'Dancing Associations and Societies in England' and
> 'Stage Dancing Competitions'.

55   NOBLE, PETER, *ed*.   British ballet.   Skelton Robinson, [c. 1950].
     358 pp.   48 pl., illus., bibliog.   21s.

> The 'Biographical Index' with Addendum (pp. 272–358) contains about
> 410 entries for mainly British and Commonwealth dancers, choreographers,
> teachers and writers; also designers, composers and conductors with reference
> to their work in ballet. Contains little-known names. Entries are normally
> confined to about 12 lines. (*See also* nos. 10 and 93.)

[56] WILSON, GEORGE BUCKLEY LAIRD.   Who's who in ballet and the
     dance.   Pitman.

> Not yet published.
> 'Questionnaire forms are going out . . . to ballet and modern dancers,
> choreographers, teachers, writers and the like . . . information has already
> been collected from most of the dancers of the Royal Ballet, London's
> Festival Ballet, the Ballet Rambert and Western Theatre Ballet . . . the book
> has a world-wide coverage.' (*The Dancing Times*, January 1964, p. 213.)

(b) General

57   Who's who. . . .   Black, 1849–.   Annual.

On a comparison of the 1964 *Who's who* and the 1957 *Who's who in the theatre* (12th ed.) it would appear that *Who's who* is more comprehensive, for it included at least 12 principal dancers of the Royal Ballet, whereas *Who's who in the theatre* included only 3. This may perhaps be an unfair comparison in view of the 7 years' difference between dates of publication. Before approximately 1950 however, *Who's who in the theatre* is more likely to provide an entry for a dancer than *Who's who*.

58   Who's who in the theatre . . . 13th ed.   Pitman, 1961.

Started as *The Green room book*, of which there were annual issues from 1906–9. From 1912 the title was changed to *Who's who in the theatre: a biographical record of the contemporary stage*. John Parker was the editor from the 2nd edition of *The Green room book* up to but not including the 12th edition of *Who's who in the theatre*. This was edited by his son, also John Parker. Freda Gay was editor for the 13th edition. The preface to the 9th edition states that 'A number of those prominently associated with ballet have now been included', although previous editions, including *The Green room book*, contained a few famous names in ballet, e.g. Diaghilev, Bedells, Dolin. Ballet biographies have been eliminated from the 13th edition, 'the popularity of ballet having increased so rapidly during recent years, a separate *Who's who in ballet and dance* (*see* no. [56]) has become necessary and will, in due course, be issued by the present publishers'. There is continual revision from one edition to another. Biographies are brought up to date, new ones are added, while the biographies of those who no longer perform are weeded out. Since the 9th edition an index has been provided for these non-performers, referring back to the last edition in which their biography appeared. In the first instance, material is obtained by questionnaire from the subject of the biography, but apparently the editor does check information independently.

III. GENERAL WORKS

THE majority of books listed below provide a general background to the ballet; other books and articles touch on the social and economic aspects of ballet in this country and the continual effort to maintain aesthetic and technical standards.

Ballet has grown from a narrowly based, exclusive entertainment to one which is reasonably popular and which may be enjoyed at regular intervals over a wide area of the country. Backed by private funds at first, it is now subsidized to a large extent by public money.

With the growth of native ballet companies and an interested audience went the growth of ballet clubs, a link between the professional and the amateur. Between 1936 and 1946 many of these clubs were formed in such contrasting towns as Manchester, Liverpool, Bala, Oxford and Cambridge (the universities), Blackburn, Burnley, Edinburgh, Bristol, and Swindon (based on the Public Library). The London Ballet Circle was founded in 1946. A. H. Franks in *Dancing as a career* published 1963 (*see* no. 154) lists, in an appendix on ballet clubs, 30 places which support a ballet club, while G. B. L. Wilson in the second edition of his *Dictionary of ballet*, 1961 (*see* no. 34) estimates that there are approximately 60 in being. Activities vary. All appear to provide lectures, demonstrations, the showing of films, and the like. Some of the more ambitious clubs put on their own entertainments; the Rudolf Steiner Hall has been taken over by one or several clubs for performances on several occasions. They draw on local dancing and possibly choreographic talent, and sometimes bring in professionals to dance the major roles and stage repertory ballets. *The Dancing Times* carries information on these activities and also reviews productions. In 1947 the Association of Ballet Clubs was formed. It acts as 'an information centre for all ballet clubs . . . and maintains links with similar organizations abroad'.[1] In April 1959 the first weekend course was arranged. Otherwise activities are much the same as those of individual ballet clubs.

Similar societies are attached to particular theatres or companies. The three main societies for ballet in this country are the Vic-Wells Association, The Friends of Covent Garden and The Friends of Festival Ballet. The Vic-

---

[1] *Ballet in Britain*, edited by P. Brinson, 1962, p. 132.

Wells Association was formed in 1923 by Lilian Baylis. Lectures, visits and holiday tours are arranged and a library is maintained at the Old Vic and the Sadler's Wells theatres. The Friends of Covent Garden was initiated in 1962 to 'augment the resources at the disposal of the Royal Opera House and . . . consolidate its support from the general public . . . such an organization can subsidize students' tickets, arrange auditions, offer prizes and scholarships, assist new composers, choreographers, and stage designers and make possible the production of ballets and operas which may not be certain of immediate commercial success'.[2] This association also sponsors lectures, demonstrations and open rehearsals for members and special performances for the young which are shared with Youth and Music. The Friends of Festival Ballet fulfils a similar purpose.

Ballet is an expensive art. Today it is very difficult, if not impossible, for any company to survive without grants from public funds or charitable foundations. The Arts Council is the body through which public grants are made. It is advised by a special sub-committee for opera and ballet. The Royal Ballet benefits through the grant received by the Royal Opera House. In the 1962/3 period the total amount given to the Opera House was £670,000 and in 1963/4 £811,963.[3] Other ballet companies assisted in 1964 were Ballet Rambert, Western Theatre Ballet and recently Festival Ballet. Two other sources of financial aid are the British Council and the Gulbenkian Foundation. The British Council arranges foreign tours and guarantees deficits to a certain sum. The Gulbenkian Foundation also patronizes ballet, and has, for example, allotted grants to the Western Theatre Ballet and the Institute of Choreology.

A continual supply of well-trained dancers is as necessary for the well-being of a ballet company as adequate financial support, and from this it follows that there must also be a supply of well-trained teachers. There are three bodies in the United Kingdom whose main concern is to do this. The first to be formed, in 1904, was the Imperial Society of Teachers of Dancing, whose interest is in all types of dancing. The headquarters is in London and there are branches in the Commonwealth. An affiliated body is the Cecchetti Society which came into being in 1922 under the guidance of Cyril Beaumont. The aim was to continue the method of teaching devised by the great Italian teacher, Enrico Cecchetti. In 1924 the Cecchetti Society joined forces with the Imperial Society, although retaining independence of action. It sponsors

---

[2] *Royal Opera House, Covent Garden: Annual Report* 1961–2, p. 3.
[3] *Royal Opera House, Covent Garden: Annual Report* 1963–4, p. 31.

a choreographic competition, the Cyril Beaumont Scholarship and the Mabel
Ryan awards for juniors and seniors.

In 1920 the Association of Operatic Dancing was formed. The name was
changed to the Royal Academy of Dancing in 1936, when a Royal Charter
was granted. The founders were Philip J. S. Richardson and Edouard
Espinosa. Its aim is to improve ballet dancing in the United Kingdom and the
Commonwealth, and to lay down a definite standard of teaching. The Royal
Academy of Dancing allots various scholarships and awards, among them
four for overseas students worth £200 each; two for Australia, one for New
Zealand and one for South Africa. It is also responsible for the Queen
Elizabeth Coronation Award, presented annually to one who has given out-
standing service to British ballet. In 1947 a Residential Teachers' Training
Course was inaugurated and a Production Club formed. Demonstrations,
lectures and classes are arranged, too. In 1930 Edouard Espinosa broke away
from the Royal Academy of Dancing to form the British Ballet Organization. All these societies set their own syllabus and examinations.

This country has been fortunate in the number of foreign dancers who
have strengthened British teaching. The majority were Russians who left
their country during the Revolution. Pavlova, Nicolas Legat, Astafieva,
Karsavina, Kyasht, Lopokova, Grigoriev and Tchernicheva, Volkova – all
these famous dancers have helped to raise standards by the example of their
virtuosity or by their actual teaching, at a time when performance and
teaching were at a low level here. Some have contributed or are contributing
more. Pavlova helped to create an audience, as well as teaching and accepting
English girls into her company. She also did something towards raising the
social standing of dancers. Lopokova gave encouragement to and danced for
the Camargo Society during its brief life, and for the Vic-Wells Ballet in its
early days. Russian tradition has been handed on to English companies by
former members of the Imperial Russian and Diaghilev companies. Tamara
Karsavina has produced ballets, and advised on the interpretation of individual roles and on ballets in which she performed in Russia. Lubov Tchernicheva and Serge Grigoriev have re-created Diaghilev ballets for the Royal
Ballet.

Others include Adeline Genée who set the highest standards in her
dancing. She was on the founding committee of the Royal Academy of
Dancing and was the first President, retiring in 1954. A new theatre named
after her was opened at East Grinstead, Sussex, in January 1967. The Italian
Enrico Cecchetti, already mentioned above, trained English dancers during

the years in which he had a school in London, and the Espinosa family, of Portuguese extraction, has provided three generations of dancers and teachers.

A public acknowledgement of the importance and discipline of ballet has recently come about. The Royal Academy of Dancing has announced that ballet has been accepted by the Associated Examining Board for the General Certificate of Education. The syllabus includes Part A, a written paper on The Historical Development of Ballet; Part B, a written paper on Stage Ballet and Theory; Part C, a project file; Part D, a practical test. (*The Dancing Times*, December 1966, p. 124.)

BIBLIOGRAPHY

Arrangement. 1. General. 2. Ballet Training and Education. 3. Children's Books. All 3 sections are arranged chronologically by date of publication.

59 HAWEIS, H. R. 'The parson, the play and the ballet.' *In: The Universal Review*, v. 1, no. 2, 15th June, 1888, pp. 248–64. 3 vignettes.
  Discusses whether clergymen should visit the theatre.

60 HEADLAM, STEWART D. The ballet. Verinder, 1894. 16 pp.
  A paper read to the Playgoers' Club, 3rd February, 1894, which argues that ballet should be regarded as a serious art. The author advocates an improvement in the social and financial status of English dancers and in the standard of criticism.

61 BRAHMS, CARYL, *ed.* Footnotes to the ballet. Davies, 1936. xx, 268 pp. front., 44 pl. 7s. 6d.
  First published 1936, there have been frequent reprints. Essays on aspects of the ballet, by specialists. 1. 'The Dancer', by Arnold Haskell; 2. 'The Choreography', by Caryl Brahms; 3a. 'The Score', by Basil Maine; 3b. 'Music and Action', by Constant Lambert; 4. 'The Décor and Costume', by Alexandre Benois; 5. 'The Role', by Lydia Sokolova; 6. 'Ballet and the Film', by Anthony Asquith; Appendix, 'The Ballet from the Front of the House', by R. C. Jenkinson.

62 HOWLETT, JASPER. Talking of ballet. Philip Allan, [1936]. 138 pp. 8 pl. 6s.
  Essays on the early days of English ballet, mainly the Vic-Wells Ballet.

63 DE VALOIS, NINETTE. Invitation to the ballet. John Lane, The
Bodley Head, 1953. 304 pp. front., 28 pl., bibliog. 21s.

> First published 1937; '. . . The reflections of an executant of the ballet',
> by the founder and first Director of the Royal Ballet (Introduction). In
> Parts 2 and 3 she discusses 'The Repertory Ballet'; in Part 4, the work of the
> ballet critic. She suggests books for 'The Ballet Lover's Library'. There are
> 36 illustrations on the plates.

64 COTON, A. V. A prejudice for ballet. Methuen, 1938. xxiii,
237 pp. front., 7 pl. 8s. 6d.

> Chapter 10, 'A Year's Achievements' (ballet activities in London in 1937).
> Critical notes are provided for the following English productions: *Les
> Patineurs*, *Wedding bouquet* and *Horoscope*, *Dark elegies*, *Checkmate*, and *Les
> Biches* and *The Beloved one* (performed by the Markova-Dolin Ballet). The
> author outlines the history of the latter company and the careers of the two
> dancers; mainly concerned with theories and the work of Russian companies.

65 HASKELL, ARNOLD LIONEL, *ed.* Ballet – to Poland. Black, 1940.
154 pp. front., 76 pl., illus. £5 5s. od.

> Included are 'A Chronology of the Ballet in England 1910–40', by Philip
> J. S. Richardson; 'Ballet and Musical Interpretation', by Constant Lambert;
> 'War, Ballet and National Culture', by A. L. Haskell. The sketches on the
> 12 plates in the text are contributed by several artists. Appended is an album
> of reproductions of photographs (91 on 64 plates), by Gordon Anthony,
> 'Baron' and Merlyn Severn, among others. The 31 illustrations and 'decora-
> tions' in the text are by Kay Ambrose.

66 HASKELL, ARNOLD LIONEL. 'The British ballet.' *In: Britain To-day*,
no. 19, 19th January, 1940, pp. 8–12. 2 pl.

67 FORD, BORIS. 'A plea for English ballet.' *In: Scrutiny*, v. 10, no. 2,
October 1941, pp. 182–9.

> Discusses the need for informed ballet criticism as an aid to the Sadler's
> Wells Ballet in shaping its policy, and for linked activity between the
> arts.

68 'DANCE CRITIC.' 'English ballet finds a patron.' *In: Penguin New
Writing, 17.* April–June 1943, pp. 129–38. 2 pl.

> C.E.M.A. as patron; Jooss Company; Ballet Rambert; Sadler's Wells
> Ballet.

69   EVANS, EDWIN. 'Ballet in Britain.' *In: Britain Today*, no. 93, January
      1944, pp. [10]–14. 6 pl.

70   ARTS COUNCIL OF GREAT BRITAIN.   Annual Report, 1945/6–.

Short reports on the activities of ballet companies subsidized by the Arts
Council are made annually. The Royal Ballet and the Ballet Rambert appear
from the 1st report (1945/6); the Sadler's Wells Theatre Ballet from the
3rd (1947/8); Western Theatre Ballet from the 14th (1958/9); the Ballets
Minerva and Harlequin Ballet from the 21st (1965/6). The retirement of
Dame Ninette de Valois from the directorship of the Royal Ballet is noted
in the 18th report. The St. James Ballet Company is mentioned briefly from
the 4th report (1948/9) to the 5th (1949/50). This company was formed by
the Arts Council under the directorship of Alan Carter. There are also
separate reports for Scotland and Wales. A detailed statement of accounts is
included in each report.

71   LEEPER, JANET. English ballet. Harmondsworth, Penguin Books,
      1945. [36] pp. 16 pl., (col.) illus. (King Penguin Series.) 2s.

Very brief but satisfactory introduction. The plates are the main interest,
reproducing costume designs and settings of English ballets.

72   AMBROSE, KAY. Ballet impromptu: variations on a theme. Golden
      Galley Press, [1946]. [96] pp. front. (col.), 7 pl. (col.), illus. 25s.

Sketches, some in colour wash, and comments including 'Twenty Years
of Ballet Rambert', 'Sketching from Action' and 'The Sadler's Wells Ballet'.
There are also reproductions of 69 photographs.

73   'Ballast for ballet: an aesthetic problem.' *In: The Times*, 12th July,
      1946, p. 8.

Discusses the need for the more serious type of ballet in general terms,
giving examples from English ballets.

74   HASKELL, ARNOLD LIONEL.   Balletomania: the story of an obsession.
      Gollancz, 1946. 350 pp. 48 pl., illus. 18s.

First published 1934.
In Chapter 10 the author gives his impressions and opinions of English
ballet in its early days, with a brief account of the Camargo Society, of which
he was a founder member.

75   HASKELL, ARNOLD LIONEL. The making of a dancer, and other papers

on the background to ballet. Black, 1946. 96 pp. front. (col.),
8 pl. 8s. 6d.

Originated in lectures to widely diverse audiences on a tour sponsored by
the Royal Academy of Dancing. The lectures were taken down in shorthand
and minimum alterations were made for the printed text. The first chapters,
'The Making of a Dancer' and 'What is Ballet', are followed by separate
chapters on the relationship of ballet to music, drama, the scenic artist and
the choreographer. The final chapter deals with ballet clubs followed by
'Any Questions'. There are 12 illustrations on plates.

76 TURNER, WALTER JAMES. English ballet. Collins, 1946. [48] pp.
12 pl. (8 col.), illus., bibliog. (Britain in Pictures: the British People
in Pictures Series). 4s. 6d.

Touches on the origins of English ballet, the elements of ballet, the male
dancer, ballet training and technique and the Sadler's Wells Company.
7 of the coloured plates reproduce décors. The bibliography contains 10
items.

77 WILLIAMSON, AUDREY. Contemporary ballet. Rockliff, 1946. xi,
184 pp. front., 62 pl. 21s.

Chapters 10–17, 'The English Scene'. The first 5 chapters deal with the
Sadler's Wells Ballet and the work of Ninette de Valois, Frederick Ashton
and Robert Helpmann for this company, followed by 'Fokine and the
English Ballet', 'Ballet Rambert' and 'Ballets Jooss'.
Chapters 1–9, 'General Aspects' and Chapters 18–20 'Ballet and the Future'.
There are 68 reproductions of photographs on plates.

78 HALL, FERNAU. Ballet. The Bodley Head, 1947. 79 pp. 2s. 6d.

'All branches of the theatre did well during the war; but the rapid growth
of interest in ballet was something un-paralleled in British theatrical history.'
Part 1 tells 'The Story up to Now', and Part 2 describes the situation at the
time of writing.

79 HASKELL, ARNOLD LIONEL. Prelude to the ballet: an analysis and a
guide to appreciation. Nelson, 1947. viii, 119 pp. illus.

'I have attempted here a practical guide to the appreciation of ballet as an
art' (Author). Appended is 'A Brief Chronological Summary of Ballet
History' and 'Glossary of Technical and Semi-Technical Terms'. Illustrations
are by Mstislav Doboujinsky.

80 SCHOLES, PERCY A. The mirror of music 1844–1944: a century of
musical life in Britain as reflected in the pages of the 'Musical Times'.

V. I. Novello and Oxford University Press, 1947. xix, 523 pp. front., 74 pp. 52s. 6d.

2 vv. 6, 'Music in the Theatre', traces 'national fluctuations of taste in opera and ballet' (ballet, pp. 264–6). I plate illustrates this section.

81 WALKER, KATHRINE SORLEY. Brief for ballet. The Pitfield Publishing Company, 1947. xx, 146 pp. front. (col.), 35 pl. (3 col.), bibliog. 10s. 6d.

In Part 3, 'Contemporary British Ballet', the author, at that time 'archivist to the London Archives of the Dance' (Foreword), covers the repertoire of the Sadler's Wells Ballet and Ballet Rambert for the period about 1930–47. The foreword is by C. W. Beaumont. The bibliography contains 35 items arranged by period or company. The frontispiece and 3 colour plates are by Sylvia Green, and the reproductions of photographs 'have been chosen to cover Parts 1 and 3 of the text'.

82 CHAPPELL, WILLIAM. Studies in ballet. Lehmann, 1948. 158 pp. front., 22 pl., illus. 15s.

Essays on a variety of subjects – choreography; *Giselle*; the Romantic Ballet; The Sadler's Wells Ballet; training; the ballet public; ballet costume and design; '*Pas de trois*' (Tamara Karsavina, Pearl Argyle, Margot Fonteyn). As well as reproductions of photographs on plates, there are line drawings by the author in the text.

83 MELVIN, DUNCAN. Background to ballet. Lantern Publication, [c. 1948]. 48 pp. illus., bibliog. 2s. 6d.

Very slight. Touches on English ballet, and some dancers and ballets. The bibliography lists 12 titles, with a note on Cyril Beaumont.

84 STOREY, ALAN. Arabesques. Newman Wolsey, 1948. [152] pp. 8 pl. 12s. 6d.

The central point of this historical survey is 'a summary of Noverre's life and an analysis of his letters', with chapters on the masque, Romantic Ballet, Petipa, Fokine and Massine. In Chapter 10 the theories and ballets of Robert Helpmann (*Adam Zero, Hamlet, Miracle in the Gorbals*), Kurt Jooss and Antony Tudor (*Dark elegies, Jardin aux lilas, Romeo and Juliet, Undertow*) are discussed. Appendix A, '*The Fairy queen*', deals with the 1946 Covent Garden production. There are 17 illustrations on plates reproducing photographs and prints. No index.

85 TENENT, ROSE. There's money in dancing. Southern Editorial Syndicate, 1948. 112 pp. front., 12 pl. 6s.

Chapter 5, 'Let's Talk of Ballet'; Chapter 1, 'What are the Prospects' (including ballet). 'Is there any Money in it, and, if so, How Best Can I Become Professional?' The author sets out to answer this question for all types of dancing. Superseded by A. H. Franks' *Dancing as a career*, 1963 (*see* no. 154).

86 WILLIAMSON, AUDREY. Ballet renaissance. Golden Galley Press, 1948. 163 pp. front., 48 pl. 15s.

Consists of periodical articles and reviews, which appeared in *The Ballet, Bandwagon, The Dancing Times, New Theatre* and *Theatre World*. They are 'substantially unaltered, but . . . several "cuts" made originally for reasons of space' have been restored. Period covered is 1945-7, and arrangement is chronological. Articles are grouped as follows – 'General Vistas'; 'Ballet in Performance' (English and foreign companies in London, mainly); 'Books, Exhibitions and Films'.

87 WILSON, GEORGE BUCKLEY LAIRD. 'Ballet clubs.' *In: The Ballet Annual 1948*, 2nd issue, p. 157–60.

88 BEAUMONT, CYRIL WILLIAM.   Dancers under my lens: essays in ballet criticism. The Author, 1949. vii, 160 pp. front., 13 pl. 18s.

Originally printed in *Ballet, Dancing World* and *Dance Journal*, 1922–48. Includes criticisms of performances by The Camarge Society, The Ballet Club and Ballet Rambert, Sadler's Wells Ballet and International Ballet.

89 MANCHESTER, PHYLLIS WINIFRED *and* MORLEY, IRIS.   The rose and the star: ballet in England and Russia compared. Gollancz, 1949. 95 pp. 32 pl. 16s.

'. . . It is the purpose of this discussion to find out where . . . affinities exist and where the two Ballets differ.' (Introduction.) Presented as a conversation between the authors. Contents – Introduction; Training; Repertoire; The Classical Ballets; Criticism; Conclusion. Plates contain 53 reproductions of photographs of ballets. Those of the Russians were taken by Iris Morley, during performances in Russia.

90 'BARON', *photographer*. 'Baron', at the ballet. Collins, 1956. 222 pp. front. (col.), 6 pl. (col.), illus. 30s.

Reprint; first published 1950. Similar are *'Baron' encore* (1952) and *'Baron's' ballet finale* (1958), both published by Collins at 42s. Arnold Haskell wrote an introduction and commentary to each, and saw the last title through the press after the death of 'Baron', who was one of the leading ballet photographers. In these 3 books he ranged widely over companies and dancers with photographs, mainly posed, of a high quality. The first volume contains a series on the Sadler's Wells Ballet's *Giselle*, 'A Gallery of British Portraits' and Ballet Rambert; the second a series on Sadler's Wells Theatre Ballet, Sadler's Wells Ballet and Festival Ballet; the third a series on Markova, Festival Ballet and pre-war Sadler's Wells Ballet. The first 2 volumes contain about 280 reproductions of photographs and the last about 200.

There are other collections of photographic reproductions which cover European ballet, if not farther afield, in much the same way. The quality of the photography is usually good, but there are wide variations in layout, choice of material and presentation. Serge Lido, of much the same standing as 'Baron', has produced several volumes, viz., *Ballet 1–5* (Paris, Art et Industrie, 1951–5); *Ballet 6–9* (Black, 1956–9, 35s.–45s.); *Ballet panorama* (Black, 1961, 63s.).

Other such publications include *Dancers of the world*, by Gordon Anthony (Phoenix House, 1952, 4s. 6d.), *Ballet in colour* (Batsford, 1959, 12s. 6d. – the colour is of poor quality) and *Beauty of ballet* (Parrish, 1961, 35s.). The last two have introductions by Arnold Haskell.

91 HALL, FERNAU. Modern English ballet: an interpretation. Melrose, [1950]. 340 pp. front., 30 pl. 20s.

'To understand its post-war trends we must examine the development of English ballet from its beginnings against the background of the great ballet tradition' (Introduction). Part 1, 'International Background'; Part 2, 'English Ballet', including chapters on the audience and on ballet clubs; and Part 3, 'Ballet in Collaboration', i.e. ballet in films, opera, musicals. . . . Appended is 'A Chronology of English Ballet (1926–48)'. There is an 'Index of Ballets, Dances, Operas, Masques, Plays, Films, etc.' and a general index. The 85 illustrations on plates are mainly photographic reproductions of scenes from ballets, occasionally of individual dancers.

92c HASKELL, ARNOLD LIONEL. Going to the ballet. Phoenix House, 1957. 124 pp. front., 32 pl. (Excursions Series for Young People). 7s. 6d.

Reprint. First published 1950; also published in America as *How to enjoy ballet*, Morrow, 1951, and by Penguin Books in 1954 at 2s. 6d., in their Puffin Story Book Series.

A simple introduction for children, in which the contribution of the dancer and choreographer is discussed; also music, and mime and acting in ballet. Appended – 'Some Ballet Terms and What They Mean' and 'Some Ballets for You to See', arranged initially by company.

93 NOBLE, PETER, *ed.* British ballet. Skelton Robinson, [c. 1950]. 358 pp. 48 pl., illus., bibliog. 21s.

Packed with information. Articles on such topics as 'English Ballet Clubs'; 'The Royal Academy of Dancing'; 'British Choreography and its Critics'; 'The Success of our National Ballet Analysed'. British companies, dancers, choreographers and designers are discussed by 16 contributors who include Cecil Beaton, C. W. Beaumont, Sir Arthur Bliss, Lionel Bradley, William Chappell, A. V. Coton, Arnold Haskell and Robert Helpmann. The reference section lists ballet companies, choreographers, designers, composers, teachers and English periodicals. Plates carry nearly 90 reproductions of photographs portraying dancers and scenes from ballets, and there are 6 sketches by Sheila Graham. No index. (*See also* nos. 10 and 55.)

94 SWINSON, CYRIL WILLIAM, *ed.* Dancers and critics. Black, 1950. 80 pp. front., 12 pl. 7s. 6d.

Included are 'Beryl Grey', by A. V. Coton, 'Robert Helpmann', by Audrey Williamson, and 'Alicia Markova', by A. H. Franks.

A number of critics were invited to contribute their views on criticism and 'to apply what they said to a dancer of their choice'. The restricted space may account for the failure of the majority to fulfil this purpose. The best essay is by Cyril Beaumont.

95 WILLIAMSON, AUDREY. 'Drama in ballet.' *In: The Ballet Annual 1950*, 4th issue, pp. 110–16.

96 BEATON, CECIL. Ballet. Wingate, [1951]. [86] pp. 64 pl., illus. 15s.

The author's impressions of ballet, as spectator, designer and photographer, including his collaboration, as designer, with Frederick Ashton on the ballets, *Apparitions, Les Sirenès* and *Les Illuminations*.

97 HASKELL, ARNOLD LIONEL. In his true centre: an interim autobiography. Black, 1951. 328 pp. front., 15 pl. 21s.

The author, besides being a writer and critic on ballet, was formerly Director of the Royal Ballet School. This autobiography contains much concerning his experiences and reminiscences of the English ballet scene particularly the Sadler's Wells Ballet and School in Part 2.

98 FRANKS, ARTHUR HENRY. Approach to the ballet. 2nd ed. Pitman, 1952. xiii, 337 pp. front., illus. 30s.

First published 1948.

Chapter 7, 'The English Companies' includes the Sadler's Wells Ballet, Ballet Rambert, International Ballet, Anglo-Polish Ballet and Pauline Grant Ballet; Chapter 9, 'A Review of some Important Ballets', discusses work by

the following English choreographers – Ashton, de Valois, Gore, Helpmann, Howard and Inglesby; also the classics and Fokine and Massine ballets; Chapter 11, 'The Literary Aspect', discusses books and periodicals in English listing some of the more important works; also, briefly, criticism in newspapers.
'I have sought to provide an introduction and to stimulate ideas.' (Author's Preface.)

99 KARSAVINA, TAMARA. 'On the interpretation of great parts.' *In: The Adelphi*, v. 29, no. 1, November 1952, pp. 12–18.

Mainly the interpretation of the character of Giselle, with comments on the Firebird and the Girl in *Spectre de la rose*.

100 BUCKLE, RICHARD. The adventures of a ballet critic. Cresset Press, 1953. viii, 296 pp. front., 22 pl., illus. 21s.

Reminiscences from end of 1945 to 1952, by the founder and editor of the periodical *Ballet*, published January 1946–October 1952. Richard Buckle was ballet critic of *The Observer* (1948–55) and has been ballet critic of *The Sunday Times* since 1960. He gives his impressions and opinions of ballet, mainly in London, performed by native and foreign companies. There are 43 illustrations. All the plates and sketches in the text are by David Thomas.

101 HALL, FERNAU. An anatomy of ballet. Melrose, 1953. 470 pp. front., 46 pl., illus. 30s.

The Introduction has material on dancers visiting London up to 1875, and on John Weaver. Part 2, 'Types of Choreography', includes Frederick Ashton, John Cranko, Ninette de Valois, Frank Staff and Antony Tudor. Part 3, 'Types of Ballet Company in the Twentieth Century', includes Markova-Dolin Ballet, Festival Ballet, International Ballet, the two Sadler's Wells Companies, Dance Theatre and London Ballet, Ballet Club and Ballet Rambert, and Margaret Barr's Dance Drama Group.
Material on English ballet has been curtailed as this subject has been dealt with in the author's *Modern English ballet* (*see* no. 91). The author has very definite views about future development of ballet and there is a certain bias. Drawings in the text are by Milein Cosman, Shiavax Chavda, Schadown and from *Traité élémentaire . . .* by Carlo Blasis. The 84 illustrations on plates are of dancers and ballets.

102 WILLIAMSON, AUDREY. The art of ballet. 2nd rev. ed. Werner Laurie, 1953. 158 pp. front., 34 pl. 18s.

First published 1950 by Elek.
In Chapters 6 and 7 some 35 English ballets are discussed; those treated in greatest detail are *Job, The Rake's progress, Miracle in the Gorbals, Checkmate,*

Adam Zero, Nocturne, Don Juan, The Prospect before us and *Pineapple Poll;* also 'An Ashton Progression' in Chapter 8.

Contents are – 'Dancing and the Dancer', 'The Foundations of Choreography', 'Music and the Ballet', 'The Function of the Designer', 'Classical Ballet', 'Modern Dance Drama', 'Comedy in Ballet', 'Abstract & Symphonic Ballet' and 'Other Frontiers'. Appended is 'A Brief Glossary of Ballet Terms'.

103   'As others see us.'   *In: The Ballet Annual 1955,* 9th issue, pp. 85–93.

1. A French view, by Olivier Merlin. 2. An American view, by John Martin. 3. A Danish view, by Svend Kragh-Jacobsen.

104   CROSLAND, MARGARET.   Ballet carnival: a companion to ballet. Arco, 1955. xii, 408 pp. front., 46 pl., illus. 21s.

There are 4 parts – 1. 'The People' (very brief biographical sketches, approximately half pertinent to English ballet); 2. 'The Stories' narrates the plot of about 160 ballets, approximately one-third created by English choreographers; 3. 'The Vocabulary'; 4. 'The Music', lists L.P. records arranged alphabetically by the name of the ballet, but does not claim to be exhaustive.

105   DE VALOIS, NINETTE. 'Arnold Haskell, C.B.E.'   *In: The Ballet Annual 1955,* 9th issue, p. 42.

106   FRANKS, ARTHUR HENRY, *ed.*   Ballet: a decade of endeavour.   Burke, 1955. 223 pp. 32 pl. 18s.

In Part 2, 'The Director Speaks', Marie Rambert writes on the Ballet Rambert, Ninette de Valois on Sadler's Wells Ballet and Anton Dolin on Festival Ballet. Part 1, 'The Scene' and Part 3, 'Dancers of Today and To-morrow' both include sections on England; the first by A. H. Franks, the second by Caryl Brahms. Other parts are as follows – 4. 'The Allied Arts', 5. 'Ballet in Two Dimensions' (cinema and television) and 6. 'The Printed Word', by Mary Clarke. Chapter 17 (Part 6) deals mainly with English critics. Rather uneven in interest, depending on the quality of the contributor.

107   FRANKS, ARTHUR HENRY.   'Ballet and reality.'   *In: The Ballet Annual 1955,* 9th issue, pp. 94–5.

The author argues that choreographers should break away from tradition and base their ballets on contemporary life.

108   HASKELL, ARNOLD LIONEL.   Ballet: a complete guide to appreciation; history, aesthetics, ballets, dancers.   4th rev. ed.   Hardmondsworth,

Penguin Books, 1955. 211 pp. front., 24 pl., illus. (Pelican). 2s. 6d.

Originally published in 1938.

Chapter 6, 'The Architects of Contemporary Ballet', contains sections on Ninette de Valois, Marie Rambert and Frederick Ashton. Chapter 7, 'Appreciation: studies of some representative ballets', includes notes on *Job, The Rake's progress, Bar aux Folies Bergère, Checkmate, Façade, Les Patineurs, Les Rendezvous, Symphonic variations, Hamlet, Miracle in the Gorbals.*

Claimed to be the 'first complete guide to ballet', this is still one of the best introductions to the subject. The text changes from one edition to another, most noticeably in the commentary on ballets where current ones have been added and those no longer performed, withdrawn. Commentaries on individual dancers were included in previous editions; here, too, dancers included change with the edition, as do the plates. In the 4th edition there are 26 reproductions of photographs on plates. Illustrations in the text and explanatory drawings in the appended 'Illustrated Glossary of some Common Terms' are by Kay Ambrose.

109 POWELL, JEANETTE. 'Philip J. S. Richardson, O.B.E.: a birthday tribute.' *In: The Ballet Annual 1956*, 10th issue, pp. 46–50.

110 DE VALOIS, NINETTE. 'The English ballet.' *In: Journal of the Royal Society of Arts*, v. 105, no. 5016, 8th November, 1957, pp. 962–73.

Includes the discussion that followed the paper.

111 DE VALOIS, NINETTE. 'English male dancing.' *In: The Ballet Annual 1957*, 11th issue, pp. 95–6.

112 'Men as the dominant sex in English ballet. Redressing the balance of power.' *In: The Times*, 26th June, 1957, p. 5.

113 SELBY-LOWNDES, JOAN. How a ballet is produced. Routledge & Kegan Paul, 1958. xi, 145 pp. 8 pl., illus. (How . . . Series). 10s. 6d.

In 145 pages, the author attempts to describe for teenagers, a production of *The Sleeping beauty* by an imaginary company; much of the information (with some history of ballet and a discussion of general principles) is in the form of rather artificial dialogue. The Introduction outlines the plot, and is followed by chapters on planning, production, choreography, scenery, costumes, music, the dancers, the business side, the theatre and final rehearsals. Neither the 22 drawings nor their captions are particularly helpful.

114 TODD, JOHN M., *ed.*   The arts, artists and thinkers: an inquiry into the
place of the arts in human life. A symposium.   Longmans, Green,
1958. [x], 345 pp. 12 pl. 35s.

> In Part 2, 'The Witness of Artists', Mary Drage, a former member of the
> Royal Ballet, writes from the dancer's point of view; in Part 3, 'Criticizing
> the Arts', A. L. Haskell '[tries] to set out what the watching of dancing has
> given to one particular spectator'.
> This book was the product of a symposium held at Downside Abbey.

115 WILLIAMSON, AUDREY.   Ballet of 3 decades. Rockliff, 1958. xi,
192 pp. front., 30 pl. 25s.

> A commentary on performances over the period 1931 to 1957; mainly
> English ballet, but includes 1. 'Ballets Russes (1931-9)' and 4. 'Ballet from
> Abroad (1946-56)'.

116 'The subject matter of ballet: a symposium.'   *In: The Ballet Annual
1959*, 13th issue, pp. 38-49.

> Contributors – Frederick Ashton, Alexander Bland, Richard Buckle,
> Anton Dolin, A. H. Franks, Arnold L. Haskell, James Monahan, Marie
> Rambert, and Peggy van Praagh.

117 'Should a ballet tell a story? Leaps and lifts towards a national choreography.'   *In: The Times Literary Supplement*, 9th September, 1960,
p. 41. 2 illus.

> This article appears in a special supplement on *The British Imagination*.

118 SWINSON, CYRIL WILLIAM. Guidebook to the ballet. English
Universities Press, 1960.   192 pp.   24 pl., illus., bibliog. (Teach
Yourself Series). 7s. 6d.

> A good introduction to the subject. Chapter 15, 'Ballet in England';
> Chapter 17, 'A Miscellany of Ballets' (a chronological list of ballets by date
> of birth of choreographer, giving year of first production, title, composer,
> librettist and designer); Chapter 19, 'Books about Ballet'. (*See* no. 12.)

119c   The author, under the pseudonym 'Hugh Fisher', has also written a
> simpler version of the above, with the same pattern (first printed 1952, latest
> impression 1965) for the *Junior Teach Yourself* series, edited by Leonard Cutts,
> under the title *Ballet*.

120 BARNES, CLIVE, *and others*. Ballet here and now. Dobson, 1961.
[188] pp. front., 16 pl. 21s.

Edited by Susan Lester, a former ballet critic of *The Sunday Telegraph*. Clive Barnes is Assistant Editor of *Dance and Dancers*; the other authors are A. V. Coton, ballet critic of *The Daily Telegraph* and Frank Jackson, a 'theatrical journalist'. Susan Lester writes the introduction giving an outline history of ballet from the end of the nineteenth century. The authors are allotted 2 chapters each, in which they examine the finance, administration and artistic guidance of English ballet. In Chapter 5, 'Critics' Forum', the authors answer questions put by the editor arising out of the previous chapters. The approach is new and interesting, but rather disjointed in effect. 21 illustrations on plates portray mainly English companies.

121   FRANKS, ARTHUR HENRY. 'Paying the piper.'   *In: The Ballet Annual 1961*, 15th issue, pp. 88–93.

Subsidies.

122   ISAACS, J. 'The ballet and the critics.'   *In: The Listener*, v. 66, no. 1697, 5th October, 1961, pp. 505–7.   3 illus.

What the author expects from a good ballet critic.

123   BRINSON, PETER, *ed.*   The ballet in Britain: eight Oxford lectures. Oxford University Press, 1962.   xii, 148 pp. front., 16 pl., illus., bibliog.   21s.

Developed from a course of lectures arranged by Peter Brinson for the Delegacy of Extra-Mural Studies, Oxford University, during autumn 1960, it describes some practical achievements and problems as well as the historical background. The introduction by Ninette de Valois is an extended version of a lecture given by her to the Royal Society of Arts in 1957. The following chapters are contributed by eminent specialists, 'The Social Setting', by Peter Brinson (historical survey); 2. 'The English School of Ballet' and 3. 'The Education of a Dancer', by Arnold Haskell; 4. 'The Education of a Choreographer', by Marie Rambert; 5. 'Reflections on British Ballet Music', by William Cole (with music examples); 6. 'Problems of Ballet Design', by William Chappell; 7. 'Folk Dance and Ballet', by Douglas Kennedy; 8. 'The Ballet in National Life', by Peter Brinson (comments on trends described in previous chapters and pleads for a greater realization of the part which ballet among the other arts can play in the life of the nation). Appendices: 1. 'Note on Extra-Mural Departments offering Ballet Lectures'; 2. 'Archives, Teaching Organizations and Ballet Clubs'; 3. 'Notes on Illustrations' (of which there are 43). The bibliography contains 40 items. 5 drawings are by William Chappell.

124C   CROSLAND, MARGARET. The young ballet lovers' companion.

Souvenir Press, 1962. 128 pp. 12 pl., illus. (The Young Companion Series). 15s.

A general introduction for children, including advice on how ballet may be studied in the British Isles, both by the amateur and the child who wishes to be a professional. This information was 'compiled with the help of the Royal Academy of Dancing, The Royal Ballet School and the Education Department of the London County Council'. (Publisher's statement.) A glossary is appended. There are 11 line-drawings which add little to the text and 20 illustrations on plates of scenes from ballets and of dancers.

125 HASKELL, ARNOLD LIONEL. 'The meaning of ballet.' *In: The British Journal of Aesthetics*, v. 2, no. 3, July 1962, pp. 259–63.

126 DE VALOIS, NINETTE. 'Ballet is my life.' *In: The Sunday Telegraph*, 17th November–1st December, 1963. Illus.

Part 1. '... Survey of the problems facing British Ballet'. (17th November, pp. 4, 5.) Part 2. What Makes a Dancer. (24th November, p. 8.) Part 3. You Can't Ignore the Public. (1st December, p. 23.)

127 DE ZOETE, BERYL. The thunder and the freshness. Spearman, 1963. 160 pp. 8 pl. 18s.

A posthumous collection of periodical articles, essays and talks. Those on English ballet are – 'The Strawberry underneath the Nettle'. Privately printed, 1953 (Ballet Rambert). 'Frederick Ashton', *Horizon*, 1942. 'The British Choreographers', *Penguin New Writing*, 1945. 'English Ballet in Wartime,' *Penguin New Writing*, 1943. 'English Ballet Finds a Patron', *Penguin New Writing*, 1943. 'Ballet in England.' 3 radio talks on the B.B.C. service to the Far East. (1, 'Introductory Talk', 1947; 2, 'What is Choreography?', 1947; 3, 'Influences on Post-War Ballet', 1948.)

128 ELLIS, DAVID. 'Some problems of touring ballet.' *In: The Ballet Annual 1963*, 17th issue, pp. 94–103.

The author is an Associate Director of Ballet Rambert.

129 WALKER, KATHRINE SORLEY. Eyes on the ballet. Methuen, 1963. [160] pp. front., illus., bibliog. 25s.

A sensible introduction, giving the usual type of information but with an unusual slant, for this book 'talk(s) about ... the audience ... what we are; and what we do and should do, and how we behave'. Part 4, 'Sharing the Ballet' covers ballet clubs, lectures, exhibitions and collecting material.

G. B. L. Wilson considers that the author has devoted 'much of her reminiscence and her comment to the Sadler's Wells Ballet' and has done 'less than justice' to other companies. (*The Dancing Times*, August 1963, p. 651.) The bibliography contains 30 unannotated items and there are about 37 reproductions of photographs.

130   BARNES, CLIVE. 'Ballet outside London.'   *In: The Ballet Annual* [*1964*], 18th issue, pp. 61–6.

131   BARNES, CLIVE. 'Ballet – plot or not?'   *In: About the House*, v. 1, no. 7, June 1964, pp. 32–3.

132   HASKELL, ARNOLD LIONEL.   Ballet retrospect.   Batsford, 1964.   172 pp.   front., 6 pl. (col.), illus.   45s.

Chapter 4, 'The New Ballet in England, France and America'. Uses material from the author's *Ballet panorama* (3rd rev. ed., 1948). A history of ballet, with chapters on criticism, the dancer as technician and artist, education through ballet, the social dance and ballet in films and television. Appended is 'A Brief Chronology'. About 130 illustrations reinforce the text.

133   GIBBONS, T. H.   'The Reverend Stewart Headlam and the emblematic dancer: 1877–94.'   *In: The British Journal of Aesthetics*, v. 5, no. 4, October 1965, pp. 329–40.

'It would be idle to claim for Stewart Headlam the status of an aesthetician of the dance: the major purpose of describing his activities has been to suggest that the poetry and the literary criticism of Arthur Symons, amongst others, may well be seen as part of a current and widespread interest in theatrical dancing' (p. 338).

134   GREGORY, JOHN.   Understanding the ballet: the steps of the dance from classroom to stage. . . .   Oldbourne, 1965.   124 pp.   illus., bibliog.   42s.

In 124 pages the author touches on several aspects of ballet – history, choreography, modern ballet, dance notation, the dancer. The 260 reproductions of photographs were by Mike Davis originally; those showing the technical steps were posed by Paula Rufina, a dancer with Harlequin Ballet. The 71 items in the bibliography give author, title, date of publication often, and the publisher sometimes. 'M.C.', reviewing the book in *The Dancing Times* (January 1966, p. 205), considers that the book falls 'between about half a dozen stools'.

135 HASKELL, ARNOLD LIONEL. What is a ballet? Macdonald, 1965.
     160 pp. 16 pl., bibliog. 16s.

> An introduction to the art. 'M.C.' considers that although some of the
> factual information is not correct 'the main body of the text is first rate'.
> (*The Dancing Times*, December 1965, p. 136.) The bibliography contains
> 29 items, and there are 20 reproductions of photographs on plates.

136 'Ensuring that British ballet has a prosperous future.' *In: The Times*,
     5th January, 1966, p. 5.

> Organization and financing of British ballet.

BALLET TRAINING AND EDUCATION

137 COOK, DUTTON. 'The Corps de ballet.' *In: Time*, March 1880,
     pp. [699]–707.

> Training and life of French and English dancers.

138 BEAUMONT, CYRIL WILLIAM. 'Cecchetti's legacy to the dance.' *In:
     Ballet Annual 1948*, 2nd issue, pp. 59–70. 2 pl., 4 illus.

> Also reprinted separately for the Cecchetti Society Branch, Imperial
> Society of Teachers of Dancing.

139 RICHARDSON, PHILIP J. S. 'Classical technique in England: its develop-
     ment under foreign teachers.' *In: The Ballet Annual 1948*, 2nd
     issue, pp. 118–25.

140 HELPMANN, ROBERT. 'How to become a ballet dancer.' *In: The
     Listener*, v. 41, no. 1055, 14th April, 1949, p. 611. 1 illus.

> Originally broadcast in the programme 'The Musician's world'.

141 GREGORY, JOHN. Light on a system of classical dance. The Federa-
     tion of Russian Classical Ballet, 1950. [16] pp. 2s. 6d.

> A lecture given at the Annual Conference of the National Association of
> Teachers of Dancing in July 1950. The author is Director of the School of
> Russian Ballet (London) and of the Harlequin Ballet Company. He bases his
> teaching on the Russian School 'finally devised by Christian Johansson and
> perfected by Nicolas Legat' who lived and taught in England from 1929 to
> 1937. Mr. Gregory endeavours 'to trace the growth of a tradition . . .

describe the finer points of the method and give some insight into the science and aesthetics of its classic form'.

142   HASKELL, ARNOLD LIONEL.   'Training for the ballet: superstition and reality.'   *In: The Adelphi*, v. 27, no. 1, November 1950, pp. 37–9.

143   SPARGER, CELIA.   'Physiotherapy at the Sadler's Wells School of Ballet.'   *In: Physiotherapy. Journal of the Chartered Society of Physiotherapy*, v. 38, no. 1, January 1952, pp. 8–13.   Illus.

144   IMPERIAL SOCIETY OF TEACHERS OF DANCING.   Golden Jubilee 1904–54. Imperial Society of Teachers of Dancing, [1954?].   15 pp.   2 pl.

A year-by-year chronology of the developing activities of the I.S.T.D.

145c   VAN PRAAGH, PEGGY.   How I became a ballet dancer.   Nelson, 1954. xi, 97 pp.   front., 6 pl.   (How I Became . . . Series).   5s.

The author has worked with the Royal Ballet as dancer, teacher and administrator. In Part 1, 'How I Became a Ballet Dancer', she writes of her early life and career so that children may know 'the kind of life they will lead' if they make ballet a career. Part 2, 'How You Become a Ballet Dancer', gives practical advice on choice of career, teacher and job.

146c   CAPON, NAOMI.   Dancers of tomorrow: the story of a girl's training at the Sadler's Wells School.   Leicester, Brockhampton Press, 1956. [95] pp.   32 pl., illus.   12s. 6d.

Based on the author's production of a B.B.C. television programme. Although written in fictional form it is based on fact. A student's career is followed through from her acceptance by the School to her first professional performance as a senior student. There are 51 illustrations on plates which are mainly from photographs.

147   CLARKE, MARY.   'Dancers – or people?'   *In: The Ballet Annual 1958*, 12th issue, pp. 84–[9].

Training and conditions of work of English dancers.

148   The Cecchetti Society: a 'Dancing Times' supplement prepared by the Cecchetti Society Branch of the Imperial Society of Teachers of Dancing. . . .   *The Dancing Times*, 1959.   16 pp.   illus.

A sketch of the main events in Cecchetti's life is followed by – 'A Class

with Cecchetti'; 'Codifying the Method'; 'The Cecchetti Society'. There is
also information on examinations; scholarships and scholarship classes; the
Choreographic Competition; The Summer School; overseas activities. The
illustrations are 21 photographs and 4 fascimiles.

149   FRANKS, ARTHUR HENRY. 'Bands of brothers or mostly sisters.' *In:*
     The Ballet Annual 1959, 13th issue, pp. 84–91.

     Dance Teachers' organizations.

150   STREATFEILD, NOEL. The Royal Ballet School. Collins, 1959.
     160 pp.   24 pl., illus.   18s.

     Part 2, 'The Royal Ballet School', begins on p. 77. There is a chapter on
the work of Ursula Moreton, Ailne Philips and Arnold Haskell for the school;
otherwise the book deals with routine and problems of the boarding school
at Richmond and the school for senior students in London. The title is misleading, for the first part of the book is concerned with ballet schools in
France, Italy and Russia, followed by chapters on 'Diaghilev', 'Dancing in
England' and 'The Camargo Society'. The 35 photographs on plates are by
Gabor Denes.

151   The Imperial Society: a 'Dancing Times' Supplement. *The Dancing
     Times*, 1960.   31 pp.   illus.

     This pamphlet was compiled from material supplied by the Imperial
Society of Teachers of Dancing. Information is given on the following
aspects of the Society – history; constitution; examinations; functions and
contests; *The Dance Journal*; history of and current information on the 11
branches of the Society; technical publications issued by the Society. 11 of
the illustrations are from photographs and 6 from drawings.

152   HASKELL, ARNOLD LIONEL. 'The Royal Ballet School: education for
     the dancer.' *In: The Yearbook of Education 1961*, ch. 9, pp. 461–6.

     Requirements of the school, curriculum, organization, problems.

153   DE MILLE, AGNES. To a young dancer: a handbook for dance stu-
     dents, parents and teachers.   Putnam, 1963.   [11], 170 pp.   front.,
     illus., bibliog.   16s.

     First published in the U.S.A. in 1962.
     Good advice for those who wish to become professional dancers, on such
themes as 'Preparation', The Dance Today', 'Professional Dancer', 'Preparation for Performance' and 'Choreography'. The author is the well-known
American choreographer and dancer, and details are geared to the American

scene. 32 titles are listed in 'Suggested Reading', some of which are not
directly concerned with dancing. Appendix 1 gives the repertoire of companies which have toured in the United States and Britain and Appendix 2,
77 Dance Films, is arranged initially by country, giving short description,
time length, date, library and size in millimetres. The illustrations are from
16 sketches by Milton Johnson.

154 FRANKS, ARTHUR HENRY. Dancing as a career. Batsford, 1963.
     120 pp. 8 pl., bibliog. (Batsford Career Books.) 12s. 6d.
>A practical guide by the late Editor of *The Dancing Times* and *The Ballroom
Dancing Times*. Includes chapters on 'So You want to be a Ballet Dancer?',
'Auditions and Agents', 'Training as a Teacher', 'Grants and Scholarships'
and 'A School of Your Own'. There are 8 appendices – Salaries; Periodicals;
Recommended Books for Students; Residential Schools; Examining Bodies;
Ballet Companies; Ballet Clubs; The Cost of Running a School. The
bibliography contains 30 items, about one-third concerned with ballet.

155 LESTER, SUSAN. Dancers and their world. Gollancz, 1965. 144 pp.
     bibliog. (. . . and their World Series.) 13s. 6d.
>' . . . Sets out to throw as much light as possible on careers in theatrical,
educational and therapeutic fields' (Preface, by Belinda Wright, p. 5).
Chapters on 'The Background of Classical Ballet'; 'Training for Classical
Ballet'; 'Dancers' Pay, Prospects, and Conditions'. Appended are 'Useful
Addresses' and 'Further Reading', (16 items).

Listed below is a selection of picturebook- and annual-type publications
for children. The contributors and editors of some of these are proved writers
on ballet. The better ones provide informative articles on history and technique as well as articles by and on dancers. Most are profusely illustrated, a
few entirely given over to illustration.

156c GRAY, F. The children's picture book of ballet. Phoenix House,
      1955. 6s. 6d.
>Contents – 'How Ballet Grew Up'; 'The Dancer's Job'; 'Dancing for
Boys and Dancing for Girls'; 'What is Ballet'.

157c CROWLE, PIGEON. Your book on ballet. Faber, 1958. (Your Book
      Series.) 9s. 6d.

158c STREATFEILD, N. Noel Streatfeild's ballet annual. Collins, [1959].
      10s. 6d.

'Two articles . . . otherwise given over to short fictional stories for the young teenager. Not enough in the book, about ballet.' (*Times Literary Supplement, Children's Book Supplement*, 4th December, 1959, p. xii.)

159c FRANKS, A. H., *ed.* Every child's book of dance and ballet. 2nd ed. Burke, 1961. 15s.

> Gives a practical approach, e.g. instruction for simple dances.

160c ROGERS, H. Ballet. Longacre Press, 1961. (Swift Picture Books Series.) 7s. 6d.

> Illustrations arranged to tell the story of 10 ballets, with captions.

161c FRANKS, A. H., *ed.* The Girl's book of ballet. 3rd rev. ed. Burke, 1962. 12s. 6d.

162c GOULDEN, S. Splendour book of ballet. W. H. Allen, 1962. (Splendour Books Series. No. 17.) 16s.

163c WINTER, G. L. The ballet book. Oldbourne, 1963. 9s. 6d.

> First published New York, Obolensky, 1962.

164c AUDSLEY, JAMES. The book of ballet. 2nd rev. ed. Warne, 1964. 10s. 6d.

> Chapters on history; famous ballets and dancers; the language of ballet.

165c DAVIS, MIKE, *ed.* 'Girl' new book of world ballet. 2nd ed. Odhams' 1964. 16s.

> Previous edition published in 1958 as *World ballet* and edited by A. L. Haskell. 1964 edition includes contributions by James Monahan, Margaret Dale, Joan and Rudolf Benesh, Grace Cone and A. V. Coton.

166c 'Princess' ballet book, no. 4. Fleetway, 1964. 12s. 6d.

IV. HISTORY TO 1920

DANCING was the pastime of aristocrats and common people from an early time, but although both classes performed the same dances at first, the court dance eventually developed from the folk dance, adapting and polishing until the origin was unrecognizable. Later the process was to be reversed and presumably borrowings were made in either direction all the time. Manuals of the art,[1] mainly French and Italian, have survived from the early fifteenth century. These enable experts to have some idea of the way in which dances were performed, but very little has been recorded in English. The earliest known reference is in Robert Copelande's French grammar published in 1521 in which he adds as an appendix, *Manner of dancynge bace daunces after the use of France*. In 1651, John Playford, a publisher, issued *The English dancing master*.[2] This provided the music for country dances and described the movement and steps. It was an extremely popular work which went into over thirty editions, and had several imitators.

The above is not irrelevant to the subject of this bibliography for it was from the technique of the social dance that ballet built up a virtuoso technique of its own. The masque, a court entertainment in England from about 1513–1640, and a predecessor of ballet incorporated dancing into its art. Edward Hall writes that 'on the daie of the Epiphanie at night, the Kyng [Henry VIII] with a xi other were disguised, after the maner of Italie, called a maske, a thyng not seen afore in Englande'.[3] He explains that the masquers wore long garments with 'visers and cappes' and that after the banquet they came in and invited ladies from among the spectators to dance and 'after thei daunced and commoned together, as the fashion of the Maske is thei took their leave'. This took place in 1513. In England masques were associated

---

[1] *See* Appendix A.

[2] M. Dean-Smith and E. J. Nicol have made a study of the editions of this work under the title of *The Dancing master 1651–1728* in v. 4, nos. 4, 5 and 6 (?) of the *Journal of the English Folk Song and Dance Society*, 1945.

[3] *Hall's Chronicle, containing The History of England, during the reign of Henry the fourth and the succeeding monarchs, to the end of the reign of Henry the Eighth, in which are particularly described the manners and customs of those periods carefully collated with the editions of 1548 and 1550.* . . . Printed for J. Johnson; F. C. and J. Rivington; T. Payne; Wilkii and Robinson; Longman, Hurst, Rees and Orme; Cadell and Davies; and J. Mawman. 1809. *In:* the third year, p. 526.

with the earlier entertainments of 'mumming' and 'disguising' and were to develop into a complex spectacle which reached its most accomplished form in the reign of James I.

No one seems to be prepared to define these terms exactly; indeed they appear to be interchangeable. The contemporary documents provide incomplete evidence but Paul Reyher, an authority on the English masque, considers that one of the main features of a 'mumming' was the silence of the participants. The disguised mummers would enter the hall 'unexpectedly', where the household was assembled, would challenge the host and his most distinguished guests to a game of dice or cards, would tactfully lose the game, present gifts to the winners, possibly dance and then withdraw, although Reyher considers that dancing was the exception, and Enid Welsford agrees with this opinion. A 'disguising' consisted of one or two groups of performers who concealed their identity. They would enter the hall, sometimes being drawn in on a 'car' and would dance. If there were two groups one would be composed of men, the other of women. Each of the sexes would dance separately, and then join together in a final dance. In both entertainments the participants were amateurs, sometimes members of the royal family and the court. Also, on the whole, they were separate from the spectators.

From the beginning of the sixteenth century the word masque gradually replaced the other two. In the early days it was difficult to pin down the essential character of the entertainment. E. K. Chambers considers that the costume used, a type of domino, he thinks, may have been the element that was 'after the maner of Italie' and never seen before in England. He points out that these costumes are described as 'long' in documents of the day. Masks were used too, to hide the face. The extract from Hall's *Chronicle* quoted above shows that the barriers between the masquers and the spectators had been broken down, for the masquers invited ladies to dance and *conversed* with them, and for a length of time this became a feature of the entertainment. This was the simple beginning but other elements were added. The masque continued to be performed during the reign of Queen Elizabeth I and was much favoured by James I's queen, Anne of Denmark. By now it had become a composite entertainment of dancing, music, speaking and towards the end singing, with elaborate scenery and costume. It could consist of any number of entries, each being introduced by a presenter who spoke to the audience. Social dances of the period had been employed in the 'mummings' and 'disguisings', and in the early masques, too, but by the end of the sixteenth century dances were being composed especially for the masquers; first one only, but in time more as this practice became popular. It was an honour to be invited to take part in the royal masques put on during the Christmas festivities and rehearsals were necessary in which some professionals took part. Inigo Jones designed scenery and costumes and Ben Jonson provided words for the actors; some other names connected with the Stuart masques were Francis Beaumont, Thomas Middleton, Samuel Daniel.

Antimasques were introduced on the suggestion of Anne of Denmark in order to provide a contrast to the grandeur of the rest of the entertainment. These included grotesque and comic interludes with country dances. Enid Welsford considers that the performance in 1609 of *The Masque of queens* was decisive in popularizing the inclusion of the antimasque. Charles I and Henrietta Maria continued the custom of creating masques, but the Civil War, culminating in the death of the king, put a stop to this type of entertainment, although attempts were made to revive it. For example William Davenant put on performances at Lincoln's Inn Field Theatre which were reminiscent of the masques but music was the most important element. Milton wrote a masque *Comus*, to be performed at Ludlow Castle but here the spoken word seems to have been the main interest. Conversely, in 1942, when Robert Helpmann created his ballet *Comus* based on Milton's work, the spoken word was represented by two speeches only. At this point it is interesting to note the first use of the word 'ballet' in the English language. In Dryden's *Essay on dramatic poesie* (1668), he describes a production as 'not a Balette or Masque, but a play'.

By the eighteenth century there were a group of well-known dancing masters, L'Abbé, Caverley, Pemberton, Isaac and others, based on London, who, not only taught social dancing, but also performed in the theatre and trained professional dancers. Kellom Tomlinson, one of the outstanding teachers, claimed in *The Art of dancing . . .* (1735) that John Shaw, a pupil of his, had done well on the stage; he also mentions a John Topham and Miss Francis. The most important man of the period was undoubtedly John Weaver, who began his career as a dancing master in Shrewsbury. He came to London and in 1702 produced *The Tavern bilkers* at Drury Lane which he claimed in his *History of mimes and pantomimes* (1728) was 'the first entertainment . . . where the Representation and the Story were carried on by Dancing Action, and Motion only was performed with Grotesque Characters after the Modern Italians such as Harlequin, Scaramouch, etc.' Thelma Niklaus[4] challenges Weaver's dating and asserts that in 1702 Weaver was at

[4] *Harlequin phoenix*, by T. Niklaus, 1956, pp. 134–5.

Lincoln's Inn Field Theatre and not at Drury Lane. Of much greater importance is *The Loves of Mars and Venus* staged in 1717. This has been claimed as
the first known *ballet d'action* in which the plot and the emotions of the
characters are portrayed by dancing and mime alone, accompanied by music.
John Weaver himself took the part of Vulcan, while Venus was Hester
Santlow and Mars, Louis Dupré. Weaver put on other ballets – *The Fable of
Orpheus and Eurydice* in 1718, *Perseus and Andromeda* in 1726 and *The Judgement of Paris* in 1732.

These activities might have laid the foundation for a tradition of ballet in
this country, but in fact the impetus petered out. London was a centre for
ballet, where Didelot put on many of his productions. There was a continuous tradition of ballet at the King's Theatre, Haymarket (called Her
Majesty's from 1838, and also known as the Italian Opera) and at Drury
Lane. Unfortunately foreign performers were allotted the main parts in the
productions. Foreign performers had, of course, been engaged during
Weaver's time to a certain extent. For example, Marie Sallé the French
ballerina had visited London as a child with her brother, performing dances
arranged by Kellom Tomlinson, and in the 1730's appearing in some of
Handel's operas. It was in London, too, that she tried out her attempted
reform in costume. Anne Cupis de Camargo, sister of the more famous
Marie, was another visitor and danced at Covent Garden and Drury Lane
between 1750 and 1754. In 1755 Noverre the French choreographer and
David Garrick agreed that Noverre should stage his *Métamorphoses Chinoises*
at Drury Lane. French dancers were engaged for this production, which was
not a great success.[5] However, Noverre visited London again in the 1780's
and put on ballets at the King's Theatre. English dancers were used mainly in
the corps de ballet but there were soloists such as the Misses Dennett, who
danced in London during the early nineteenth century. The movement of
dancers was not entirely one way, for Simon Slingsby, an Englishman, performed at the Opéra in Paris towards the end of the century.

In 1832 *La Sylphide* was first performed in Paris with Marie Taglioni in the
leading part. This introduced the era of the Romantic Ballet, of which possibly *Giselle* is the best known creation. The work of Jules Perrot at the
King's Theatre from 1842 to 1848 and productions at Drury Lane ensured
that London was still a centre for ballet, but the chief performers were still

---

[5] An account of the riots caused by this production, mainly for political reasons, is given in
The History of the theatres of London and Dublin from the year 1730 to the present time ... 1761.
pp. 131–6.

drawn from France and Italy. Benjamin Lumley had been connected with
the King's Theatre since 1836, becoming manager in 1842. He engaged the
famous ballerinas of the period, perhaps his greatest triumph being the *Pas de
quatre* danced by Taglioni, Cerrito, Grisi and Grahn in 1845 and arranged by
Perrot. Carlo Blasis, another great name of the Romantic Ballet, had danced
at the King's Theatre in 1827, and was the choreographer in 1847. Lumley
also attempted to found a school in order that he could obtain fresh dancers
for his theatre, but unfortunately this excellent idea came to nothing and in
1858 he withdrew from management. Drury Lane adopted the same policy
of engaging foreign personnel, but did at least encourage one native dancer,
Clara Webster, who was beginning to make a name for herself at the time of
her death in 1844 as the result of being burned during a performance.

After about 1850 the Romantic Ballet declined and in London public
interest turned to the opera. The main outlet for dancers appears to have been
the interludes of dancing in opera, until in 1871 the Alhambra Theatre and
in 1884 the Empire Theatre began to include short ballets in their variety
programmes. The Empire was fortunate in having Adeline Genée as ballerina from 1897 to 1907. She was extremely popular and helped to maintain
standards. After 1907, Topsy Sinden, Lydia Kyasht and Phyllis Bedells in
turn filled her place. Other names associated with the Empire Ballets were
Katti Lanner, Fred Farren and C. Wilhelm. The Alhambra relied on several
choreographers and among the dancers who appeared were Pierina Legnani,
Catherine Geltzer and Vasili Tikhomiroff. The costumes were designed by
Monsieur Alias and the musical director was Georges Jacobi.

Both theatres closed regular performances of ballet about the beginning of
the First World War, but by this time Diaghilev had brought his company to
London (1911) and some Russian dancers, including Anna Pavlova and
Lydia Kyasht, had appeared independently. Diaghilev's company and his
entire conception of ballet made a great impact and helped to revive an
interest in the art. The company made regular visits to London apart from
the period of the First World War; the last being in 1929, the year of
Diaghilev's death. C. W. Beaumont has written about these London seasons
in his book *The Diaghilev Ballet in London: a personal record* (2nd ed., 1951).
From 1912 Pavlova made London her base and performed there at intervals.
She spent a great deal of time in touring, but when in London would teach,
and also took English dancers into her company. One of these was Algeranoff,
who wrote of his experiences in *My years with Pavlova* (1957).

Apart from this there had been a revival of interest in all types of dancing during the period. For instance, Isadora Duncan's interpretation of the ancient classical dance had been admired, and in 1911 Cecil Sharp founded the English Folk Dance and Song Society. By the 1920's it was possible for ballet, previously a foreign importation, to take root in this country.

The following books were used in writing the Introduction to this section:

FRANKS, A. H.   Social dance: a short history.   Routledge and Kegan Paul, 1963.

GUEST, I.   The dancer's heritage: a short history of ballet.   Rev. ed. Harmondsworth, Penguin Books, 1962.

REYHER, P.   Les masques anglaises.   Paris, Librairies Hachette, 1909.

SWINSON, C. W.   Guidebook to the ballet.   English Universities Press, 1960.

WELSFORD, E.   The court masque.   New York, Russell and Russell, 1962.

WICKHAM, G.   Early English stages, 1300–1660.   V. 1 (1959) and v. 2, pt. 1 (1963).   Routledge and Kegan Paul.

BIBLIOGRAPHY

Arrangement.   1. Ballet in England to 1830. 2. The Romantic Ballet. 3. The Alhambra and Empire Ballets. 4. Surveys of more than one period. Within each division the arrangement is chronological by date of publication.

BALLET IN ENGLAND TO 1830

167   WEAVER, JOHN.   An essay towards an history of dancing, in which the whole art and its various excellencies are in some measure explain'd. Containing the several sorts of dancing, antique and modern, serious, scenical, grotesque, etc. . . .   Printed for Jacob Tonson, 1712.   [9], 2–172 pp.

In Chapter 7, 'Of the Modern Dancing', John Weaver discusses 'stage dancing'. The first 6 chapters deal with the advantages of dancing; objections to dancing and Weaver's answer; history of the ancient dance; mimes and pantomimes.

168   NOVERRE, JEAN GEORGES.   Letters on dancing and ballets.   Beaumont, 1930.   xiii, 169 pp.   front., 11 pl.   25s.

A translation by C. W. Beaumont of *Lettres sur la danse et sur les ballets*, first published in 4 vv. in 1760, 'printed in Lyon, and issued almost simultaneously in Lyon and Stuttgart' (Ivor Guest in *Ballet: an exhibition* . . . , 1957. *See* no. 7). A paperback reprint was issued by Dance Horizons, New York, 1966, at 28s. The above translation appeared first in *The Dancing Times*, in serial form, and has been revised with added notes for this translation. *Lettres sur la danse* . . . is a key work on the aesthetics of ballet-making. In it Noverre claimed that the plot of a ballet should be explicit and continually carried forward by the dancing without the aid of elaborate programme notes. This was the main reform, among others, that he advocated. An earlier

169   translation, *The Works of monsieur Noverre translated from the French*, London, 1783, in 3 vv., is listed in the British Museum Catalogue, but appears to have been mislaid (it was reported missing on application November 1965). A

170   biography of Noverre has been written by Deryck Lynham, *The Chevalier Noverre, father of modern ballet* (Sylvan Press, 1950, 21s.), in which is appended 'Some Scenarios of Noverre' and 'The Known Productions of Noverre'.

171   Charles Edwin Noverre, a descendant of Noverre's brother wrote a life, *The Life and works of the chevalier Noverre* published in 1882, too, for which he had 'access to family papers', (*Chevalier Noverre*, by D. Lynham . . . Preface, p. 9).

172 GALLINI, GIOVANNI-ANDREA. A treatise on the art of dancing. Printed for the author; and sold by R. and J. Dodsley . . . T. Becket, . . . and W. Nicholl, 1762. 292 pp.

On the title page, the author is described as Director of the dances at the Royal Theatre, Haymarket. Covers a wide range. Chapters 2 and 3 include aspects of theatrical dancing, e.g., the use of masks; costume; scenery; characteristics needed to be a choreographer; the difference between male and female dancing; the need for mime.

173 An heroic epistle, from Monsieur Vestris, Sen.: in England, to Mademoiselle Heinel, in France: with notes. Printed for R. Faulder . . . 1781. 24 pp.

A satirical description, in verse, of a benefit for the younger Vestris, and of his success, in London.

174 OULTON, W. C. A history of the theatres of London containing an annual register of new pieces, revivals, pantomimes . . . being a continuation of Victor's and Oulton's histories from the year 1795 to 1817 inclusive. . . . C. Chapple . . . W. Simpkin and R. Marshall, 1818.

V. 1.   Theatre Royal, Drury Lane.   iv, 384 pp.

V. 2.   Theatre Royal, Covent Garden.   [1], 360 pp.

V. 3.   Theatre Royal, Haymarket, and English Opera.   [1], 265 pp.

> Some 70 ballets are listed. Entries are mostly brief, but usually indicate how the ballets were received by the audience.

175   EBERS, JOHN.   Seven years of the King's Theatre.   Harrison Ainsworth, 1828.   xxviii, 395 pp.   front., 5 pl.

> A year by year account of seasons from 1821–7. The author was Manager during this period except in 1824, even then being still 'involved in the concerns of that year'. There are 6 appendices; 2 are concerned with ballet, viz. no. 4 'Agreement between the French Administration and Mr. Ebers' (concerning the engagement of dancers from the Paris Opéra) and no. 6, 'Statement of Engagements', which gives separate tables for opera and ballet, of performers employed and the amount paid to them. The plates show portraits of singers.

176   [YATES, G.]   The ball: or, a glance at Almack's in 1829.   Henry Colburn, 1829.   xv, 206 pp.   7s. 6d.

> Mainly social dancing, but does make the odd reference to foreign dancers performing in London, e.g. Vestris, father and son, Le Picq and Gallini.

177   COOK, DUTTON.   'Ballets and ballet-dancers.'   *In: Belgravia*, February 1875, pp. [522]–32.

> Morris dance; Sir William Davenant; *Mars and Venus*; ballet dancers from France; Garrick's *Chinese festival* with its French dancers. . . .

178   COOK, DUTTON.   A book of the play: studies and illustrations of histrionic story, life and character.   3rd rev. ed.   Sampson Low, Marston, Searle & Rivington, 1881.   viii, 391 pp.

> Chapter 32, 'Ballets and Ballet-Dancers' touches on a variety of subjects including *Mars and Venus*, *Chinese festival* and the dancer, Miss Rose.

179   AVERY, EMMETT L.   'Two French children on the English stage (1716–19).'   *In: Philological Quarterly*, v. 13, no. 1, January 1934, pp. 78–82.

> Marie Sallé and her brother.

180   AVERY, EMMETT L.   'Dancing and pantomime on the English stage

1700–37.' *In: Studies in Philology*, v. 31, no. 3, July 1934, pp. 417–52.

Mitchell P. Wells in 'Some Notes on the Early Eighteenth-Century Pantomime', in *Studies in Philology* (v. 32, no. 4, October 1935, pp. 598–607), challenges those parts of the above which deal with eighteenth-century pantomime.

181   AVERY, EMMETT L.   'Foreign performances in the London theaters in the early eighteenth century.' *In: Philological Quarterly*, v. 16, no. 2, April 1937, pp. 105–23.

Includes dancers.

182   SMITH, WILLIAM CHARLES, *comp.*   The Italian opera and contemporary ballet in London 1789–1820: a record of performances and players with reports from the journals of the time.   The Society for Theatre Research, 1955.   xviii, 191 pp.   front., 2 pl.   Private circulation.

The following is given under each year – introduction; company (opera and ballet performers separately); operas performed and ballets performed; for individual ballets – title, choreographer, composer, date and number of performances. The author has not attempted 'to produce a personally critical history of the period' but has gleaned material from newspapers, newspaper cuttings, libretti and personal memoirs in the British Museum Library and the Bodleian Library. There are 5 indexes, of which the second is 'Ballets and Divertissements', and the fourth 'Ballet-Dancers, Choreographers, Ballet-Masters'.

183   VINCE, STANLEY W. E.   'Marie Sallé, 1707–56.'   *In: Theatre Notebook*, v. 12, no. 1, autumn 1957, pp. 7–14.

Includes information on London seasons.

184   VINCE, STANLEY W. E.   'Camargo in London, 1750–4.'   *In: Theatre Notebook*, v. 12, no. 4, summer 1958, pp. 117–26.

The author wrote in *Theatre Notebook* (v. 13, no. 1, autumn 1958, pp. 26–7), 'Miss Lillian Moore has suggested that the Camargo whose London appearance from 1750–4 were described in the last issue of *Theatre Notebook* (i.e. the article referred to above) was, in fact, not the great Marie Anne Cupis de Camargo, but her younger sister Anne. She supports her contention with some telling references.'

[185] Famed for dance: essays on the theory and practice of theatrical dancing in England, 1660–1740.   New York, New York Public Library, 1960.   64 pp.   8 pl., illus.

To celebrate 'the bicentenary of the death of John Weaver. . . . It has done this by republishing, in brochure form, a series of scholarly articles on the early stirrings of the art of ballet in England which had previously appeared in its Bulletin. The greater part of the brochure is devoted to a masterly study by Selma Jeanne Cohen, 'Theory and Practice of Theatrical Dancing', in which she discusses at length the theory of Weaver, examines the choreographic achievements of Josias Priest . . . and closes with a sketch of the life and career of the incomparable Hester Santlow, the first English ballerina. Ifan Kyrle Fletcher's Woodward lecture on 'Ballet in England, 1660–1740', delivered at Yale last year, is an informative introduction to a hitherto almost uncharted period in dance history, and in conclusion, Roger Lonsdale contributes an interesting article on 'Dr. Burney, John Weaver and the *Spectator*'. Excellently illustrated and produced, this work is indispensable for anyone studying the origins of the art of ballet.'

The annotation for this entry has been copied from a review of the work by Ivor Guest in *The Dancing Times*, December 1960, p. 171.

186   The London stage 1660–1800: a calendar of plays, entertainments and afterpieces together with casts, box office receipts and contemporary comment compiled from the playbills, newspapers and theatrical diaries of the period. Carbondale, Illinois, Southern Illinois University, 1960–.

Edited, with critical introduction, as follows:

Part 1.   1660–1700, by William van Lennep.   1963. $25.

Part 2.   1700–29, by Emmett L. Avery.   1960.   2 vv. $50.

Part 3.   1729–47, by Arthur H. Scouten.   1961, 2 vv. $50.

Part 4.   1747–76, by George Winchester Stone, Jun.   1962. 3 vv. $75.

Part 5.   1776–1800, by C. Beecher Hogan.   Not yet published.

The Introduction to each part includes a section on dancing – Part 2, 'Dancers and Dancing' (pp. cxxx–cxxxv); Part 3, 'Dancing, Music, Singing and Speciality Acts' (pp. clv–clix); Part 4, 'The Theatrical Dance' (pp. cxxxv–cxliv). ' . . . an indispensable work of reference. Much more, however, has been presented here than dates, play-titles, cast-lists and, where known, nightly receipts. A great deal of pertinent information, culled both from newspaper notices and from contemporary correspondence has been added. . . . These two volumes, together with the previously published volumes . . . amply show that *The London Stage*, when completed, will indeed be a noble record of the theatrical activities from Betterton's days to those of Mrs. Siddons.' (*Times Literary Supplement*, 25th May, 1962, p. 368.) A list of references precedes the text, in each part published.

187 CHATWIN, AMINA, *and* RICHARDSON, PHILIP J. S. 'The father of
English ballet: John Weaver (1673–1760).' *In: The Ballet Annual
1961*, 15th issue, pp. 60–4.

188 NETTL, PAUL. The dance in classical music. Owen, 1964. vii,
168 pp. 4 pl. 25s.

> Copyright date 1963, New York, Philosophical Library.
> Based on part of a course held at Indiana University. The first 20 pages
> give some account of Marie Sallé's appearances in London in operas by
> Handel.

THE ROMANTIC BALLET

189 CHALON, ALFRED EDWARD. Six sketches of Mademoiselle Taglioni in
the characters in which she has appeared during the present season,
drawn from the life. J. Dickinson, 1831. 6 pp. 6 pl.

> The dancer is portrayed in the characters of Flore, La Tyrolienne, La
> Naiade, La Bayadère, La Napolitaine. Poems by F. W. N. Bayley accompany
> the sketches, which were 'drawn on stone' by R. J. Lane.

190 SMITH, ALBERT. The natural history of the ballet girl. Bogue, 1847.
103 pp. front., illus. 1s.

> '... We shall knock over theatrical romance for common-place reality.'
> The imaginary life of a dancer of the *corps de ballet*, 'inside information
> supplied by Miss Lonsdale, a member of the Drury Lane *corps de ballet*'
> (Catalogue of The National Book League Exhibition ... on Ballet, by Ivor
> Guest, no. 59). About 30 engravings by A. Henning; also music.

191 LUMLEY, BENJAMIN. Reminiscences of the opera. Hurst and
Blackett, 1864. xx, 448 pp. front.

> '... A record of the administration, vicissitudes, splendours ... decline
> of ... Her Majesty's Theatre' during the seasons 1842–52 and 1856–8.
> References to the ballet are fairly numerous to 1847, but there is little after
> this. Included is an account of the staging of the 1845 *Pas de quatre* with
> Taglioni, Cerrito, Grisi and Grahn.

192 BEAUMONT, CYRIL WILLIAM. 'Some prints of the romantic ballet.'
In: The Print Collector's Quarterly, v. 18, no. 3, July 1931, pp. 220–43.
12 illus after the original prints.

193   FLETCHER, IFAN KYRLE. 'Early prints of the ballet.' *In: The Connois-*
      seur, June 1937, pp. 323–8.   10 illus.

> Eighteenth century and the Romantic Ballet.

194   BEAUMONT, CYRIL WILLIAM, *and* SITWELL, Sacheverell.   The romantic
      ballet in lithographs of the time.   Faber, 1938.   316 pp.   81 pl.
      (9 col.)   50s.

> ' . . . Contains . . . almost every single print that is worth reproduction. . . .
> Some ninety per cent of the ballet prints are here reproduced, together with,
> perhaps seventy per cent of the known music titles' (Introduction, by
> Sacheverell Sitwell). This is followed by 'The Dancers of the Romantic
> Ballet' and 'The Lithographs of the Romantic Ballet: an annotated catalogue',
> by Cyril Beaumont in which he lists 120 lithographs (81 have been repro-
> duced here) providing the name of the original delineator and the litho-
> grapher, size, whether coloured and a description of the print; also place of
> publication, publisher and date where possible. The plates are divided into 2
> sections – the prints proper, and music titles, arranged chronologically by
> dancer.

195   CHAFFEE, GEORGE.   The   romantic ballet in   London 1821–58.   Some
      hitherto   unremarked   aspects.   New York, Dance Index – Ballet
      Caravan Inc., 1943.   120–99 pp.   illus.

> *Dance Index* first appeared in January 1942 and ended publication in 1947.
> Its purpose 'was to make an attempt to provide an historical and critical basis
> for judging the present and future of dancing. For this purpose *Dance Index*
> gathers, arranges and contrasts material of factual nature heretofore un-
> available in the United States. Generally, each issue of the magazine is
> devoted to a monograph either on one subject or by one writer.' (*The Dance
> encyclopaedia,* edited by Anatole Chujoy, 1949, p. 361). The above work
> comprises nos. 9, 10, 11 and 12 of v. 2, issued September–December 1943.
> George Chaffee states in his introduction that 'this (brief) monograph makes
> no pretence of being a formal history of the Romantic Ballet in London. Its
> interests are purely exploratory, documentary and critical.' Part 1, 'The
> Continental Ballet in London'; Part 2, 'The English Ballet in London'; and
> Part 3, 'Iconography', 'Catalogue of Souvenir Prints' and 'Tables of Dancers
> and Ballets'. The 28 illustrations are taken from prints of the period under
> discussion.

196   EVANS, M. STEWART.   'The romantic ballet print.'   *In: Country Life,*
      v. 113, no. 2927, 20th February, 1953, pp. 484–5.   7 illus.

> In this field 'London reigned supreme'.

197 GUEST, IVOR. The romantic ballet in England: its development, fulfil-
ment and decline. Phoenix House, 1954. 176 pp. front. (col.),
24 pl. 25s.

The theme is 'the development of ballet in London principally at the
Opera House in the Haymarket, until the great flowering of the Romantic
Ballet in the eighteen-thirties and forties and its subsequent decline to virtual
extinction as a companion to opera'. (Introduction.) The period covered is
about 1770–1880, foreign visitors to London being the main interest. The
author has drawn his material from newspapers and periodicals of the period
and gives references to these at the end of each chapter. Appendices – A,
'Ballet-masters at the King's (later Her Majesty's) Theatre 1770–1881';
B, 'Ballets given at the King's (. . .) Theatre 1772–1881'; C, 'Principal
Dancers and Choreographers at the King's (. . .) Theatre 1750–1881'; D,
'Selected List of Ballets Performed at other London Theatres (except the
Alhambra)'; E, 'Selected List of Principal Dancers appearing at other London
Theatres (except the Alhambra)'. 42 illustrations on plates make 'extensive
use' of the engravings in the illustrated periodicals of the time.

198 GUEST, IVOR. Victorian ballet-girl: the tragic story of Clara Webster.
Black, 1957. [8], 136 pp. front., 22 pl., illus., bibliog. 21s.

A biography of one of the few English dancers to make a name during
the period of the Romantic Ballet, with an account of the Webster family
and of the conditions under which English dancers worked during this
period. The bibliography contains references to 34 periodicals and 15 books.
27 illustrations on plates and 31 text illustrations are reproductions of contemporary prints, playbills, etc.

199 GUEST, IVOR. A gallery of the romantic ballet: a catalogue of the
collection of dance prints at the Mercury Theatre. New Mercury,
1965. 56 pp. 32 pl. 19s.

The Preface by Marie Rambert describes how the collection was built up.
The Introduction traces the course of the Romantic Ballet, then turns to the
prints – 'Most . . . were published between 1831 and 1847, thus spanning,
but for one year, the series of seasons in which the great Taglioni danced in
London. Let us therefore imagine these pictures to be the golden memories
of a ballet-lover of that time, and share his experiences in the theatre as we
survey them' (p. 13). 145 prints are listed in the catalogue, which gives the
names of the dancers and the ballet in which each is portrayed, the type of
print and the artists involved. There are indexes of artists, dancers . . . with
key dates, ballets, giving choreographer, composer and place and date of
first performance; 64 prints are reproduced on plates. The cover was designed
by Christopher and Robin Ironside.

200 MOORE, LILLIAN. Bournonville's London spring. New York, New
York Public Library . . . 1965. 26 pp. front. (col.), 2 pl., illus.
8s. 6d.

> An account of a visit to London, by August Bournonville. He had been
> engaged to dance in a gala season of ballet and opera at the King's Theatre
> (1828). This essay provides information about the English ballet scene and
> particularly about an English dancer, Louisa Court, with whom Bournonville
> was in love. It is based on letters owned by the Royal Library, Copenhagen.
> There are 5 illustrations in the text, 1 photographic reproduction and 2
> facsimiles of prints on plates.

THE ALHAMBRA AND EMPIRE BALLETS

201 EDWARDS, HENRY SUTHERLAND. The lyrical drama: essays on subjects, composers and executants of modern opera. V. 1. W. H.
Allen, 1881. iv, 312 pp.

> Chapter 35, 'Extinction of the Ballet', describes the position at the time
> of writing, and gives reasons why interest in ballet had declined in England.

202 [BYRNE, MRS. WILLIAM PITT]. Gossip of the century: personal and
traditional memories – social, literary, artistic, etc. V. 2. Ward
and Downey, 1892. xx, 619 pp. front., 7 pl., illus.

> Chapter 5, 'Choreography', includes some recollections of London seasons.

203 MAYHEW, ATHOL. 'The building of the ballet.' *In: The Idler*, v. 2,
August 1892, pp. [60]–9.

> The rehearsal and organization for a new ballet at the Alhambra.

204 FLITCH, JOHN ERNEST CRAWFORD. Modern dancing and dancers.
Grant Richards, 1912. 228 pp. front. (col.), 47 pl. (8 col.). 15s.

> 2nd edition 1913. (This edition not examined.)
> Chapter 12, 'The English Ballet', provides material on Adeline Genée, and
> the ballets at the Empire and Alhambra Theatres.

205 PERUGINI, MARK EDWARD. 'Why not British ballet?' *In: Proceedings
of the Musical Association*, 10th February, 1920, pp. [43]–58.

> The ballets at the Alhambra and Empire theatres are mentioned in passing.
> The discussion is also of some interest.

206 WALKER, KATHRINE SORLEY. 'Georges Jacobi and the Alhambra
     ballet.' *In: Theatre Notebook*, v. 1, no. 6, January 1947, pp. 82–3.

207 GUEST, IVOR.   The Alhambra ballet.   New York, Dance Perspectives,
     1959.   72 pp.   front., illus., bibliog. (Dance Perspectives 4.)
     $1.50.

   A history of ballet at the Alhambra Theatre from 1864 to about 1912, with
   a short account of visiting companies after that date. There are 3 appendices –
   1, 'Ballets Produced at the Alhambra, 1860–1912'; 2, 'Divertissements in
   Light Operas given at the Alhambra 1872–4'; 3, 'Principal Dancers in the
   Alhambra Ballets . . .'. The bibliography lists 21 items. Illustrations consist
   of reproductions of 14 photographs and 11 sketches, costume designs and
   caricatures.

208 GUEST, IVOR.   The Empire ballet.   The Society for Theatre Research,
     1962.   111 pp.   8 pl.   21s.

   Covers the period from 1884 to 1916, when the ballet company was dis-
   banded, and, very briefly, visiting dancers to 1927. There are chapters on
   Katti Lanner (who was engaged as ballet mistress in 1887 and who choreo-
   graphed many of the Empire ballets) and on Adeline Genée. The 6 appendices are as follows – A, 'Ballets Produced at the Empire Theatre 1884–1915';
   B, 'Principal Dancers in the Empire Ballets 1884–1915'; C, 'Some Empire
   Ballets: selected scenarios'; D, 'Wilhelm's Scenarios for *High jinks*'; E,
   'Lighting Plot for *Orfeo* (1891)'; F, 'Property Plot for *Dolly* (1890)'. There
   are separate indexes for 'Persons', 'Ballets, Musical Comedies, Operas, etc.'
   and 'Theatres'. The 16 illustrations on 8 plates are reproduced mainly from
   contemporary sources.

SURVEYS OF MORE THAN ONE PERIOD

209 'The Columbine question.'   *In: All the Year Round*, no. 373, new
     series, 22nd January, 1876, pp. 390–4.

   Disturbances at the Surrey Theatre caused by admirers of rival dancers of
   Columbine; the Misses Bennett; the *Pas de quatre* danced by Taglioni, Grisi,
   Grahn and Cerrito.

210 COCHRAN, CHARLES BLAKE.   Showman looks on.   Dent, 1945.   viii,
     323 pp.   front. (col.), 32 pl. (1 col.), illus., bibliog.   18s.

   In Chapter 12, 'Ballet Memories', the author recalls ballet at the Alhambra
   and Empire Theatres, the Diaghilev Ballet, the dancers Genée, Bedells,

Kyasht, de Valois and Helpmann, and some of the choreographers and dancers he employed for his own revues. The bibliography contains 20 items, author and title only.

211 LYNHAM, DERYCK. Ballet then and now: a history of the ballet in Europe. Sylvan Press, 1947. 214 pp. illus., bibliog. 30s.

Chapter 9, 'The Decline of the Romantic Movement', has material on ballet at the Alhambra and Empire Theatres; Chapter 14, 'British Ballet', concentrates on Ballet Rambert and the Sadler's Wells Ballet. Appendices – A, 'Music for Ballets and Divertissements composed by G. Jacobi'; B, 'Letter from Fokine to the Editor of *The Times* (1914)'; C, 'Letter from Diaghilev to *The Times* (1929)'; F, 'The Productions of the Sadler's Wells (and Vic-Wells) Ballet'. The bibliography contains about 120 items, arranged alphabetically by author's name; not all have a direct bearing on ballet. The 61 illustrations are reproductions of photographs of dancers, and ballets, and of prints and sketches for costume and décor.

212 RICHARDSON, PHILIP J. S. 'Chronology of the ballet in England, 1910–45.' *In: The Ballet Annual* [1947], 1st issue, pp. 115–36.

213 HASKELL, ARNOLD LIONEL. A picture history of ballet. Rev. and reprinted. Hulton Press, 1957. 24, [168] pp. illus. (Hulton's Picture Histories Series.) 25s.

First published 1954.

The introduction aims at giving 'A sketch of the development of ballet as a background to the illustrations' which trace its 'long journey ... in time and space ... with a linking commentary'. As the continuous history of English ballet has been short, it is only allotted a small proportion of space in text and illustration. The latter includes 'Great Britain: the Alhambra and Empire' (illus. nos. 236–46); 'The Birth of British Ballet' (462–92); 'Artistic Directors of the Sadler's Wells Ballet' (512–14); 'Some Dancers of Today (English)' (515–30); 'The Romantic Ballet: the Golden Age' (128–222) – many of these dancers and ballets were seen in London. The 558 illustrations include reproductions of photographs by about 35 photographers, contemporary prints and sketches for décor and costume.

214c RYAN, JUNE. Ballet history. Methuen, 1960. 72 pp. front., illus., bibliog. (Methuen Outlines Series.) 10s. 6d.

A brief but clear historical outline for children. English ballet, 1914 to about 1958, is covered in 14 pages, most space being devoted to the Royal Ballet. Appended is a Glossary and 'A Select Book List' of 12 items, by Jennifer Solomon. There are indexes of persons, and of ballets and companies. Drawings are by the author.

215 GUEST, IVOR. The dancer's heritage: a short history of ballet. Rev.
     ed. Harmondsworth, Penguin Books, 1962. [171] pp. front.,
     24 pl., bibliog. 6s.

>   First published 1960, by Black. Foreword by Margot Fonteyn.
>   Chapter 10, 'Contemporary Ballet: Britain' (pp. 129–39), deals mainly
>   with Ballet Rambert, Camargo Society, Royal Ballet (which receives most
>   space) and Festival Ballet. A chronology (1400–1961) is appended. For
>   bibliography *see* no. 13.

216 REYNA, FERDINANDO. A concise history of ballet. Thames and
     Hudson, 1965. 255 pp. front. (col.), illus. (col.). 35s.

>   Published in 1964 by Éditions Aimery Somogy, Paris, as *Histoire du ballet*.
>   Chapter 16, 'Ballet In England'. Separate indexes under Ballets and Names
>   are appended. 232 illustrations include reproductions of photographs, and
>   of drawings, prints and costume designs.

V. HISTORY FROM 1920; BALLET COMPANIES

ALTHOUGH the main interest during the 1920's was in the Russians, there had been a movement towards creating a truly English ballet. A beginning had been made in 1921 when Marian Wilson organized a season of ballet at the Kingsway Theatre, with English dancers. Another short-lived company formed in 1926 was the Cremorne Ballet whose Director was C. W. Beaumont. More important, Marie Rambert came to London in 1914 and later took lessons with Serafina Astafieva. She opened a school in 1920; six years later she encouraged Frederick Ashton to create the choreography for *A Tragedy of fashion* and herself danced in it. It was a short ballet included in a Nigel Playfair revue called *Riverside nights* and has been claimed as the first modern English ballet.

1930 was a key year for English ballet; the Camargo Society came into being; Ninette de Valois moved permanently to the Old Vic Theatre with her school; the Ballet Club gave its first performance. A. L. Haskell and P. J. S. Richardson organized the Camargo Society as a measure to keep ballet alive in Great Britain after the death of Diaghilev. Ballets were presented to subscription audiences. The performers were drawn mainly from the Rambert and Vic-Wells companies with guest dancers of the calibre of Lydia Lopokova, Olga Spessivtseva and Alicia Markova. Sixteen ballets were commissioned, among them *Job*, with choreography by Ninette de Valois, and several by Frederick Ashton. The Camargo Society lasted for three years only, but during this time Ballet Club and the Vic-Wells Ballet had the opportunity to establish themselves and when the Society was wound up in 1933 the ballets which it owned were handed over to the Vic-Wells Ballet. From the early 1930's to the beginning of the Second World War the history of English ballet becomes the history of Ballet Rambert and the Vic-Wells Ballet. During this period both companies consolidated their position, surviving the impact that the various foreign companies, mainly the 'ballet russe' companies of René Blum and Colonel de Basil, had on English audiences. In 1935 Alicia Markova left Sadler's Wells and joined Anton Dolin in forming the Markova-Dolin Ballet which was backed by Mrs. Laura Henderson. This company toured England and Europe with seasons in London until 1938.

BALLET RAMBERT 1931–

The Ballet Rambert is the oldest English ballet company in existence. It was founded by Marie Rambert, who, after a training in Dalcroze eurhythmics and a year or two spent with the Diaghilev Company, came to London after the First World War. She taught ballet almost at once, and in 1920 opened a school. Her pupils performed in isolated ballets which were created for a variety of purposes, or shown privately in Marie Rambert's studio. In time this group of students came to be known as the Marie Rambert dancers. In 1930 a public matinée was organized, and later in the year a two-week season was held at the Lyric Theatre, Hammersmith, with Karsavina as a guest dancer. A second season at Christmas followed. Eventually it was decided to form a club for lovers of ballet. The Rambert dancers performed twice a week at the Mercury Theatre which had been converted from the dance studio. The first performance was on 16th February, 1931. The Ballet Club was successful and continued until 1939. At the outbreak of war the Rambert School was evacuated to the country and the company was disbanded for a short while. It soon re-formed, however, and in 1940 Marie Rambert decided to accept the offer of Harold Rubin to dance at the Arts Theatre. This ensured the company regular employment and a London base. Apart from the performances in London, Ballet Rambert also toured on the outskirts of London. In 1941 the link with Harold Rubin and the Arts Theatre was broken, due to a disagreement over dancers' salaries. To all intents the Ballet Rambert no longer existed, as Harold Rubin had a legal right to present the company. It was not until 1943 that it was re-formed again under the sponsorship of the Council for the Encouragement of Music and the Arts. For the remainder of the war Ballet Rambert spent most of its time in touring the country, visiting many factory hostels, with occasional London seasons.

This pattern was maintained for about twenty years. Ballet Rambert spent most of the year touring, not only in the United Kingdom but also abroad; perhaps the most spectacular tour being that to China in 1957. The company had a short summer season of two to three weeks in London at the Sadler's Wells Theatre. In the autumn of 1966 a major re-organization took place. The company was limited to about twenty dancers under the direction of Dame Marie Rambert and Norman Morrice. It concentrates now on presenting works by new choreographers who are interested in experimenting with the medium. The company obtained a London base at the Jeannetta

Cochrane Theatre, where it gave a two-week season in November and December 1966.

In the 1930's the Ballet Rambert evolved the chamber ballet. It showed that it was possible to provide a satisfying artistic experience on a small stage with adequate costumes and scenery. The Company has always been noted for the style and production of its work due mainly to its founder, and Marie Rambert has been noted for her flair in discovering and developing the talent of dancers and choreographers.

Possibly the finest modern works in the repertoire are the Antony Tudor ballets – *Jardin aux lilas, Dark elegies, Gala performance, Judgement of Paris, Soirées musicales* – Ballet Rambert is the only English company to dance these ballets.

ROYAL BALLET 1931–

The national company is of course the Royal Ballet. Its first beginnings were in the School of Choreographic Art founded by Ninette de Valois as a school of dancing in 1926. In the same year she contacted and met Lilian Baylis, and agreed to create the dances required for the operas put on at the Old Vic, to provide dancers from her school, and to teach. In 1931 Ninette de Valois was engaged as Director and ballerina of a newly formed company. Her school was disbanded, and she moved to the Sadler's Wells Theatre. On 5th May, 1931, the first whole evening of ballet was presented, and proved successful. This led to another, then a fortnightly and finally twice-weekly perform-ances. Alicia Markova was the ballerina from 1932 to 1935. In the latter year Frederick Ashton was appointed as choreographer and Margot Fonteyn took over some of Markova's roles. Between 1935 and 1939 the company estab-lished itself firmly and increased its repertoire of new ballets, and also over the years added the great classical ballets to its repertoire.

During the war years the Vic-Wells Ballet followed the routine of other companies. It spent a great part of its time in touring interspersed with London seasons, mainly at the New Theatre. It was in 1940 that the Company was first styled the Sadler's Wells Ballet.[1] At the end of the war it was invited to become the resident ballet company at the Royal Opera House, Covent Garden, which after being used for other purposes in war-time, was reverting to its proper function of providing opera and ballet throughout the year. *The*

[1] *Complete book of ballets*, by C. W. Beaumont. Rev. ed. 1951, p. 930, note.

Sleeping beauty was performed in the presence of an illustrious audience headed by King George VI and Queen Elizabeth, the Prime Minister and representatives of foreign countries. A highlight of the post-war years was the visit of Massine. He taught the company his two best known works, *The Three-cornered hat* and *La Boutique fantasque*, and created *Donald of the burthens*. In 1949 the company made its first tour of America. American tours have become a regular part of the Company's life, taking place at two to three-yearly intervals.

In 1956 the Sadler's Wells Ballet was granted a Royal Charter and its name changed to the Royal Ballet. It was in this year, too, that the Company was to have danced for the first time in Russia, but the visit was cancelled due to the uneasiness felt in this country over Russian intervention in the Hungarian Revolution. The visit took place in 1961, with some success. In 1962 Ninette de Valois retired from the Directorship of the Royal Ballet and her place was taken by Frederick Ashton.

The repertory of the company is based on the classical ballet with revivals of Fokine, Massine and Balanchine ballets. There are always several Ashton ballets in performance with occasional revivals of works by de Valois, Helpmann and Cranko. Kenneth Macmillan, formerly the resident choreographer, produced new works each year. Norman Morrice, mainly a 'Rambert' choreographer, has created a ballet for the touring section of the Royal Ballet.

The Royal Ballet is noted for its well-schooled dancers, and in fact has been criticized for placing too much emphasis on this aspect of the dancers' training. It has produced in Margot Fonteyn an internationally known ballerina of the first rank.

When the Sadler's Wells Ballet moved to Covent Garden it was decided to form a second company to be based on the Sadler's Wells Theatre under the direction of Peggy Van Praagh; first named the Sadler's Wells Opera Ballet, this was later changed to the Sadler's Wells Theatre Ballet. The function of this company was to provide a testing ground for young dancers before they graduated to the bigger company. It was hoped, too, that inexperienced choreographers would be able to work with the company. For ten years it fulfilled these purposes, but in 1956 the Sadler's Wells Theatre Trust decided that it could no longer support the company financially. The Royal Opera House took over the responsibility for the Sadler's Wells Theatre Ballet. At first it became the touring company of the Royal Ballet organization. Gradually the two companies became fully integrated and now there

FATAL AND DISTRESSING ACCIDENT TO MISS CLARA WEBSTER.

Last Saturday night a very lamentable accident took place at Drury-lane Theatre, during the performance of "The Revolt of the Harem," which has proved fatal to Miss Clara Webster, the dancer. In the second act of the ballet, the ladies of the Harem are discovered bathing, among whom Zulica, the royal slave (Miss Webster), is one. During the scene, the gas placed at the bottom of the stage, or under the sunken portion of it, where the water pieces, or waves, are placed, caught the light drapery of Miss Webster's dress, and in an instant her whole person was enveloped in flames.

This frightful event, taking place on the stage, in sight of the audience, the whole house was in a state of consternation, and screams issued from the ladies in front of the boxes and pit, who were the first to perceive the appalling accident.

The whole corps de ballet, who were on the stage with her, closed round her, to extinguish the flames, but, terrified at the appearance which presented itself, they retreated, and she rushed forward alone towards the front of the stage. Mrs. Plunkett alone endeavoured to extinguish the flames, and in so doing was herself nearly falling a victim to her intrepidity and good feelings. At this moment a carpenter belonging to the theatre sprang from the wing of the stage, and throwing himself up on the young lady, extinguished the fire by rolling upon her. In doing so, however, he severely cut her upper lip, and received some slight injury himself from the burning clothes. Miss Webster was immediately taken into the green-room, and placed upon a sofa. Her clothes were nearly all consumed, at least all her external garments. Fortunately, Dr. Marsden was in the theatre, and his assistance was rendered without delay. The usual applications of spirits of wine and water, flour, &c., were had recourse to, and every as-

THE LATE MISS CLARA WEBSTER.

sistance was rendered. Miss Webster's face was much blistered, and in some parts scorched, the eye-lashes and eye brows burnt off; but the hair of the head was untouched. The lower extremities were much scorched, and the flesh of the hips was also much burnt. The hands also suffered dreadfully. Miss Webster never lost her recollection, but exhibited, notwithstanding the dreadful agony under which she laboured, great physical power, and extraordinary moral fort-

Portrait of Clara Webster, with an account of the accident which caused her death, taken from *The Illustrated London News* for December 21st, 1844, pp. 397-8.

PLATE I

The first project for the Camargo Society's *Job*. Gwen Raverat's toy theatre figures made to illustrate a scene from Geoffrey Keynes' ballet. The photograph for this reproduction was kindly lent by Miss Mary Clarke, Editor of *The Dancing Times*.

PLATE 2

is a regular exchange of dancers. The second company performs at Covent Garden, when the resident company is performing elsewhere. There has been less choreographic experiment, but it is still used as a trying out ground for choreographers new to the Royal Ballet.

LONDON BALLET 1937-40

A short-lived company was the London Ballet. Antony Tudor left Ballet Rambert in 1937 and with Agnes de Mille formed a company based on the Oxford Playhouse. In 1938 it moved to London putting on Tudor ballets such as *Jardin aux lilas*, *Dark elegies* and *Gala performance*. The following year the choreographer left for America, the direction of the company passing to Peggy van Praagh and Maude Lloyd.

WAR-TIME BALLET COMPANIES 1939-46

Ballet companies had certain difficulties to overcome during the war – the loss of experienced male dancers; the hardships of touring in war-time; the insufficiency of the food ration for dancers who undertook hard physical exercise; the scarcity of materials for effective costumes and scenery. Another problem, not as immediate as the others, was the loss of contact with foreign companies, which meant that an effective means of comparing standards of performance was lost. In spite of all this ballet was a popular entertainment. There was a demand for it and several new companies were organized during the 1939-41 period including Ballet de la Jeunesse Anglaise, Anglo-Polish Ballet, International Ballet and Ballet des Trois Arts. The Anglo-Polish Ballet was one of the more successful war-time companies. Its repertoire was based on a number of ballets displaying Polish national dances and themes, the best known being *Cracow wedding*. The company was led by Jan Cobel and among the dancers were Alicja Halima, Alexis Rassine and Sally Gilmour. Ballet de la Jeunesse Anglaise was directed by Lydia Kyasht, the former ballerina of the Empire Theatre. It performed at irregular intervals during the war, the last appearance being in 1946. Another company which survived only a short while was the Metropolitan Ballet directed by Cecilia Blatch and Leon Hepner. It was formed in 1947 while the war-time interest in ballet still provided impetus. It was this company which introduced Svetlana Beriosova to English audiences.

INTERNATIONAL BALLET 1941–53

The International Ballet was formed in 1941 by Mona Inglesby, who directed the company, too. Its policy was to tour with the full-length classics as the mainstay of the repertoire. In this Mona Inglesby had the advice of Nicholas Sergueeff, the regisseur of the company who had brought out of Russia very full notes on the classical ballets performed there. She herself also composed the choreography of several ballets, including *Everyman* and *Comus*.

FESTIVAL BALLET 1950–

Festival Ballet was originally formed for the purpose of exploiting the partnership of Alicia Markova and Anton Dolin. These two dancers returned to England from America in 1948, to appear as guest dancers with the Sadler's Wells Ballet. In 1949 a company was brought together for touring purposes, and a year later it became the Festival Ballet under the direction of Julian Braunsweg. In 1952 Alicia Markova left the company but returned several times as guest dancer, and in 1960 Anton Dolin, who had been Artistic Director, also left, his place eventually being taken by John Gilpin. For several years the company has worked under financial difficulties. In 1965 it went bankrupt. Immediate grants were obtained from private sources in order to keep the company together until help could be obtained from public bodies. Donald Albery was appointed Chairman and Administrator and Norman McDowell as Artistic Director. The latter brought with him some of the dancers from London Dance Theatre, which he had formerly directed.[2] He has since resigned from this post.

On the whole the company has commissioned a lighter type of ballet than the other two big companies. For example the regular Christmas production for some years has been *Casse-Noisette* with costumes by Alexandre Benois and spectacular changes of scenery. It has also been the policy of Festival Ballet to engage guest dancers from other countries.

BALLETS MINERVA 1954–

Ballets Minerva was formed in 1954 by Kathleen Gray and Edward

[2] '*What happened to Festival Ballet?*', by G. B. L. Wilson. *In: The Dancing Times*, November 1965, pp. 72–3.

Gaillard. It has a London base, but performs mainly in remote parts of the country with a repertoire based mainly on the classical style.

WESTERN THEATRE BALLET 1957–

A very different type of company is Western Theatre Ballet. It is a small company of about twenty dancers, formed in Bristol in 1957, by Elizabeth West and Peter Darrell. For the most part it is a touring company both at home and abroad, and has performed at the Jacob's Pillow Festival. The repertoire consists of experimental ballets with some classical *pas de deux* and its chief choreographer is Peter Darrell. In the future Western Theatre Ballet will have a close link with Sadler's Wells Theatre, for in *The Times* for 6th January, 1965, it was announced that the company had been invited to take over responsibility for the Opera Ballet in London and on tour. In June and July 1966 they had their first season at Sadler's Wells Theatre.

HARLEQUIN BALLET 1961–

There are other smaller companies. The Harlequin Ballet was founded by Barbara Vernon and John Gregory as an outlet for the dancers trained in their School of Russian Ballet. Performances are given in schools, clubs, seaside theatres and in the open air. The repertoire ranges from classical ballet to folk and jazz ballet, and includes *Les Millions d'Harlequin* produced by Tamara Karsavina.

LONDON BALLET AND LONDON DANCE THEATRE

Two other recently formed and short-lived companies were London Ballet formed in 1961 and directed by Walter Gore, and London Dance Theatre directed by Norman McDowell. The former company survived for about a year only. London Dance Theatre made its first provincial tour in 1964 and in 1965 had a London season at the Vaudeville Theatre, but has since disbanded.

BIBLIOGRAPHY

Arrangement. 1. Developments 1920–35. 2. Surveys from 1935. 3. Individual Companies, arranged chronologically, by date of formation of Company; within each

Company, by date of publication. 4. Other Companies. 1, 2 and 4 are arranged chronologically by date of publication.

DEVELOPMENTS 1920–35

217 HENRY, LEIGH. 'Dancers and the dance.' *In: The Musical Standard,* v. 17, no. 358 (new illustrated series), 4th June, 1921, pp. 193–4.
> English ballet at the Coliseum.

218 SHIPP, HORACE. 'The problem of British ballet.' *In: The Sackbut,* v. 6, no. 9, April 1926, pp. 257–8.
> The Cremorne Ballet Company.

219 MONTAGU-NATHAN, MONTAGU. 'The Camargo Society: its probable influence on British music.' *In: The Musical Times,* v. 71, no. 1051, September 1930, pp. 798–9.
> The author was Honorary Secretary of the Camargo Society.

220 HASKELL, ARNOLD LIONEL. 'The ballet in England.' *In: New English Weekly,* 2nd June–7th July, 1932, v. 1, nos. 7–12.
> 1. Introductory. No. 7, pp. 162–3.
> 2. The Camargo Ballet season. (*High yellow, Job, Swan lake*), no. 8, pp. 185–6.
> 3. The Camargo Ballet Season. (*The Enchanted grove, Façade, Mars and Venus*); also considers 'what standards of criticism one can apply', no. 9, pp. 208–9.
> 4. The Camargo Ballet Season. (*Origin of design*); also the male dancer, organization of The Association of Operatic Dancing and the Cecchetti Ninette Society; de Valois, no. 10, pp. 232–4.
> 5. The Making of Dancers; décor, No. 11, pp. 255–6.
> 6. The Camargo Ballet Season. (*Giselle, Rio Grande*), no. 12, pp. 283–4.

221 SHIPP, HORACE. 'The ballet renews itself.' *In: The Sackbut,* v. 12, no. 4, July 1932, pp. 219–22.
> Camargo Society; Ballet Club; Vic-Wells Ballet.

222 DE ZOETE, BERYL. 'The Camargo ballet season.' *In: Monthly Musical Record,* v. 62, no. 738, July–August 1932, pp. 132–3.

223 HERRING, ROBERT. 'The undying swan.' *In: The London Mercury*, v. 28, no. 168, October 1933, pp. 536–41.

About 500 words devoted to the early days of Ballet Club, the Camargo Society and Vic-Wells Ballet.

224 HEPPENSTALL, RAYNER. 'The year in ballet.' *In: The Criterion*, v. 15, no. 58, October 1935, p. 57–64.

Includes companies performing in London during the preceding year and an appraisal of Antony Tudor's *Descent of Hebe* in about 250 words.

SURVEYS FROM 1935

225 PERUGINI, MARK EDWARD. A pageant of the dance and ballet. Jarrolds, 1935. 318 pp. front., 38 pl. 18s.

Based on the author's *Art of ballet* (1915), the above is 'largely re-written with new chapters, new illustrations and a chronology added'. Chapter 30, 'Memories – Russian and Otherwise' (companies visiting London); Chapter 31, 'The Pageant of Recent Years' (influence of the Russians, English dancers, Vic-Wells Ballet and Ballet Rambert); Chapter 32, 'Finale and – the Future'. 'A Bibliographical Note' precedes the text, with 21 items ranging more widely than the dance, and a chronology is appended (3500 B.C.–A.D. 1935). There are 40 illustrations on plates.

226 HASKELL, ARNOLD LIONEL. Dancing round the world: memoirs of an attempted escape from ballet. Gollancz, 1937. 352 pp. 48 pl., illus. 18s.

In Chapter 16, 'The English Scene Three Years After; amende honorable . . .', the author re-assesses more favourably his judgement on English ballet, particularly the Vic-Wells and Rambert Companies, published in *Balletomania* (*see* no. 74) as Chapter 10, 'English Interlude'. The following chapter, 'Other Organizations and Visitors to London', includes the Markova-Dolin Ballet. The appendix lists the repertoire of the leading companies to appear in London 1933–7.

227 'Dance Critic.' 'English ballet in wartime.' *In: Penguin New Writing* 13, April–June 1942, pp. 108–15. 4 pl.

Late 1939–41.

228 HASKELL, ARNOLD LIONEL. Ballet since 1939. Longmans Green for

The British Council, 1946.   47 pp.   front. (col.), 16 pl., bibliog. (The Arts in Britain Series. No. 2.)   2s.

> Devoted to English ballet. Information on the Sadler's Wells Company (productions 1939–44), Ballet Club, International Ballet and the Royal Academy of Dancing; also Chapter 1, 'The Birth of British Ballet' and, Chapter 4, 'Nationalism in Ballet' (British dancing and choreography). There are 5 appendices – A, 'The Artistic Pedigree . . .'; B, 'Some Key Dates . . .'; C, 'Creations . . . 1939–44'; D, 'British Composers whose Works have been Performed. British Painters Responsible for Décor'; E, 'Bibliography . . . published since 1939' (7 titles).

229   WINKWORTH, FRANCIS, *comp.*   A pageant of ballet. Jeans, 1947. [35] pp.   illus.   6s.

> A booklet largely composed of 64 reproductions of photographs of the Sadler's Wells Ballet; Sadler's Wells Opera Ballet; International Ballet; Ballet Rambert; Ballets Nègres.

230   'THE TIMES.'   Musical Britain 1951.   Oxford University Press, 1951. [8], 256 pp.   24 pl.   21s.

> Compiled by the music critic of *The Times*, to cover the musical events of the Festival of Britain, both in London and the provinces. The reviews are written by 'some dozen pens'. Chapter 10, 'Ballet', contains reviews of *Daphnis and Chloe*, *Harlequin in April* and *Tiresias* (Sadler's Wells companies), *Le Beau Danube*, *Impressions* and *Pas de quatre* (Festival Ballet) and *Orlando's silver wedding* (Battersea Festival Gardens). Folk dance and visiting Spanish companies are covered; also, in Part 2, ballet at the Edinburgh Festival. There are 6 illustrations on the plates illustrating Chapter 10.

[231]   HASKELL, ARNOLD LIONEL.   Ballet 1945–50.   Longmans Green, for The British Council, 1952.   48 pp.   front., 14 pl., bibliog. (Arts in Britain Series.)   2s. 6d.

232   TREWIN, JOHN COURTENAY.   'United Kingdom: ballet.'   *In: World Theatre*, v. 4, no. 2, [summer 1955], pp. 78–81.   2 illus.

> 1954–1955[?] London season including foreign visiting companies.

233   TREWIN, JOHN COURTENAY.   'United Kingdom: ballet.'   *In: World Theatre*, v. 5, no. 4, autumn 1956, pp. [330]–2.   2 illus.

> Royal Ballet and Festival Ballet season.

234 TREWIN, JOHN COURTENAY. 'United Kingdom: ballet.' *In: World Theatre*, v. 8, no. 2, summer 1959, pp. 156–8. 1 illus.

> Mainly the 1958 Royal Ballet season in London.

BALLET RAMBERT, 1931–

235 HASKELL, ARNOLD LIONEL. The Marie Rambert ballet. 3rd enl. ed. British Continental Press, 1931. 55 pp. 8 pl. (Artists of the Dance Series. No. 6.) 2s. 6d.

> First published 1930. 3rd ed. has been increased by 10 pages.
> The early history of Ballet Rambert, with short critical studies of dancers including Pearl Argyle, William Chappell, Diana Gould, Andrée Howard, Prudence Hyman and Harold Turner; also Frederick Ashton and Susan Salaman as choreographers. Chapter 2, 'Marie Rambert and her Methods'. A foreword by Tamara Karsavina is followed by an appendix listing the repertoire.

236 BRADLEY, LIONEL. Sixteen years of Ballet Rambert. Hinrichsen, 1946. [83] pp. front., illus. 15s.

> A short history of the company, now superseded by Mary Clarke's *Dancers of Mercury* (*see* no. 247), introduces the 73 reproductions of photographs which are 'a record of the work of Ballet Rambert during 16 years, with brief comments on the choreographers and the music, the designer and the dancers'. (Preface.) Appended are 'Complete Repertoire (revised to 30th November, 1945)' and separate indexes with notes, for choreographers, composers, designers and dancers.

237 RAMBERT, MARIE. 'Twenty years after.' *In: The Ballet Annual* [*1947*], 1st issue, pp. 82–[9].

238 COAST, JOHN. 'The Ballet Rambert.' *In: The Ballet Annual 1948*, 2nd issue, pp. 126–8.

239 GORE, WALTER. 'Ballet Rambert comes of age.' *In: Souvenirs de Ballet, no. 1*, 1949, pp. 40–[7]. 7 illus.

> Includes a list of the repertoire, creations but not revivals, arranged chronologically.

240 MILLER, TATLOCK. 'The Ballet Rambert in Australia.' *In: The Ballet Annual 1949*, 3rd issue, pp. 132–4.

241 DE MILLE, AGNES. Dance to the piper: memoirs of the ballet. Hamilton, 1951. viii, 318 pp. front., 14 pl. 18s.

 Chapter 18, 'Marie Rambert'; Chapter 19, 'Antony Tudor and Hugh Laing'. The author, the American choreographer and dancer, was a student at the Rambert School during the 1930's.

242 DE ZOETE, BERYL. The strawberry underneath the nettle. Priv. print. 1953.

 'I want here to consider what it was in those productions of the Ballet Rambert that drew one again and again to Sadler's Wells Theatre.' (*See also* no. 127.)

243 LANDSTONE, CHARLES. Off-stage: a personal record of the first twelve years of state sponsored drama in Great Britain. Elek, 1953, 204 pp. 6 pl. 18s.

 In Chapter 4, 'Miners, Mummers and Mim' (pp. 61–5), the author, an Associate Drama Director of the Arts Council, 1942–52, writes of his association with Ballet Rambert. He was responsible for the company on its tours of hostels during and immediately after the Second World War.

244 WILSON, GEORGE BUCKLEY LAIRD. 'The Ballet Rambert.' *In: The Ballet Annual 1953*, 7th issue, p. 101.

245 BLAND, ALEXANDER. 'Marie Rambert.' *In The Ballet Annual 1955*, 9th issue, pp. 58–63.

246 'Ballet Rambert's new standing.' *In: The Times*, 2nd August, 1962, p. 7.

247 CLARKE, MARY. Dancers of Mercury: the story of Ballet Rambert. Black, 1962. xv, 240 pp. front., 34 pl., illus. 40s.

 The standard history of the Ballet Club, later the Ballet Rambert; also a sketch of Marie Rambert's early life in Warsaw and Paris, her years with Dalcroze (1910–12) and the Diaghilev Ballet (1912–13). There are 2 appendices – 'Ballet Workshop' and 'List of Ballets Produced by the Ballet Rambert'. '. . . Sources of information are acknowledged in footnotes' (Acknowledgements). There are 85 reproductions of photographs on plates and 11 drawings in the text by Richard Ziegler (6) and Loudon Sainthill (1); the remainder are reproductions of posters and programmes.

THE ROYAL BALLET, 1931–

248 NEATBY, KATE. Ninette de Valois and the Vic-Wells Ballet. British Continental Press, 1934. 46 pp. front., 6 pl. (Artists of the Dance Series. No. 11.) 2s. 6d.

> Edited by Edwin Evans, who also wrote the 'Conclusion'. Includes 2 chapters on Ninette de Valois as a performer, and as producer and choreographer, and an appendix 'Programme Note for *Job*'. 'One of the earliest appreciations of the work of the company and its founder' (*Ballet: an exhibition . . . organised by Ivor Guest*. National Book League, 1957, p. 38).

249 BEAUMONT, CYRIL WILLIAM. The Vic-Wells Ballet. The author, 1935. 45 pp. front., 11 pl. 3s. 6d.

> A brief history of the company to 1935, with notes on the following ballets – *Job, Fête polonaise, Les Rendezvous, The Haunted ballroom, The Jar, Création du monde, Rake's progress, Les Sylphides, Carnaval, Giselle, Cassenoisette, Coppélia*, and *Lac des cygnes*. Appended is 'Repertory of the Vic-Wells Ballet, January 1931–June 1935'. No index.

ABER, ADOLF. 'Checkmate: Arthur Bliss's ballet in Paris.' July 1937. *See* no. 356.

250 ANTHONY, GORDON, *photographer*. Ballet: camera studies. Bles, 1937. 241 pp. front., 95 pl. 42s.

> Most of the photographic reproductions (33 plates) portray individual dancers, of the Vic-Wells Ballet, and Markova and Dolin (7 plates); also of the de Basil and René Blum Companies and the Ballets Jooss. Arnold Haskell provides an introduction to each company and notes on the dancers.

'Checkmate': a new ballet by Arthur Bliss.' June 1937. *See* no. 355.

251 ANTHONY, GORDON, *photographer*. The Vic-Wells Ballet: camera studies. Routledge, 1938. xiv, 24 pp. front., 55 pl. 10s. 6d.

> The introduction by Ninette de Valois indicates the growth of the company and assesses some of the dancers photographed. These studies originally appeared in *The Bystander*; the majority, of individual dancers, are posed.

252 SEVERN, MERLYN, *photographer*. Ballet in action. John Lane, The Bodley Head, 1938. xxix, 128 pp. front., illus. 42s.

'Every moment that ends in a set pose . . . even if . . . only held for a split second, must be photographed at the precise moment when the pose is at its tensest and most expressive – *the significant moment.*' (*Double exposure*, by M. Severn. Faber, 1956, p. 63.) ' . . . Capital reproductions of photographs taken at actual performances.' The photographer has 'the unusual knack of catching the dancers at the critical point in their movements' (*The Times Literary Supplement*, 16th July, 1938, p. 481). The photographs show the Sadler's Wells Ballet in *Apparitions*, *Le Baiser de la fée*, *Carnaval*, *Casse-Noisette*, *Checkmate*, *Giselle*, *Les Rendezvous*, *Swan lake* and *Wedding bouquet*. There is an introductory essay and critical notes by Arnold L. Haskell and appended are 'Notes on the Ballets' and 'Photographic Data'. There are 237 reproductions of photographs.

ANTHONY, GORDON, *photographer.* 'The Sleeping princess': camera studies. 1940.

    See no. 373.

253 DENT, EDWARD JOSEPH. A theatre for everybody: the story of the Old Vic and Sadler's Wells. Boardman, 1945. [152] pp. front. (col.), 18 pl., illus., bibliog. 12s. 6d.

    Chapter 7, 'Ballet', sketches the work done by the Sadler's Wells Company at the Sadler's Wells Theatre. 36 illustrations are by Kay Ambrose and the bibliography contains 27 items.

The English ballet folios. 1945.

    See no. 331.

254 TURNER, WALTER JAMES. 'The Sadler's Wells ballet.' *In: Future Books*, v. 2, *The Stage is Set*, [c. 1945], pp. 101–[104]. 9 illus. (3 col.)

255 WILLIAMSON, AUDREY. 'Theatre World' guide to the Sadler's Wells ballet. [TheatreWorld, c. 1945.] [21] pp. illus. 1s.

    General information on the company.

CHAPPELL, WILLIAM. 'The Sleeping beauty.' July 1946.

    See no. 374.

256 Covent Garden books no. 1–, 1946–. illus. 5s.–15s.

    A photographic record over the years of new productions at the Royal

Opera House, with information about and photographs of personnel and occasional articles and appreciations. Those quoted below are devoted to The Royal Ballet; each contains about 50 pages and about 6 illustrations in colour.

No. 1. 1946–7, edited by Anthony Gishford.

Includes *'The Sleeping beauty'* (5 col. illus. 4 photos.) and *'Giselle'* (4 col. illus. 4 photos., 4 costume designs in col.), by Sacheverell Sitwell.

No. 2. 1947–8, edited by Michael Wood.

Includes 'British Council Tours of the Sadler's Wells Ballet 1946–7', by Evelyn Williams.

No. 3. 1948–9, edited by Michael Wood.

No. 5. 1949–50, edited by Michael Wood.

No. 6. 1950–2, edited by Michael Wood.

Includes 'Constant Lambert 1905–51: an appreciation', by Edward J. Dent.

No. 8. 3rd September, 1952–23rd August, 1954, edited by Michael Wood.

Includes 'Sadler's Wells Ballet Repertory' (February 1946–August 1954).

No. 9. Edited by Michael Wood.

This is the 25th Anniversary issue entitled 'The Sadler's Wells Ballet 1931–56: a record of twenty-five years', and gives information on artists of the Sadler's Wells Ballet and the Sadler's Wells Theatre Ballet in 1956; the programme and cast of the first performances at The Old Vic 5th May, 1931, the Sadler's Wells Theatre 15th May, 1931, and The Royal Opera House, Covent Garden, 20th February, 1946; the staff of the Sadler's Wells School; past members of the company; composers who have created special works or whose music has been used; conductors, and choreographers and designers who have worked with the companies. It also includes maps showing the towns visited by both companies in Great Britain, Northern Ireland and the Republic of Ireland 1931–55, in Europe 1931–56, and in the United States and Canada 1949–55. There is also a 'Full List of Ballets since 1931' that gives date, ballet, theatre, composer, choreographer and designer.

No. 11. 23rd August, 1954–1st January, 1957, edited by Michael Wood.

No. 13. 26th March, 1957–4th April, 1961, edited by William Beresford.

Includes 'The Royal Ballet. The Company as at 1st September, 1961'.

No. 15. September 1961–May 1964, edited by Clement Crisp.

HASKELL, ARNOLD LIONEL. 'Miracle in the Gorbals': a study. 1946.

See no. 368.

257 MANCHESTER, PHYLLIS WINIFRED. Vic-Wells: a ballet's progress. Gollancz, 1946. 114 pp. 24 pl. 6s.

First published in 1942, this is the 3rd impression with a 3-page epilogue to bring the material up to date.

An individual account of the first 10 years of the company's existence 'written entirely from the point of view of an onlooker who has not, and has never had, any inside knowledge of the policies and plans which have guided the Vic-Wells Ballet' (author's note). Chapters include 'English and Russian – a contrast'; 'Vic-Wells and the Russian Classics'; 'The Audience'; 'Some Artists'. Still interesting to read for the opinions expressed although factually superseded by Mary Clarke's *The Sadler's Wells Ballet* (*see* no. 278), 35 illustrations on plates.

MANDINIAN, EDWARD, *photographer.* 'The Sleeping beauty', as presented by The Sadler's Wells Ballet 1946: a photographic record.

> *See* no. 375.

258   ANTHONY, GORDON, *photographer.* Studies of the Sadler's Wells Ballet Company at Covent Garden. Home & Van Thal, 1947. [8] pp. front., 64 pl. 42s.

> Reproductions of studio photographs of 28 dancers of the company.

259   BEAUMONT, CYRIL WILLIAM. The Sadler's Wells Ballet: a detailed account of works in the permanent repertory, with critical notes. Rev. and enl. ed. The author, 1947. 214 pp. front., 48 pl. 21s.

> First published 1946, the subsequent edition was enlarged by 7 pages; ballets included are the same in both editions.
> The author has concentrated on descriptions of the ballets followed by a short historical or critical commentary. Choreographers represented – Ninette de Valois; Frederick Ashton; Robert Helpmann; Andrée Howard. Of historical rather than current interest. Reproductions of photographs on plates depict the ballets described.

260   HASKELL, ARNOLD LIONEL. The National ballet: a history and a manifesto. 2nd ed. Black, 1947. viii, 96 pp. front. (col.), 8 pl., 1 illus., bibliog. 10s. 6d.

> First published 1943; the Introduction is by Ninette de Valois.
> The history and achievements of the Sadler's Wells Ballet, with emphasis on its 'national' aspect. Post-war material was added and the bibliography brought up to date, although the pagination was unaltered. The 8 appendices are 1, 'A Critic's Path' (A. L. Haskell); 3, 'Key Dates . . . with Commentary'; 4, 'The Choreography of Frederick Ashton'; 5, 'A Note on the Classics in the Wells Repertoire'; 6, 'The Company in 1931, 1935, 1943 and 1946'; 7, 'Notes on the Music of the Wells Productions'; 8, 'The Yearly Repertoire from 1935'. The Bibliography (Appendix 2) contains 44 items arranged chronologically, with annotations.

261 LEE-ELLIOTT, THEYRE. Paintings of the ballet. Collins, [1947].
     [18] pp. front. (col.), 74 pl. (22 col.), illus. 18s.
         The artist has concentrated on atmosphere rather than realism, taking his
     impressions mainly from dancers of the Sadler's Wells Ballet. The intro-
     duction, 'Painting the Ballet', is by A. L. Haskell.

262 LEITH, EVELEIGH. 'Its own mechanism.' *In: The Ballet Annual*
     [*1947*], 1st issue, pp. 137–51.
         Behind the scenes personnel of the Sadler's Wells Company and School.

263 MARSHALL, NORMAN. The other theatre. Lehmann, 1947. 240 pp.
     front., 24 pl. 15s.
         Chapter 10, 'Ninette de Valois and the English Ballet', (pp. 139–61).

'Miracle in the Gorbals.' February 1947.
     See no. 369.

SEDGWICK, RUSSELL, *photographer.* The 'Swan lake', as presented by
     the Sadler's Wells Ballet: a photographic record. The story of the
     ballet, by Cyril W. Beaumont. 1947.
     See no. 379.

264 SEVERN, MERLYN, *photographer.* Sadler's Wells Ballet at Covent
     Garden. John Lane, The Bodley Head, 1947. 10 pp. front.,
     [80] pl. 21s.
         Action photographs of the company in the following ballets – *The Sleeping
     beauty; Miracle in the Gorbals; The Rake's progress; Symphonic variations; Adam
     Zero*. The photographer was formerly on the staff of *Picture Post*, and was the
     first and one of the most successful photographers to catch dancers in action.

265 ANTHONY, GORDON, *photographer.* The Sadler's Wells Ballet: camera
     studies. 2nd ed. Bles, 1948. xvi pp. front., 47 pl. 21s.
         First published 1942. The introduction is by Eveleigh Leith.
         The 2nd ed. is, in fact, a reprint. 'The pictures . . . are mainly selected for
     their merit as action studies, giving as much as possible the spirit of the dance
     as well as the personality of the dancer' (Foreword by the author).

266 BENNETT, VIVIENNE. 'Ninette de Valois and the Sadler's Wells
     Ballet.' *In: The New English Review Magazine*, v. 1 (new series),
     no. 4, December 1948, pp. 231–6. 3 illus.

MANDINIAN, EDWARD, *photographer*. Purcell's 'The Fairy queen' as presented by the Sadler's Wells Ballet and the Covent Garden Opera: a photographic record.   1948.

    See no. 359.

MIDDLETON, M. H.   'The Fairy queen', [1948].

    See no. 360.

267 'Profile – Ninette de Valois.'   *In: The Ballet Annual 1948*, 2nd issue, pp. 54–8.

    Reprinted from *The Observer*.

268 THOMAS, STEPHEN.   'The Sadler's Wells Ballet and The British Council.'   *In: The Ballet Annual 1948*, 2nd issue, pp. 148–53.

BENTHALL, MICHAEL, *and others*.   'Hamlet' and 'Miracle in the Gorbals'.   1949.

    See no. 337.

269 DE VALOIS, NINETTE.   'The Sadler's Wells Ballet.'   *In: The Year's Work in the Theatre 1948–1949*, pp. 38–41.

KIRSTEIN, LINCOLN, *and others*.   'Carnaval', 'Le Spectre de la rose' and 'Les Sylphides'.   1949.

    See no. 339.

LAWSON, JOAN, *and others*.   'Job' and 'The Rake's progress'.   1949.

    See no. 340.

SITWELL, SACHEVERELL, *and others*.   The Sleeping beauty.   1949.

    See no. 376.

270 KLEMANTASKI, LOUIS, *photographer*.   Background to a ballet.   Klemantaski, [1951].   [32] pp.   illus.   3s. 6d.

    '... We present [60] original photographs illustrating something of life behind the curtain at the Royal Opera House, Covent Garden'; also backstage shots of ballets in performance. John F. Speed wrote the captions.

271 'Sadler's Wells in the U.S.A. and Canada 1949.' *In: The Ballet Annual 1951*, 5th issue, pp. 54–5.

Excerpts from local newspapers.

'Tiresias: a symposium of views.' Autumn 1951.

See no. 386.

272 WHITE, FRANKLIN. Sadler's Wells Ballet goes abroad. Faber, 1951. xvi, 108 pp. front. (col.), 48 pl., illus., map. 25s.

An informal account of the second tour of America and Canada (1950–1) by one of the dancers. The photographer was Bryan Ashbridge, also a member of the company. The repertoire, dancers and staff for the tour are listed. 137 illustrations on 48 plates.

273 WOOD, ROGER, *photographer*. The Sadler's Wells Ballet . . . at the Royal Opera House, Covent Garden. Saturn Press, 1951. [32] pp. front., illus. 6s.

46 reproductions of photographs of members of the company posed in different parts of the Opera House

274 KENNEDY, LUDOVIC. 'With the Sadler's Wells Ballet in America.' *In: The Ballet Annual 1952*, 6th issue, pp. 64–6.

MONAHAN, JAMES. 'Donald of the burthens.' Winter 1951–2.

See no. 358.

275 'The Sadler's Wells Ballet at the Royal Opera House, Covent Garden. A statistical survey 1946 – 5th July, 1952.' *In: The Ballet Annual 1953*. 7th issue, p. 141.

276 CLARKE, MARY. 'Building a national ballet.' *In: The National and English Review*, v. 142, no. 854, April 1954, pp. 229–33.

277 CLARKE, MARY. 'The Corps de ballet of Sadler's Wells.' *In: The Ballet Annual 1954*, 8th issue, pp. 78–84.

278 CLARKE, MARY. The Sadler's Wells Ballet: a history and an appreciation. Black, 1955. xv, 336 pp. front., 30 pl., bibliog. 21s.

The standard history of the company, giving a year by year account and assessment of work done. The 5 appendices are A, 'The Sadler's Wells School'; B, 'The Sadler's Wells Theatre Ballet'; C, 'The Work of the Sadler's Wells Overseas'; D, 'The Sadler's Wells Benevolent Fund'; E, 'List of Ballets produced by The Sadler's Wells Ballet'. There are reproductions of 46 photographs on plates and 5 posters.

For bibliography *see* no. 11.

279 HASKELL, ARNOLD LIONEL, *and others, eds.* Gala performance. Collins, 1955. 248 pp. front. (col.), 7 pl. (col.), illus. 42s.

   Co-editors were Mark Bonham Carter and Michael Wood.

   Published for the 25th anniversary of the Sadler's Wells Ballet. The main appeal is in the photographic reproductions illustrating the work of the Sadler's Wells Theatre Ballet and School, as well as the main company. There are also articles which include 'The Sadler's Wells School', by Arnold Haskell; 'The Sadler's Wells Ballet', by James Monahan; 'Music and Ballet', by Robert Irving; 'Ballet Décors', by Sir Kenneth Clark'; Some Problems of Ballet Today', by Ninette de Valois. An appendix gives 'A Record of First Productions, Revivals and their Casts from the Foundation of the Sadler's Wells Ballet until the Present Day'. The coloured plates are of designs for costumes, scenery and front cloths of ballets presented by Sadler's Wells, and there are about 200 photographs.

280 HUROK, SALOMON. S. Hurok presents . . . the world of ballet. Hale, 1955. 317 pp. front., 24 pl. 18s.

   Chapter 12, 'Ballet Climax – Sadler's Wells and after . . .'.

   Account of the first two American tours of Sadler's Wells Ballet, by the impresario who was responsible for them; his opinions of the dancers and ballets.

281 HART, JOHN, *photographer.* Ballet & camera: Sadler's Wells dancers behind and on stage. Chatto & Windus, 1956. 48 pp. front., illus. 10s. 6d.

   74 photographic reproductions, with explanatory captions, portray the Royal Ballet at rehearsal, and judging by the immediacy of the photographs, in actual performance. Among other ballets *Madame Chrysanthème*, *Le Lac des cygnes* and *The Firebird* are represented. The photographer is an Assistant Director of the Royal Ballet who has been with the company since 1938, formerly as a dancer.

282 'The Sadler's Wells Ballet on tour: a statistical survey 1946–54.' *In: The Ballet Annual 1956*, 10th issue, pp. [132–3].

Roger Wood

Margot Fonteyn as Ondine (centre), Michael Somes as Palemon (left) and Alexander Grant as Tirrenio (right) in a scene from the ballet *Ondine*, with choreography by Frederick Ashton and music by Hans Werner Henze.

PLATE 3

The Shadow, choreography by John Cranko, music by Dohnanyi. An example of Benesh dance notation, with corresponding musical score, reproduced from *Introduction to Benesh Dance Notation*, by Rudolf and Joan Benesh, by kind permission of The Institute of Choreology.

PLATE 4

283 'Twenty-five years of Sadler's Wells Ballet. Evolution of a national company.' *In: The Times*, 4th May, 1956, p. 3.

284 'Britain's Royal Ballet. Questions of policy and future development.' *In: The Times*, 21st June, 1957. p. 3.

285 DE VALOIS, NINETTE. Come dance with me: a memoir 1898–1956. Hamilton, 1957. xvi, 234 pp. front., 34 pl. 25s.
    Reminiscences of the Director of The Royal Ballet, with much on the founding and development of the national ballet company. 64 reproductions of photographs on plates.

286 MONAHAN, JAMES. 'The first twenty-five years.' *In: The Ballet Annual 1957*, 11th issue, pp. 54–62.

    'Royal Ballet's problems in staging "Petrouchka".' 18th March, 1957.
    See no. 372.

287 'The Sadler's Wells Ballet at the Royal Opera House, Covent Garden. A statistical table, 3rd September, 1952 – 23rd June, 1956.' *In: The Ballet Annual 1957*, 11th issue, p. [146].

288 'Charter of Incorporation of the Royal Ballet.' *In: The Ballet Annual 1958*, 12th issue, pp. 45–55.

289 DAVIS, MIKE, *photographer*. Mike Davis at the Royal Ballet. Old-bourne, 1958. [144] pp. front., illus. 25s.
    Essays include 'Classical Dancing', by Mary Clarke; 'On Being a Choreographer', by Frederick Ashton; 'Ballet and its Audience', by Noël Goodwin; 'The Royal Ballet School', by Arnold Haskell; 'B.B.C. Television and the Royal Ballet', by Margaret Dale. About 180 photographs show the company in rehearsal and performance, also portraits.

290 'Male dancers in the Royal Ballet.' *In: The Times*, 14th January, 1958, p. 3.

291 'A greater Royal Ballet in the making.' *In: The Times*, 3rd February, 1958, p. 12.

292 ROYAL OPERA HOUSE, COVENT GARDEN. Annual Report, 1957/8-.
1s.

> Some 35 pages of information on the Royal Ballet and the Opera Company
> – the year's work; new productions; ballet performances during the year;
> appearances of guest artists; guest appearances by Royal Ballet dancers;
> tours; finance; personnel.

293 SWINSON, CYRIL WILLIAM. The Royal Ballet Today. Black, 1958.
32 pp. front., illus. (Dancers of To-day Series. No. 14.) 7s. 6d.

> Includes 'A Brief Chronology of Outstanding Events', 'Covent Garden
> Opera Ballet' and 'The Royal Ballet School'. (*See also* no. 432.)

294c SWINSON, CYRIL WILLIAM. The story of the Royal Ballet. Rev. ed.
Black, 1959. [83] pp. front., illus. 7s. 6d.

> First published as *The Story of the Sadler's Wells Ballet*, in 1954. A simple
> history of the company for children; about 20 pages have been added to
> bring the story up to 1959. The rather small illustrations consist of 38
> reproductions of photographs mainly of ballets in the repertoire.

GUEST, IVOR, *ed.* La Fille mal gardée. 1960.

> *See* no. 361.

295 'Dancing as an extra. A student has a chance to appear with the Royal
Ballet.' *In: The Times*, 30th August, 1961, p. 10.

> The ballet was *The Sleeping beauty.*

296 LAWSON, JOAN. 'The new generation of the Royal Ballet.' *In: The
Ballet Annual 1961*, 15th issue, pp. 94–103.

297 MANCHESTER, PHYLLIS WINIFRED. 'The Royal Ballet in the U.S.A.'
In: The Ballet Annual 1962, 16th issue, pp. 47–50.

298 'Need to bring on young dancers. Royal Ballet living on its capital.'
In: The Times, 1st February, 1962, p. 5.

> Questions whether young dancers on tour have proper opportunities for
> training, and untried choreographers opportunity for experiment.

299 'Royal Ballet could use Ballet Rambert.' *In: The Times*, 2nd February, 1962, p. 13.

Continuation of article in *The Times*, 1st February, 1962, p. 5, 'Need to Bring on Young Dancers . . .'. Suggests that Ballet Rambert could be used as a training ground for the Royal Ballet.

300 ROSLAVLEVA, NATALIE. 'The Royal Ballet in the U.S.S.R.' *In: The Ballet Annual 1962*, 16th issue, pp. 38–46, 145–6.

301 MONAHAN, JAMES. 'Ballet today.' *In: Aspect*, No. 6, July 1963, p. [69]–76. 8 illus.

Reviews the development of ballet from Diaghilev and relates the work of the Royal Ballet to it.

302 MONAHAN, JAMES. 'Madam Ninette.' *In: The Ballet Annual [1963]*, 18th issue, pp. 32–4.

Reprint of an article from *The Guardian*.

303 [MONAHAN, JAMES], KENNEDY, JAMES, *pseud.* 'Nureyev and the Royal Ballet: a study in reciprocal influences.' *In: The Guardian*, 19th December, 1963, p. 7.

304 PETO, MICHAEL, *and* BLAND, ALEXANDER. The dancer's world. Collins, 1963. [192] pp. front., illus. 45s.

About 170 reproductions of photographs of dancers of the Royal Ballet and guest artists, mainly at practice and rehearsal, in which the dancers appear to be unaware of the camera. There is a section on the Kirov Ballet, which visited Covent Garden in 1961. Alexander Bland, ballet critic of *The Observer*, has written the notes, and an introduction discussing the appeal of ballet and the problems and satisfactions of being a dancer. The 10 drawings are by Josef Herman.

' "The Swan lake" that nobody knows.' 11th December, 1963.

See no. 382.

'Divided loyalties for the producer of "Swan lake".' 6th January, 1964.

See no. 383.

305 MONEY, KEITH, *photographer*. The art of the Royal Ballet. Harrap, [1964]. 272 pp. fronts. (1 col.), 11 pl. (col.), illus. 65s.

The photographer, who 'worked almost continuously with the company for 6 months', covers the period from *Marguerite and Armand* in 1963 to *The Dream* in 1964. In some 450 photographs and 15 sketches, the majority taken unposed at rehearsal and during performance, he attempts 'to suggest a sequence of events'; and writes the introduction and captions. Other ballets recorded at some length are – *Elektra, Petrushka, Sylvia, Les Sylphides, The Two pigeons, Bournonville extracts, House of birds, The Rake's progress, The Invitation, Coppélia* and *La Fille mal gardée*. In an adverse review in *The Dancing Times* for August 1964, (p. 586) 'M.C.' considers that there is 'a haphazard scrapbook air about the whole book'.

'A Russian ballet which has been adopted by the British.'   24th February, 1964.

> *See* no. 377.

WRIGHT, PETER.   'Quintet & Summer's night.'   Christmas 1964.

> *See* no. 354.

306   AMAYA, MARIO.   'Royal Ballet USA.'   *In: About the House*, v. 1, no. 10, June 1965, pp. [4]–[7].   2 illus.

> 1965 tour.

307   ARUNDELL, DENNIS.   The story of Sadler's Wells 1683–1964.   Hamilton, 1965.   xiv, 306 pp.   front., 16 pl., illus.   35s.

> Although ballet was performed at this theatre during the earlier periods, the following chapters are of greatest interest, containing material on Sadler's Wells Ballet and Sadler's Wells Theatre Ballet – 16, 'Enter "The Lady" 1925–33'; 17, 'Years of Achievement 1933–9'; 18, 'Opera and Ballet 1939–51'; 19, 'Success Again 1951–7'.

BRINSON, PETER.   'The new old "Swan lake".'   August 1965.

> *See* no. 384.

SADLER'S WELLS THEATRE BALLET, 1946–57

308   NOBLE, PETER.   'Sadler's Wells Theatre Ballet: the junior company makes good.'   *In: Theatre World*, v. 43, no. 273, October 1947, pp. 22, 35, 36.   1 illus.

FROST, HONOR. How a ballet is made. 1948.

See no. 366.

309 WILLIAMS, PETER. 'The Sadler's Wells Theatre Ballet.' *In: Souvenirs de Ballet*, no. 1, 1949, pp. 64–[7]. 3 illus.

310 WOOD, ROGER, *photographer.* The Theatre Ballet of Sadler's Wells, in photographs. Phoenix House, 1952. 32 pp. front., illus. 7s. 6d.

The introduction by Arnold Haskell explains the function of the company, and notes outstanding productions. 53 reproductions of photographs, with comments by John Hall, portray the company and individual dancers at rehearsal and in performance.

311 CHUJOY, ANATOLE. 'The Sadler's Wells Theatre Ballet.' *In: The Ballet Annual 1953*, 7th issue, pp. 78–85.

312 'The Sadler's Wells Theatre Ballet – a statistical survey from the first performance of the company on 8th April, 1946, until 31st March, 1954.' *In: The Ballet Annual 1955*, 9th issue, pp. [136]–[7].

313 Sadler's Wells Theatre Ballet, no. 1. Sadler's Wells Foundation, [1956?]. 56 pp. illus.

Edited by Russell Brown.

The text deals mainly with ballets performed by the company, and statistics. About 66 illustrations are reproductions of photographs, costume designs and 2 facsimiles of Hogarth's 'Rake's progress'.

314 [SWINSON, CYRIL WILLIAM], FISHER, HUGH, *pseud.* The Sadler's Wells Theatre Ballet. Black, 1956. 82 pp. front., 31 pl. 12s. 6d.

For reference only, apart from the introduction which reviews the work and aims of the company. The period covered is 1945–56. The main text lists the repertoire from 1946, arranged chronologically by first performance by the Sadler's Wells Theatre Ballet, giving first cast. It is preceded by a yearly account of the personnel of the company. Appended are separate indexes of composers, choreographers, designers and dancers who have worked with the company, a list of tours undertaken and ... 'A Statistical Survey from the First Performance of the Company ... until 31st March, 1956'. 86 reproductions of photographs on plates depict scenes from ballets performed.

MARKOVA-DOLIN BALLET, 1935-8

315   VAN DAMM, VIVIAN.   Tonight and every night.   Paul, 1952.   206 pp.
front., 22 pl.   15s.

> Chapter 9, 'Ballet through Britain', the formation and first tour of the
> Markova-Dolin Ballet [c.1935]. The author was associated with Laura
> Henderson, who financed the company.

INTERNATIONAL BALLET, 1941-53

316   'International Ballet.'   *In: The Ballet Annual 1948*, 2nd issue, pp. 160-1.

> Check list of ballets performed by this company, giving choreographers,
> composers, designers and principal dancers.

317   ROSOMUND, FRANCIS.   'The International Ballet.'   *In: Souvenirs de
Ballet*, no. 1, 1949, pp. 48-53.   8 illus.

318   FRANKS, ARTHUR HENRY.   'The Inglesby legend: a short factual survey
of the International Ballet.'   *In: The Ballet Annual 1950*, 4th issue,
pp. 104-8.

319   International Ballet. [c. 1951].   [32] pp.   illus.

> Brochure containing photographs of dancers, and ballets in the repertoire
> including sequences of the ballets *Everyman* and *The Masque of Comus*. No
> title-page. Title taken from cover.

320   International Ballet 1941-51.   [International Ballet Company, 1951.]
[36] pp.   illus.   5s.

> A brochure presenting 'a pictorial record and impression of the present
> rather than . . . the past', with a tribute to Nicolai Sergueeff, by Mona
> Inglesby. Some 60 photographs portray the company in posed studies and
> portraits. An appendix lists the Council of Management and members of the
> company. There are reproductions of 13 sketches by Fred Daniels.

METROPOLITAN BALLET, 1947-9

321   COTON, A. V.   'The Metropolitan Ballet.'   *In: Souvenirs de Ballet*,
no. 1, 1949, pp. 54-[9].   10 illus.

FESTIVAL BALLET, 1950–

322 WILSON, GEORGE BUCKLEY LAIRD. 'The Festival Ballet in Monte Carlo.' *In: The Ballet Annual 1952*, 6th issue, pp. 137–8.

323 HALL, ALFRED GEORGE, *ed.* London's Festival Ballet Annual 1956–7. Grays Inn Press, [1956]. 151 pp. illus. 21s.
 'Background to a Ballet: the story of how a ballet is staged' is the most substantial article. There is also information on and reproductions of about 140 photographs of ballets in the repertoire, tours, guest dancers and personnel of the company; also about 20 portrait sketches.

[324] DAVIS, MIKE, *photographer.* Mike Davis looks at London's Festival Ballet. C. P. Enterprises, 1957. [48] pp. illus. 7s. 6d.

 CROWLE, PIGEON. The Nutcracker ballet: a Christmas fantasy and its history. 1958.
 See no. 370.

324a SWINSON, CYRIL WILLIAM. London's Festival Ballet. [Rev. ed.] Black, 1958. 32 pp. front., illus. (Dancers of To-day Series. No. 4.) 7s. 6d.
 First published in 1953 as *Festival ballet*. (*See also* no. 432.)

WESTERN THEATRE BALLET, 1957–

325 MASSIE, ANNETTE. 'Creating a new audience for the ballet.' *In: The Guardian*, 22nd April, 1960, p. 8. Illus.

326 Western Theatre Ballet. [1963?] [16] pp. illus.
 A publicity booklet with 28 reproductions of photographs of ballets in the repertoire, and individual dancers. There is a brief introduction to the work of the company and the repertoire is listed, giving composer, choreographer designer and duration of ballet, with a few words setting the scene of the ballets.

OTHER COMPANIES

327 CLARKE, MARY. 'Ballets on a smaller stage.' *In: The Ballet Annual 1954*, 8th issue, pp. 132–3.

Ballet Workshop, New-Ballet Company and the John Cranko season at Henley-on-Thames.

328 FROSTICK, MICHAEL. 'Ballet premieres – Edinburgh International Ballet.' *In: The Ballet Annual 1959,* 13th issue, pp. 91–3.

329 'Significant new ballet company.' *In: The Times,* 2nd October, 1961, p. 16.

Formation and repertoire of Walter Gore's London Ballet.

VI. BALLETS

THE items included in this chapter are those which treat of a number of ballets or individual ballets *per se*. Some of these productions are presented by or associated with one company in particular, and are an illustration of the work of that company at a certain period. In such cases a reference has been made in the preceding chapter on companies.

The Complete book of ballets and its three supplements, by Cyril Beaumont, are the outstanding works in this chapter. They cover a wide range historically and topographically, and are more detailed than any of the other works listed below. The latter tend to deal with the present (at time of publication) and immediate past repertoire.

Some American books have been included. On the whole these cover ballets in the repertoire of American companies but are useful for information on the works of English choreographers performed only by American companies; for instance, the later work of Antony Tudor.

BIBLIOGRAPHY

Arrangement. 1. Works on more than one ballet arranged chronologically by date of publication. 2. Works on individual ballets arranged alphabetically by title of ballet, and then chronologically. 3. Children's books arranged chronologically by date of publication.

WORKS ON MORE THAN ONE BALLET

330 Beauties of the opera and the ballet. Bogue, 1845. xiv, 160 pp. 10 pl., illus.

> The plots of the following ballets are given – *Giselle, Le Diable boiteux, Ondine* and *La Sylphide*; also the history of Her Majesty's Theatre. There are 10 steel engraved portraits, and wood engravings of scenes from the works described, carried out under the supervision of Charles Heath.

331 The English ballet folios. [Kelgee Publications, 1945]. illus.
> 1. *The Rake's progress;* 2. *Les Patineurs;* 3. *The Prospect before us.*

Each booklet is about 4 pages; the introduction is by P. W. Manchester. The illustrations are of members of the Sadler's Wells Company in poses from the above ballets, drawn by Sheila Graham.

332 Ballet Pocket Series. Black, 1949–60. 96 pp. illus. 4s. each.

Gives the background and narrates the plot briefly.

332a POSNER, SANDY.

Coppélia, 4th ed. 1953; *Giselle*, 5th ed. 1953; *Petrouchka*, 3rd ed. 1957; *The Sleeping princess*, 2nd ed. 1953.

332b ROBERTSON, MARION.

Le Beau Danube and *Le Tricorne*, 2nd ed. 1949; *La Boutique fantasque*, 2nd ed. 1949; *Hamlet* and *Miracle in the Gorbals*, 1949; *L'Oiseau de feu* and *Schéhérazade*, 2nd ed. 1953; *The Rake's progress* and *Checkmate*, 1949; *Swan lake*, 3rd ed. 1959.

332c SANDON, JOSEPH.

Façade and other early Ashton ballets, 1954; *Les Sylphides, Le Carnaval* and *Le Spectre de la rose*, 1954.

332d SWINSON, CYRIL.

The Nutcracker (Casse Noisette), 1960.

333 BEAUMONT, CYRIL WILLIAM. Complete book of ballets: a guide to the principal ballets of the nineteenth and twentieth centuries. Rev. ed. Putnam, 1949. xxi, 1106 pp. front., 158 pl. 42s.

First published 1937; this revised edition was reprinted with additions in 1951.

English choreographers represented are Ninette de Valois (also 1st and 2nd supplements), Anton Dolin, Keith Lester, Frederick Ashton (also 1st, 2nd and 3rd supplements) and Antony Tudor (also 1st supplement), and some Empire and Alhambra ballets as well. This is a standard work. The contents are arranged chronologically by date of birth of choreographer. Biographical information on the choreographer is given followed by origin, history and plot of the ballets; also original cast, choreographer, designer, composer and writer of scenario. Many ballets after 1910 'have been described from observation or from information supplied by the choreographer'. Three supplements, following the plan of the original volume, bring it up to date to 1955.

334   — — Supplement to Complete Book of Ballets (Putnam, 1952. 21s.)

335   — — Ballets of Today, . . . (2nd supplement, Putnam, 1954. 21s.)

336   — — Ballets, Past and Present (3rd supplement, Putnam, 1955. 21s.)

> These include the following choreographers – Andrée Howard (1st, 2nd, 3rd), Frank Staff (1st), John Cranko (2nd, 3rd), Walter Gore (2nd) and Robert Helpmann (3rd).

337 BENTHALL, MICHAEL, *and others*. 'Hamlet' and 'Miracle in the Gorbals'. Bodley Head, for the Governors of Sadler's Wells Foundations, 1949. 46 pp. front., 12 pl. (Sadler's Wells Ballet Books. No. 3.) 2s. 6d.

> 'The Dance-Drama', by Michael Benthall; 'The Dancer's *Hamlet*', by Clemence Dane; 'A Note on the Décors', by M. H. Middleton; 'The Place of *Miracle in the Gorbals* in Contemporary Choreography', by A. L. Haskell; 'The Music of *Miracle in the Gorbals*', by Eric Blom. The appendix gives the casts of the 2 ballets, in the original production.

338 DAVIDSON, GLADYS. Stories of the ballets. Werner Laurie, 1949. xvi, 486 pp. front. (col.), 16 pl. 15s.

> ' . . . Romantic stories derived from some of the most famous ballets . . . [from] the nineteenth century to the present day' (Author's Preface), with no critical analysis of choreography or performers. Arrangement is alphabetical by choreographer; some 20 are represented, including Frederick Ashton, Adeline Genée, Walter Gore, Robert Helpmann, Andrée Howard, Mona Inglesby, Susan Salaman, Antony Tudor and Ninette de Valois. Appended is an index of ballets giving information on book, music, scenery, costume, choreography and first production.

339 KIRSTEIN, LINCOLN, *and others*. 'Carnaval', 'Le Spectre de la rose' and 'Les Sylphides'. Bodley Head for the Governors of Sadler's Wells Foundations, 1949. 40 pp. front., 12 pl. (Sadler's Wells Ballet Books. No. 4.) 2s. 6d.

> 'Fokine', by Lincoln Kirstein; 'Michael Fokine, Choreographer', by Arnold L. Haskell; 'The Music of *Les Sylphides*, *Carnaval* and *Le Spectre de la rose*', by Stewart Deas. The appendix lists casts of first production by Sadler's Wells Ballet and revivals of the 3 ballets with alternative casts.

340 LAWSON, JOAN, *and others*. 'Job' and 'The Rake's progress'. Bodley
Head for the Governors of the Sadler's Wells Foundations, 1949.
48 pp. front., 12 pl. (Sadler's Wells Ballet Books. No. 2.) 2s. 6d.

> 'Ninette de Valois as Choreographer', by Joan Lawson; 'Imaginary Land-
> scape with Figures' (Rex Whistler's designs and costumes for *The Rake's
> progress*), by James Laver; '*Job*', by Geoffrey Keynes; 'The Music of *Job*', by
> Frank Howes. The appendix lists the cast of the original productions for
> both ballets.

341 LAWRENCE, ROBERT. The Victor book of ballets and ballet music.
New York, Simon and Schuster, 1950. xviii, 531 pp. illus. $5.

> 'Ballet Perspectives', a short history, introduces the main text, which is
> arranged alphabetically under the name of the ballet, with information on
> composers, designers of scenery and costume, librettist, details of first per-
> formance; the pattern and/or plot being described, in some cases with
> musical examples. English choreographers represented are – Frederick
> Ashton (*Cinderella*, *Façade* and *The Wise virgins*), Ninette de Valois (*The
> Prospect before us*), Anton Dolin (*Romantic age*, *Scènes de ballet*) and Antony
> Tudor (*Dark elegies*, *Dim lustre*, *Gala performance*, *Jardin aux lilas*, *Pillar of
> fire*, *Romeo and Juliet*, *Shadow of the wind* and *Undertow*). Appended is a
> 'Selective Discography of RCA Victor Recordings' covering 71 ballets;
> also indexes for choreographers, and for composers and a general index.
> About 200 illustrations are rather small and indistinct.

342 GUEST, IVOR. 'The miracles of Jules Perrot.' *In: Opera Ballet Music-
Hall in the World 2*. [1952], pp. [51]–[60].

> Perrot's divertissements performed at Her Majesty's Theatre in the Hay-
> market, by some of the leading ballerinas of the Romantic Ballet. The text
> is in French and English. The 14 illustrations are facsimiles of letters and
> contemporary prints.

343 WHITE, ERIC WALTER. 'The great choreographical creations during
the winter: new British ballets. *In: Opera Ballet Music-Hall in the
World 1*, 1952, pp. 5–[14]. 11 illus.

> *Donald of the burthens; Mirror for witches; Tiresias; Pineapple Poll; Harlequin
> in April.*

344 HASKELL, ARNOLD LIONEL. 'English ballet: recent works.' *In: Opera
Ballet Music-Hall in the World 3*, 1953, pp. 55–[9]. 7 illus.

345 BALANCHINE, GEORGE. Balanchine's complete stories of the great

ballets. New York, Doubleday, 1954. 615 pp. 24 pl., illus., bibliog. $5.95.

Edited by Francis Mason.

Naturally this has an American slant but Part 1, 'Stories of the Great Ballets', describes some 130 ballets of which approximately a quarter have a particular current or historical interest for ballet-goers in the United Kingdom. Composer, choreographer, designer of scenery and costume, lighting, company first presenting and in which theatre and principal dancers are given first. Then follows a description of plot or theme related to the movement of the ballet. Finally a note gives circumstances of creation, quotations from reviews, information concerning revivals. Parts 2–11 include information on history; careers; dancers; a chronology; a glossary (Part 9); 'Annotated Selection of Ballet Recordings', by Jacques Fray (Part 10); 'Selected Reading Guide' (Part 11), which contains about 90 items arranged alphabetically by title. Publisher is given, but no date. Drawings are by Marta Becket.

346 KROKOVER, ROSALYN. The new Borzoi book of ballets. New York, Knopf, 1956. xvii, 320, xii, [2] pp. 32 pl. $6.

Deals with ballets in the repertory of American companies; includes *Daphnis and Chloe* (among other productions) and *Illuminations*, by Frederick Ashton and *Dim lustre, Gala performance, Judgement of Paris, Lilac garden, Pillar of fire* and *Romeo and Juliet*, by Antony Tudor. The plot of each ballet is described, with information on date of first production, music, setting and

347   principal dancers. This book replaces *The Borzoi book of ballets*, by Grace Roberts published in 1946, which included *The Devil's holiday*, by Frederick Ashton and *Undertow*, by Antony Tudor. Ivor Guest considers that *The New Borzoi book of ballets* is 'more popular and less informative in approach' (*Ballet: an exhibition . . . 1957, see* no. 7). There are 53 illustrations on plates.

348 CROWLE, PIGEON. Come to the ballet. Faber, 1957. 132 pp. front. (col.), 16 pl., illus. 15s.

The plot of 10 ballets in the past and present repertoire of English companies is given, with information on the choreographer and his collaborators, origin of ballet, revivals etc. Text illustrations are drawn by Charles Stewart and there are 20 reproductions of photographs on plates. A glossary is appended.

349 DREW, DAVID, ed. The Decca book of ballet. Muller, 1958. xxix, 572 pp. front., 36 pl., illus. 63s.

The introduction is by Ansermet. The aim is to 'provide guidance for those who listen to ballet music on gramophone records, in the concert hall, and on the radio', and to help the ballet-goer to follow the action. It is also claimed that 'a complete record (of ballets) now in the repertoire of the two Royal Ballet companies' is given. The main sections covering pp. 25–487 are Part 2, 'Ballets to Specially Composed Scores', and Part 3, 'Symphonic Ballets', each being arranged alphabetically by composer, sub-divided by ballets. The following information is provided – arranger and orchestrator; writer of the book; choreographer; designer of scenery and costume; place of first production and which company; where appropriate, revivals; first British production; table of musical numbers and conductor. The remaining sections are Part 1, 'Short History of Ballet', by A. L. Haskell, Part 4, 'Some Famous Dancers and Choreographers', by G. B. L. Wilson and K. I. Newby, and Part 5, 'Some Famous Ballet Companies' (including Ballet Rambert, London's Festival Ballet and the two Royal Ballet companies). Appended is a discography compiled by the Decca Recording Company.

Contributors are drawn from the world of music and ballet and include Felix Aprahamian, Richard Arnell, Clive Barnes, Eric Blom, Joan Chissell, Mary Clarke, John Lanchbery, Edward Lockspeiser, Leighton Lucas, M. Montagu-Nathan and J. A. Westrup. This wide range may account for unevenness in the approach and details of the articles. There are musical examples. The 45 reproductions of photographs on plates depict scenes and dancers from the ballets discussed.

350   HART, JOHN, *photographer*. The Royal Ballet in performance at Covent Garden. Faber, 1958. 160 pp. illus. 36s.

About 220 excellent action photographs arranged to illustrate the plots of the following ballets – *The Sleeping beauty; Job; La Péri; Cinderella; Birthday offering; The Lady and the fool; Prince of the Pagodas; Noctambules; Miraculous mandarin; Giselle; Lac des cygnes.* There is a short introduction to each ballet and choreographer represented.

351   HALL, ALFRED GEORGE. The story of the ballet [series]. Ballet Books, [1961.] 25 pp. illus. 2s. 6d. each.

Coppélia; Giselle; The Nutcracker; Sleeping beauty; Swan lake; Les Sylphides. Each booklet contains a brief introduction to and plot of the ballet, with many photographs drawn from different sources.

352   BARNES, CLIVE. 'Ballets down the drain. 2 . . . ballets seen in Britain.' *In: The Ballet Annual 1963.* 17th issue, pp. 87–93.

Ballets, presented by foreign companies, which the author would like to see in the repertoire of English companies, and native ballets which he would like to see revived.

353 COTON, A. V. 'Shakespeare and the ballet.' *In: The Listener*, v. 71, no. 1,830, 23rd April, 1964, pp. 667–9. 3 illus.
   Among others *The Dream* (Ashton) and *Images of love* (Macmillan).

354 WRIGHT, PETER. 'Quintet & Summer's night.' *In: About the House*, v. 1, no. 8, Christmas 1964, pp. [14]–16. 6 illus.

WORKS ON INDIVIDUAL BALLETS

Checkmate

355 'Checkmate: a new ballet by Arthur Bliss.' *In: The Musical Times*, v. 78, no. 1,132, June 1937, pp. 522–3.

356 ABER, ADOLF. 'Checkmate: Arthur Bliss's ballet in Paris.' *In: The Musical Times*, v. 78, no. 1,133, July 1937, pp. 648–9. 1 illus.

Doktor Faust

357 HEINE, HEINRICH. Doktor Faust: a dance poem. . . . Nevill, 1952. v, [64] pp. illus., 10s. 6d.
   Edited and translated by Basil Ashmore. 'Mr. Ashmore went to the British Museum, and here now is his find.' (J. C. Trewin, in the introduction.)
   This scenario was written at the request of Benjamin Lumley who was Manager of Her Majesty's Theatre from 1842–58. The ballet was never staged owing to the prolonged appearance of the singer Jenny Lind and the hostility of the ballet master, according to Heine. Also translated is a letter from Heine to Lumley on the history of the Faust story, dated 1st October, 1851. 12 wood engravings are by Hellmuth Weissenborn.

Donald of the Burthens

358 MONAHAN, JAMES. 'Donald of the burthens.' *In: Foyer*, no. 2, winter 1951–2, p. 47. 1 illus.

Fairy Queen

359 MANDINIAN, EDWARD, *photographer*. Purcell's 'The fairy queen', as presented by the Sadler's Wells Ballet and the Covent Garden Opera: a photographic record. Lehmann, 1948. 96 pp. 53 pl.; illus.
   The preface is by Edward J. Dent.

16 plates depict the ballet (4, 7, 9, 12, 13, 30–2, 36–40, 44–6). Constant Lambert contributes an article on 'The Music of *The Fairy queen*' with an appendix listing the pieces used in his adaptation of Purcell's music; Michael Ayrton writes on 'The Design and the Device'. 60 illustrations on plates and 12 smaller illustrations include reproductions of photographs of the production and of costume and décor sketches.

360   MIDDLETON, M. H.   'The Fairy queen.'   *In: The Ballet Annual* [1948], 2nd issue, pp. 141–3.

Fille mal Gardée

361   GUEST, IVOR, *ed.*   La Fille mal gardée.   *The Dancing Times*, 1960. 71 pp.   16 pl., illus., bibliog.   (Famous Ballets 1.)   7s. 6d.

A history of one of the oldest ballets in performance. Chapters 2–5 inclusive deal with the Royal Ballet production, and are written by Frederick Ashton, the choreographer, John Lanchbery, who arranged the music, Nadia Nerina, who danced the role of Lise, and Osbert Lancaster, who designed the sets. Other chapters deal with foreign productions. The bibliography contains 12 items; there are music examples and the 26 illustrations on plates are reproductions of prints and photographs.

Giselle

362   BEAUMONT, CYRIL WILLIAM.   The ballet called 'Giselle'.   The Author, 1944.   140 pp.   front., 46 pl., diagr.   21s.

'First attempt . . . to study the evolution of a ballet from conception to realization, and to follow it through its main phases of production [also an endeavour] to view the ballet from both sides of the curtain' (Author's Preface). A detailed work divided into Part 1, 'Historical and Biographical', and Part 2, 'Technical and Critical'. The latter includes a simplified choreographic script of the ballet and the author's remarks on production. The illustrations are reproductions of photographs of scenes from different productions, and of lithographs and costume designs.

363   GUEST, IVOR.   'Parodies of "Giselle" on the English stage (1841–71).'   *In: Theatre Notebook Bulletin*, v. 9, no. 2, January–March 1955, pp. 38–46.   4 pl.

Invitation

364   CRISP, CLEMENT.   'The Invitation.'   *In: The Musical Times*, v. 102, no. 1,416, February 1961, pp. 88–[9].

Some information on the collaboration of composer and choreographer.

Judgement of Paris

365 WEAVER, JOHN. The Judgement of Paris. A dramatic entertainment
in dancing and singing, after the manner of the ancient Greeks and
Romans. As it is perform'd at the Theatre-Royal in Drury Lane. . . .
Printed for J. Tonson . . . 1733. 12 pp.

> On title-page 'Words by Mr. Congreve. Set to Musick by Mr. Seedo'.
> A libretto which gives the placing of the dances, and the stage directions.

Khadra

366 FROST, HONOR. How a ballet is made. Golden Galley Press, 1948.
[3], 27 pp. front. (col.), 4 pl. (col.), illus. (Ballet Series. No. 1.)
10s. 6d.

> Staged by the Sadler's Wells Theatre Ballet. The choreographer was
> Celia Franca, with whom the author, who designed the costumes and décor,
> worked closely. 33 illustrations are reproduced from photographs by
> Churton Fairman and Roger Wood.

Loves of Mars and Venus

367 WEAVER, JOHN.   The Loves of Mars and Venus: a dramatick entertainment of dancing, attempted in imitation of the pantomimes of the
ancient Greeks and Romans: as perform'd at the theatre in Drury-
Lane. W. Mears . . . J. Browne . . . 1717. [2], ix–29 pp.

> The scenario of Weaver's first serious attempt at the *ballet d'action*. He
> indicates the placing of the dances and mime, listing in scene 2 the emotions
> to be displayed and the appropriate gestures. (B.M. C.121. C.19.)

Miracle in the Gorbals

368 HASKELL, ARNOLD LIONEL. Miracle in the Gorbals: a study. Edinburgh, The Albyn Press, 1946. 63 pp. 15 pl. 8s. 6d.

> The history of the ballet, with an assessment of dancers' interpretations
> and a description written while attending a performance. The ballet was first
> produced in 1944, with choreography by Robert Helpmann, music by
> Arthur Bliss and scenario by Michael Benthall.

369 'Miracle in the Gorbals.' *In: Scotlands SMT Magazine*, v. 39, no. 2,
February 1947, pp. 12–14. 6 illus.

Nutcracker

370 CROWLE, PIGEON. The Nutcracker ballet: a Christmas fantasy and its
history. Faber, 1958. 52 pp. front. (col.), 40 pl. 21s.

> Alexandre Benois wrote the foreword and David Lichine the preface.
> The plot, with an account of the 1892 Russian production and some re-
> vivals, and of the 1957 Festival Ballet production.

Orpheus and Eurydice

371 WEAVER, JOHN. The Fable of Orpheus and Eurydice, with a dramatick
entertainment in dancing thereupon: attempted in imitation of the
ancient Greeks and Romans. As perform'd at the Theatre Royal in
Drury-Lane. Printed for W. Mears . . . J. Browne . . . and W.
Chetwood . . . 1718. [1], 25 pp. front.

> The plot without indication of dances or stage directions, interspersed
> with verses and notes on the characters. The frontispiece is signed E. Kirkall.
> (B.M. 1343. d.44.)

Petrouchka

372 'Royal Ballet's problems in staging "Petrouchka".' *In: The Times,*
18th March, 1957, p. 12.

Sleeping Beauty

373 ANTHONY, GORDON, *photographer.* 'The Sleeping princess': camera
studies. Routledge, 1940. 49 pp. 63 pl. 42s.

> 'A collection of 'Action' pictures taken in my studio of the chief characters
> from the story, in poses which are as near as possible characteristic ones,
> taken from the dances they illustrate, and are placed in the order of their
> appearance'. The majority appeared in *The Bystander.* Articles – 'Tchaikowsky
> and the Ballet', by Constant Lambert; 'Décor and Costume', by Nadia
> Benois; a study of the choreography, by A. L. Haskell.

374 CHAPPELL, WILLIAM. 'The Sleeping beauty.' *In: Penguin New
Writing* 28, July 1946, pp. 87–100. 4 pl.

> First production by Sadler's Wells Ballet at Covent Garden.

375 MANDINIAN, EDWARD, *photographer.* 'The Sleeping beauty' as presented by The Sadler's Wells Ballet 1946: a photographic record.
C. W. Beaumont, 1946. [8], [16] pp. front., 39 pl. 25s.

A record of the first production to be presented in the Royal Opera House after the Second World War. Cyril Beaumont narrates the story of the ballet and gives his impressions of the production.

376   SITWELL, SACHEVERELL, *and others*.   The Sleeping beauty.   Bodley Head, for the Governors of Sadler's Wells Foundations, 1949. 56 pp. front., 12 pl.   (Sadler's Wells Ballet Books. No. 1.)   2s. 6d.

'*The Sleeping beauty*', by Sacheverell Sitwell; 'A Backstage View', by Joy Newton; 'First Performance', by Tamara Karsavina; 'The Composer and the Music', by Dyneley Hussey. The appendix lists the cast for the first Sadler's Wells production and the 1946 revival.

377   'A Russian ballet which has been adopted by the British.'   *In: The Times*, 24th February, 1964, p. 14.

Royal Ballet production of *The Sleeping beauty*.

Song of the Earth

378   PORTER, ANDREW.   'The Song of the earth.'   *In: About the House*, v. 2, no. 2, June 1966, pp. 16–18.

Swan Lake

379   SEDGWICK, RUSSELL, *photographer*.   The 'Swan lake' as presented by the Sadler's Wells Ballet: a photographic record. The story of the ballet, by Cyril W. Beaumont.   C. W. Beaumont, 1947, [8], 8pp.   front., 29 pl.   21s.

A record of the production first presented on 7th September, 1943, including the cast list for the first performance. Margot Fonteyn and Robert Helpmann are portrayed in the principal roles.

[380] DERRINGTON, E. G.   The story of 'Swan lake', the ballet.   St. Clements Press, 1948.   28 pp.   illus.   2s.

Edited by W. G. Raffé.

381   BEAUMONT, CYRIL WILLIAM.   The ballet called 'Swan lake'.   The Author, 1952.   176 pp.   front., 42 pl., diagr., bibliog.   25s.

A study similar to the author's *The Ballet called Giselle* (*see* no. 362). There are 3 appendices – A, 'Alternative Choreographic Versions of certain Steps and Variations'; B, 'Original Sequence of Numbers in Tchaikowsky's Score . . . first Production at Moscow 1877'; C, 'Bibliography' ,which con-

tains 33 items including Russian material. The 60 illustrations on plates are
reproductions of photographs and facsimiles.

382   'The "Swan lake" that nobody knows.'   *In: The Times*, 11th December, 1963, p. 17.

   Resumé of the early history of the ballet, leading up to the Royal Ballet
   versions. This article was occasioned by Robert Helpmann's new production
   for the company, and outlines the major changes he made.

383   'Divided loyalties for the producer of "Swan lake".'   *In: The Times*,
6th January, 1964, p. 6.

   Royal Ballet's new 1963 production.

384   BRINSON, PETER.   'The new old "Swan lake".'   *In: About the House*,
v. 1, no. 11, August 1965, pp. [2]–5.   3 illus.

   Production of the Royal Ballet touring company.

Sylvia

385   HUSSEY, DYNELEY.   'A classic of ballet.'   *In: Britain To-day*, no. 200,
December 1952, pp. 36–9.   1 pl.

Tiresias

386   ' "Tiresias": a symposium of views.'   *In: Foyer*, no. 1, autumn 1951,
pp. 41–[5].   10 illus.

   Alan Rawsthorne writes on the music; James Monahan and C. B. Mortlock
   on the choreography. The illustrations include 7 musical quotations.

CHILDREN'S BOOKS

'Stories of the ballet' is a popular type of publication in children's books.
The following give a straightforward account of the plot of selected ballets
with factual information on the choreographer and his collaborators, and
are illustrated.

387c   DAVIDSON, GLADYS.   Ballet stories for young people. 2nd ed.
Cassell, 1960.   12s. 6d.

388c   CROWLE, PIGEON.   Tales from the ballet.   Faber, 1960.   15s.

389c DAVIDSON, GLADYS. More ballet stories for young people. Cassell, 1961. 13s. 6d.

There is also the fictional type of publication with dialogue and descriptions, often with coloured illustrations. Some concentrate on one or two ballets only. In this category are the following, except the books by U. Roseveare and C. Viveash.

390c BRAHMS, CARYL. 'Coppélia': the story of the ballet told for the young. Haverstock, 1946. 3s.

391c LYNHAM, DEREK. Tales from the ballet: 'Swan lake', 'Petrouchka'. Sylvan Press, 1946. 6s. 6d.

392c ROSEVEARE, URSULA. Selected stories from the ballet. Pitman, 1955. (Based on a B.B.C. programme.) 8s. 6d.

393c VIVEASH, CHERRY. Tales from the ballet. Ronald, 1958. 10s.

394c APPLEBY, WILLIAM, and FOWLER, FREDERICK. 'Nutcraker' and 'Swan lake'. Oxford University Press, 1960. 8s. 6d.

395c APPLEBY, WILLIAM, and FOWLER, FREDERICK. 'The Sleeping beauty' and 'The Firebird'. Oxford University Press, 1964. 8s. 6d.

396c 'The Nutcracker' Oldbourne Press, 1963. (Stories from the ballet for Children Series.) 10s. 6d.

397c SHAD, W. H. 'Coppélia.' Oldbourne Press, 1964. (Stories from the Ballet for Children Series.) 10s. 6d.

VII. CHOREOGRAPHERS

THE first English choreographer of note was John Weaver (1673–1760). He does not appear to have recorded the choreography of his ballets *The Loves of Mars and Venus* and *The Fable of Orpheus and Eurydice* in the notation of the time, but the scenarios have been preserved (*see* nos. 367, 371) and these do give an idea of the action and sequence of the dances. English dancing masters, notably Kellom Tomlinson and Mr. Isaac, also composed theatrical as well as social dances. In the second half of the eighteenth century James d'Egville[1], an Englishman of French extraction, made a name as a choreographer. In 1799 he was ballet master at the King's Theatre and retained this post until 1809, with breaks during the seasons 1803, 1806 and 1807.[2] In the nineteenth century, while the Romantic Ballet flourished, London was one of the main centres for this art, but relied almost entirely on foreign choreographers; among these Jules Perrot was outstanding. He mounted many of his ballets in London. Other foreign choreographers working in London included Deshayes[1], Filippo Taglioni, Albert and Saint Léon. Afterwards there was practically nothing for about fifty years until the Alhambra and Empire provided a stage for the short spectacular ballets associated with these theatres. The Empire Theatre depended to a large extent on the Austrian Katti Lanner as choreographer. She was engaged in 1867 as ballet mistress and was responsible for some of the choreography. She was an Austrian dancer who had performed with Elssler and Cerrito, thus forming a link with the Romantic Ballet. The Alhambra employed several choreographers including Bertrand, Carlo Coppi and Alfredo Curti.

From the nineteen-twenties, a number of English choreographers have developed their talent, mainly with Ballet Rambert and the Royal Ballet. Ballet Rambert was the company on which Frederick Ashton, Antony Tudor, Andrée Howard, Walter Gore, Frank Staff and Norman Morrice created their first ballets, although almost all eventually worked for other companies. In 1935 Frederick Ashton was appointed choreographer to what was then the Vic-Wells Ballet; Antony Tudor after a period with the Vic-Wells

---

[1] The British Museum Library holds scenarios of ballets by d'Egville and Deshayes. They are listed in *A bibliography of dancing*, compiled by C. W. Beaumont (*see* no. 1).

[2] *The Romantic ballet in England*, by I. Guest, 1954, Chapter 3, pp. 22–3.

Ballet, and the London Ballet, which he directed, went to the United States; Norman Morrice has worked almost entirely with Ballet Rambert, but recently created *The Tribute* for the touring company of the Royal Ballet.

Apart from Ninette de Valois and Frederick Ashton, the most successful 'Royal Ballet choreographers' have been Robert Helpmann, John Cranko and Kenneth Macmillan. Robert Helpmann produced most of his ballets during and immediately after the Second World War, although in 1963 he returned to the Royal Ballet to create *Elektra*. John Cranko worked with the Sadler's Wells Theatre Ballet and the Royal Ballet from about 1949 to 1960 before joining the Stuttgart Ballet in 1961, while Kenneth Macmillan became a member of the Sadler's Wells Theatre Ballet in 1946 and remained with the Royal Ballet until autumn 1966, when he took over the direction of the ballet company in Berlin. From 1955 he had created ballets for the Royal Ballet and the Sadler's Wells Theatre Ballet. Other English choreographers include Jack Carter, Michael Charnley, Peter Wright and Peter Darrell; all have worked for several companies although the name of Peter Darrell is associated particularly with Western Theatre Ballet.

There is as much need for experiment in choreography as in any other art form, but because of the economic fact that ballet is an expensive entertainment it is always a problem to supply the means. Groups have been formed at different times to try to overcome this difficulty. Ballet Workshop had its headquarters at the Mercury Theatre, although independent of Ballet Rambert. It was formed by Angela and David Ellis in 1951 and survived for four years. A subscription membership formed the audience and performances were on Sundays. 'Forty choreographers were given a chance during these four years. . . . Not many of them showed talent but all their ideas were faithfully presented, and often a conventional piece of choreography would be made tolerable by a pretty set and costumes. . . . Above all, the programmes were musically interesting.'[3] By 1955 the directors were having difficulty in arranging programmes and finding dancers, so Ballet Workshop was discontinued. In 1952 Sadler's Wells Ballet backed a similar venture. Eventually 'its function was taken over by the Sunday Ballet Club',[4] which in 1958 put on its first production. It had been formed by Francis Sitwell and James Ranger 'to promote new ballets especially by as yet unrecognized choreographers and artists'.[5] Four to five performances were to be given

[3] *Dancers of Mercury*, by M. Clarke, 1962, Appendix A, p. 229.
[4] *A Dictionary of ballet*, by G. B. L. Wilson. Rev. ed. 1961, p. 254.
[5] 'Sunday ballet'. In: *The Dancing Times*, January 1958, p. 199.

annually and finances were to come from box office receipts, donations and sponsoring by ballet clubs and individuals. The Club survived until about 1962. A recent development has been the formation of Balletmakers Ltd. in 1963, a non-profit-making company with a Council of Management. It is 'open for active membership to dance students and young professionals in ballet and the allied arts. . . . At first . . . the work of the group [was concentrated] almost entirely in the classroom. . . . [The aim was] to present one annual production'.[6] The first public performance of this group was reviewed in *The Dancing Times* for August 1964 (p. 597).

BIBLIOGRAPHY

Arrangement. 1. General, and items dealing with more than one choreographer, arranged chronologically by date of publication. 2. Experimental Group: Ballet Workshop, arranged chronologically by date of item. 3. Individual choreographers arranged alphabetically by name of choreographer then chronologically by date of publication of item.

GENERAL, AND ITEMS DEALING WITH MORE THAN ONE CHOREOGRAPHER

398   'DANCE CRITIC.' 'Three British choreographers.' *In: Penguin New Writing 24,* 1945, pp. 116–27.   4 pl.
> Ninette de Valois; Andrée Howard, Frederick Ashton.

399   'Choreography. The place of mime.' *In: The Times,* 14th December, 1951, p. 2.

400   JACKSON, FRANK.   They make tomorrow's ballet: a study of the work of Jack Carter, Michael Charnley, John Cranko.   Meridian Books, 1953.   viii, [43] pp.   24 pl.
> Reviews the career and ballets of each choreographer to early 1953. The last chapter discusses the problems of the young choreographer. 44 reproductions on plates are from photographs by Paul Wilson.

401   FRANKS, ARTHUR HENRY.   Twentieth century ballet.   Burke, 1954. xii, 228 pp.   24 pl.

---

[6] '*The Birth of Balletmakers Limited*', by T. Early. *In: The Dancing Times,* September 1963, p. 705.

Chapter 7, 'Ninette de Valois'; Chapter 8, 'Frederick Ashton'; Chapter 9, Antony Tudor'; Chapter 10, 'Walter Gore'; Chapter 11, 'Robert Helpmann'; Chapter 12, 'Andrée Howard'; Chapter 16, 'John Cranko'; Chapter 18, '... and others' (includes Frank Staff, Celia Franca, Michael Charnley and Kenneth Macmillan). 36 reproductions of photographs on plates.

402 'Chance for the English choreographer. Dominant figure in our ballets.' *In: The Times*, 28th August, 1957, p. 11.

403 BRINSON, PETER. 'The choreographer to-day.' *In: The Ballet Annual 1958*, 12th issue, pp. 62–7.

404 RAMBERT, MARIE. 'The art of the choreographer.' *In: Journal of the Royal Society of Arts*, v. 110, no. 5,074, September 1962, pp. 741–51.

About 900 words devoted to English choreographers, particularly Walter Gore. The introduction of the speaker by Cyril Beaumont as Chairman, and the discussion, are also printed.

405 VAN PRAAGH, PEGGY, *and* BRINSON, PETER. The choreographic art: an outline of its principles and craft. Black, 1963. xxiv, 387 pp. 39 pl., illus. 60s.

The foreword is by Cyril Beaumont.
The authors collaborated for 6 years on this book. Peggy van Praagh worked for the Royal Ballet for many years as dancer, teacher and Assistant Director of the Sadler's Wells Theatre Ballet (1952–5) and is now Director of the Australian Ballet. Peter Brinson has written and lectured on ballet, and organizes and introduces 'Ballet for All'. A Research Fellowship awarded by the Council of Europe enabled him to study the archives of ballet in Europe (*see* no. 663).
7 parts present the choreographer in his historical setting, at work and in the theatre, and in relation to his collaborators – the librettist, composer, designer and dancer. There are 11 appendices. The first 3 reproduce ballet scenarios of the eighteenth, nineteenth and twentieth centuries. 4–11 are as follows – The Collaborators at Work; The Composer at Work; The Choreographer's Technical Inheritance; The Preservation of Ballets; Film; The Training of Choreographers; The Education of Critics and Audiences. The University Contribution; Glossary of Ballets; Suggestions for Further Study (*see also* no. 14).
This, the first comprehensive work in English on the subject, obtained a front-page review in *The Times Literary Supplement* (16th January, 1964, pp. 37–8). The anonymous reviewer considers that it contains 'much in-

formation available in more specific studies, some clear pictures and interesting documentary appendices, forming a quarter of the whole. To the
amateur of ballet who wishes to penetrate the mysteries of dance design, or
to the apprentice dance-designer who, having danced, wishes to design
dances, there is little help.' James Monahan (*The Dancing Times*, November
1963, p. 80), agrees with this point of view but considers that the book is
likely to remain the standard work for many years. The plates include
facsimiles of designs, manuscripts, scenes from ballets, also reproductions of
photographs of nineteenth- and twentieth-century ballets and dancers.

406 LAWSON, JOAN. A history of ballet and its makers. Pitman, 1964.
viii, 202 pp. 32 pl., bibliog. 50s.

   Chapter 3, 'The English Scene', includes John Weaver and foreign artists
in England; Chapter 10, 'The Search for Expression', includes Margaret
Morris; Chapter 11, 'English Ballet', – Marie Rambert, Ninette de Valois,
Frederick Ashton, Antony Tudor, Andrée Howard, Walter Gore, Robert
Helpmann, John Cranko, Kenneth Macmillan.
   'Choice of choreographers to discuss has been decided by reading accounts
of their works by their contemporaries and their own personal letters, plans
and other data, and by the fact that they are choreographers whose work is
of special interest to performers'. (Preface.) 68 illustrations on plates are
reproductions of photographs and facsimiles of original prints from other
books and title-pages. Cyril Beaumont considers that this book is 'A valuable
contribution to dance literature'. (*The Dancing Times*, December 1964, p.
133.)

EXPERIMENTAL GROUP: BALLET WORKSHOP

407 MANCHESTER, PHYLLIS WINIFRED. 'Ballet Workshop.'   *In: The Ballet
Annual 1952*, 6th issue, pp. 110–11.

408 CLARKE, MARY. 'Ballet Workshop.'   *In: The Ballet Annual 1953*, 7th
issue, pp. 119–23.
   Includes check list of productions.

409 WILSON, GEORGE BUCKLEY LAIRD. 'Report on Ballet Workshop.'
In: The Ballet Annual 1955, 9th issue, pp. 118–21.

410 WILSON, GEORGE BUCKLEY LAIRD. 'Ballet Workshop.'   *In: The
Ballet Annual 1956*, 10th issue, p. 115.

INDIVIDUAL CHOREOGRAPHERS

Ashton

411 DE ZOETE, BERYL. 'Frederick Ashton: background of a choreo-
     grapher.' *In: Horizon*, v. 6, no. 31, July 1942, pp. [8]–15.

412 BEAUMONT, CYRIL WILLIAM. 'Frederick Ashton – English choreo-
     grapher.' *In: Souvenirs de Ballet, no. 1*, 1949, pp. 6–[13].   3 illus.
     Includes a list of works arranged chronologically.

413 KRAGH-JACOBSEN, SVEND. 'International choreography takes the lead
     in Copenhagen . . . "Romeo and Juliet".' *In: The Ballet Annual
     1956*, 10th issue, pp. 105–8.

414 'Homage to Ashton.' *In: The Ballet Annual 1961*, 15th issue, pp.
     43–[59].
     Contributors – Arnold L. Haskell, Marie Rambert, Margot Fonteyn,
     Michael Somes, Vera Volkova.

415 WILLIAMS, PETER. 'Sir Fred.' *In: About the House*, v. 1, no. 6,
     March 1964, pp. 4–13.   15 illus.

Cranko

416 HASKELL, ARNOLD LIONEL. 'The ballets of John Cranko.' *In: Foyer*,
     no. 1, autumn 1951, pp. 38–40. 3 illus.

417 WILLIAMS, PETER. 'John Cranko: development of a choreographer.'
     In: The Ballet Annual 1954, 8th issue, pp. 90–5.

418 [MONAHAN, JAMES], KENNEDY, JAMES, *pseud.* 'In his own tradition.'
     In: The Guardian, 20th November, 1965, p. 7.   1 illus.

de Valois

419 LAWSON, JOAN. Choreography and Ninette de Valois. [Fitzroy
     Publications, c. 1947]. [1], 32 pp.   4 pl., illus., diagrs. (Makers
     of English Ballet Series. No. 1.)

The work of the choreographer in general, followed by a study of Ninette de Valois, and her ballets, which are illustrated by reproductions of photographs on plates. The drawings are by Wadlow.

Helpmann

420 BRAHMS, CARYL. Robert Helpmann, choreographer. Batsford, 1945. [43] pp. front., 62 pl. 18s.

> First published 1943.
> On page 22 the author begins her assessment of Robert Helpmann as choreographer of *The Birds, Comus* and *Hamlet*. 72 reproductions of photographs by Russell Sedgwick illustrate the ballets; an unusual feature is the number of photographs portraying *The Birds*.

WALKER, KATHRINE SORLEY.   Robert Helpmann . . . 1957.

> *See* no. 483.

Macmillan

421 'The germ of a ballet: Kenneth Macmillan's scenario for "Noctambules".'   *In: The Ballet Annual 1957*, 11th issue, pp. 86–94.   8 pl.

> Choreographer's scenario with 'a photographic record of the creation of the ballet'. The photographer is John Hart.

422 'A choreographer's progress.'   *In: The Times*, 29th December, 1960, p. 9.

> Interview with Kenneth Macmillan, then Resident Choreographer, of the Royal Ballet.

423 'Talking to Kenneth Macmillan.'   *In: About the House*, v. 2, no. 2, June 1966, pp. 19–20.   8 illus.

Morrice

424 'Norman Morrice – choreographer of the here and now.'   *In: The Times*, 24th July, 1963, p. 15.

Rodrigues

425 RODRIGUES, ALFRED. 'British choreographer in Italy.'   *In: The Ballet Annual 1957*, 11th issue, pp. 100–3.

VIII. DANCERS

The majority of books listed in this chapter are rather light-weight biographies or collections of photographs. The only serious study is James Monahan's book on Margot Fonteyn. In the field of autobiography there is nothing to compare with *Theatre street*, by Tamara Karsavina or *Dancing for Diaghilev*, by Lydia Sokolova. The reason for this may be that English ballet has established itself only during the last thirty years or so, and few of the dancers involved in this growth have retired yet.

There has been a two-way traffic in dancers in the past as well as the present. English dancers were accepted into Diaghilev's and Pavlova's companies, and there are English dancers working with Continental companies now. On the other hand there are dancers, foreign by birth, not to mention dancers from the Commonwealth, who have been associated with English companies, for example, Adeline Genée, Svetlana Beriosova, Rudolf Nureyev. Books by, or about such dancers during the period of their work in England, have been included.

BIBLIOGRAPHY

Arrangement. 1. General works and works on more than one dancer, arranged chronologically by date of publication. 2. Works on individual dancers arranged alphabetically by the professional name of the dancer. Where there is more than one work under the name of a dancer, the entries have been arranged chronologically by date of publication.

GENERAL WORKS AND WORKS ON MORE THAN ONE DANCER

426 Haskell, Arnold Lionel. Our dancers (first series) . . . British Continental Press, [193?]. [6] pp. front., 49 pl. (Artists of the Dance Series. No. 9.) 2s. 6d.

   Includes English 'dancers of international reputation and comparative newcomers of the post Diaghileff era'. (Editor's note.)

427 Haskell, Arnold Lionel. Ballet vignettes. Edinburgh, Albyn Press, 1948. 80 pp. 16 pl. 10s. 6d.

4, 'Alicia Markova . . .'; 5, 'Pearl Argyle . . .'; 9, 'Margot Fonteyn'; 10,
'. . . Helpmann'; 11, 'Some British Dancers'; 12, 'Some British Male
Dancers'; 13, 'British Dancers: the future'. The achievements and capabilities
of each dancer are discussed in the compass of about 2 pages. 24 reproductions
of photographs on plates.

428 BEAUMONT, CYRIL WILLIAM. 'The return of Markova and Dolin.'
In: The Ballet Annual 1949, 3rd issue, pp. 53–5.

429 BEAUMONT, CYRIL WILLIAM. 'Some dancers of the Sadler's Wells
Theatre Ballet'. *In: Foyer*, no. 1, autumn 1951, pp. [58]–60, 62.
10 illus.

Svetlana Beriosova; Elaine Fifield; Maryon Lane; Patricia Miller; Sheilah
O'Reilly.

430 BEAUMONT, CYRIL WILLIAM. 'Some dancers of the Sadler's Wells
Theatre Ballet. Part 2. *In: Foyer*, no. 2, winter 1951–2, pp. 53–4,
56, 58, 60. illus.

David Blair; Stanley Holden; David Poole; Pirmin Trecu.

431 ANTHONY, GORDON, *photographer*. The Sadler's Wells Ballet. Phoenix
House, 1952. 10 pp. 10 pl. (col.). (Dancers in Colour: first
series.) 4s. 6d.

12 dancers are portrayed. Notes on each of the 10 plates precede the text.

432 Dancers of To-day Series. Black, 1952–64. Illus.

1. *Margot Fonteyn*. First published 1952; 3rd ed. 1964. 2. *Moira Shearer*.
1952; reprint 1958. 3. *Violetta Elvin*. 1953. 4. *London's Festival Ballet*. First
published 1953; rev. ed. 1958. 5. *Ballerinas of Sadler's Wells*. First published
1954; reprint with corrections 1956. 6. *Alicia Markova*. 2nd ed. 1958. 7.
Michael Somes. 1955. 8. *Beryl Grey*. 1955. 9. *Svetlana Beriosova*. 1956. 10. *Six
dancers of Sadler's Wells*, 1956. 11. *Nadia Nerina*. 1957. 12. *John Gilpin*. 1957.
13. *Rowena Jackson and Philip Chatfield*. 1958. 14. *The Royal Ballet today*.
1958. 15. *Great ballerinas of to-day*. 1960. 16. *Great male dancers*. 1964.
All the volumes in this series were written by Cyril Swinson (*pseud.* Hugh
Fisher) with the exception of nos. 1 (3rd ed.) and 16, which, after Cyril
Swinson's death, were completed by Mary Clarke and Ivor Guest respectively. A short introduction is followed by about 50 clear but in some cases
rather small reproductions of photographs by such well-known photographers as Gordon Anthony, 'Baron', Andrew McBean, Houston Rogers
and Roger Wood. The dancer is shown in a variety of roles, with a brief

commentary on his or her life and career. Where more than one edition has been issued, the illustrations have been changed to include new roles. The volumes on the Royal Ballet and Festival Ballet follow a similar pattern providing a pictorial record of repertoire and personnel, with commentary. With the exception of no. 16, these volumes are not indexed.

See also nos. 293, 324a, 436–7, 439–40, 442, 444, 453, 470, 479, 491, 495, 499, 500.

433 DAVIDSON, GLADYS. Ballet biographies. Rev. ed. Werner Laurie, 1954. xvi, [336] pp. front., 8 pl., bibliog. 15s.

New information has been added within the existing space and earlier material has been revised (note to Preface). The contents list shows no change in headings or pagination. The 'biographies' vary from one to eight pages according to the importance of the subject. There are about 73 entries of which roughly half deal with well-known figures in English ballet. The bibliography precedes the text and lists 49 un-annotated items arranged alphabetically by author giving author and title only. There are 14 reproductions of photographs.

434C CROWLE, PIGEON. Enter the ballerina. Faber, 1955. 178 pp. front. (col.), 32 pl., illus. 15s.

3, 'Alicia Markova'; 4, 'Margot Fonteyn'; 5, 'Violetta Elvin'; 7, 'Svetlana Beriosova'.
A sketch of the training and career, of each dancer. 38 reproductions of photographs on plates, with 2 drawings, by the author, in the text.

435 McCONNELL, JANE. Famous ballet dancers. New York, Crowell, 1955. [xiii], 176 pp. 16 pl., bibliog. $2.75.

Also published by Toronto, Ambassador Books at $3.50.
'Anton Dolin', pp. 49–61; 'Alicia Markova', pp. 62–75; 'Moira Shearer', pp. 76–85; 'Margot Fonteyn', pp. 86–94. The bibliography contains 54 items.

436 [SWINSON, CYRIL WILLIAM]. Fisher Hugh, *pseud.* Ballerinas of Sadler's Wells. Black, 1956. 32 pp. front., illus. (Dancers of To-day Series. No. 5.) 6s.

First published 1954, this impression was reprinted with corrections and some new illustrations.
Pearl Argyle; Svetlana Beriosova; Violetta Elvin; Margot Fonteyn; Beryl Grey; Mary Honer; Rowena Jackson; Alicia Markova; Pamela May; Nadia Nerina; Moira Shearer. (*See also* no. 432.)

437 SWINSON, CYRIL WILLIAM. Six dancers of Sadler's Wells: Julia
     Farron, Leslie Edwards, Rosemary Lindsay, Alexander Grant,
     Elaine Fifield, David Blair. Black, 1956. 32 pp. front., illus.
     (Dancers of To-day Series. No. 10.) 6s. 6d.
     See also no. 432.

438 HALL, ALFRED GEORGE, *ed.* A legend of British ballet. Alicia Markova
     and Anton Dolin: a collection of portraits. Hall Publications,
     [1957]. [39] pp. illus. 5s.
     Peter Williams wrote a short introduction to the 51 reproductions of
     photographs.

439 SWINSON, CYRIL WILLIAM. Rowena Jackson and Philip Chatfield.
     Black, 1958. 32 pp. front., illus. (Dancers of To-day Series.
     No. 13.) 7s. 6d.
     See also no. 432.

440 SWINSON, CYRIL WILLIAM. Great ballerinas of today. Black, 1960.
     32 pp. front., illus. (Dancers of To-day Series. No. 15.) 7s. 6d.
     Includes Margot Fonteyn and Alicia Markova. *See also* no. 432.

441 'Shake-speares ladyes: Antoinette Sibley, Merle Park, Lynn Seymour.'
     In: About the House, v. 1, no. 7, June 1964, pp. 13–[15]. 3 illus.

442 SWINSON, CYRIL WILLIAM. Great male dancers. Black, 1964.
     40 pp. front., illus. (Dancers of To-day Series. No. 16.) 10s. 6d.
     Survey of male dancing from the sixteenth century to the present day,
     with a mention of the greatest dancers and their contribution to ballet. A
     section on English dancers appears in the last 5 pages. Contains an index of
     dancers. *See also* no. 432.

INDIVIDUAL DANCERS

Bedells

443 BEDELLS, PHYLLIS. My dancing days. Phoenix House, 1954. 224 pp.
     front., 32 pl. 21s.
     Phyllis Bedells danced at the Empire Theatre, following Lydia Kyasht as
     ballerina in 1914. She danced for the Camargo Society too and was partnered

by Anton Dolin, retiring in 1935. She is on the Committee of the Royal
Academy of Dancing. 62 reproductions of photographs on the plates.

Beriosova

444 SWINSON, CYRIL WILLIAM.   Svetlana Beriosova.   Black, 1956.   32 pp.
front., illus.   (Dancers of To-day Series. No. 9.)   6s. 6d.
See also no. 432.

445 FRANKS, ARTHUR HENRY.   Svetlana Beriosova: a biography.   Burke,
1958.   144 pp.   front., 30 pl.   25s.
A popular biography, with some assessment of the dancer's style. There
are 60 reproductions of photographs on plates, and 2 portraits by Juliet
Pannett in the text.

Dolin

446 HASKELL, ARNOLD LIONEL.   Some studies in ballet.   Lamley, [1928].
198 pp.   12 pl., illus.   21s.
Black issued this title in 1941. Apparently there is no new material, for
the pagination and number of illustrations are the same as for the 1928 issue.
'Anton Dolin' (pp. 53–60).

447 DOLIN, ANTON.   Divertissement.   Sampson Low, Marston, [1931].
xii, 244 pp.   front., 47 pl.   12s. 6d.
Autobiography covering the dancer's childhood, training and early career,
which was mainly with Diaghilev Ballet and his own company the Nem-
chinova-Dolin Ballet, also some performances in revues.

448 HASKELL, ARNOLD LIONEL.   Anton Dolin: 'the first chapter'.   2nd
ed.   British Continental Press, 1934.   31 pp.   5 pl. (Artists of the
Dance Series. No. 3.)   2s. 6d.
First published 1929.
An account of Anton Dolin's career, with chapters on 'The Male Dancer';
'Roles and Creations with the Russian Ballet'; 'Dolin and Nemchinova';
'Dolin and the Art of Partnering'. An appendix lists roles danced.

449 DOLIN, ANTON.   Ballet go round.   Joseph, 1938.   355 pp.   front.,
31 pl.   15s.
A second volume of autobiography covering the years 1937 and 1938.
There are several chapters on the Markova-Dolin Ballet and some material
on Camargo Society productions.

[450]c SELBY-LOWNDES, JOAN. The blue train: the story of Anton Dolin. Collins, 1953. 252 pp. illus., bibliog. 8s. 6d.

> '...Fictional narrative of the life of...the young Anton Dolin... reasonably told, with very little sentiment and probably a closeness to fact.' (*Times Literary Supplement, Children's Book Section*, 27th November, 1953, p. vi.)

451 DOLIN, ANTON. Autobiography. Oldbourne, 1960. 336 pp. front., 32 pl. 30s.

> Anton Dolin's third autobiographical volume which deals mainly with his career from 1939 onwards. There are 60 reproductions of photographs on plates, and separate indexes for names, and ballets and plays.

Edwards

452 'Familiar personage of the Royal Ballet.' *In: The Times*, 16th June, 1964, p. 14. 1 illus.

> Leslie Edwards.

Elvin

453 [SWINSON, CYRIL WILLIAM, *ed.*] Fisher, Hugh, *pseud. ed.* Violetta Elvin. Black, 1953. 32 pp. front., illus. (Dancers of To-day Series. No. 3.) 6s.

> *See also* no. 432.

Espinosa

454 ESPINOSA, EDOUARD. And then he danced: the life of Espinosa by himself. Sampson Low, Marston, [1948]. xxxi, [1], 187 pp. front., 18 pl. 18s.

> Edited by Rachel Ferguson, who also wrote the foreword, 'Edwardian Legend: a study of Edouard Espinosa'. This and a glossary precede the text.

Fonteyn

455 ANTHONY, GORDON, *photographer*. Ballerina: further studies of Margot Fonteyn. Home & van Thal, 1945. 16 pp. 31 pl. 21s.

> An introduction by Eveleigh Leith, sketching the ballerina's career, is followed by photographic studies in 8 roles.

456 BEAUMONT, CYRIL WILLIAM. Margot Fonteyn. The Author, 1948.

20 pp. front., 8 pl. (Essays on Dancing and Dancers Series. No. 11.) 6s.

A brief review of the main roles danced by Margot Fonteyn from the beginning of her career to 1946, followed by comments on the quality of her performances.

457 FONTEYN, MARGOT. ' . . . on ballet dancing.' *In: The Listener*, v. 39, no. 1,009, 27th May, 1948, p. 849. 1 illus.

Originally broadcast in *Woman's Hour* and printed in *Did You Hear That?*

458 WILLIAMS, PETER. 'Margot Fonteyn – English ballerina.' *In: Souvenirs de Ballet, no. 1*, 1949, pp. 24–[7]. 3 illus.

459 ANTHONY, GORDON, *photographer*. Margot Fonteyn. Phoenix House, 1950. [132] pp. front. (col.), 60 pl. 12s. 6d.

Also limited autographed edition at 63s.
A study, by Ninette de Valois, is followed by a photographic record of roles danced, to 1946 (all taken in the studio, unless stated otherwise). Comments on performances are added by the photographer.

460 CHAPPELL, WILLIAM. Fonteyn: impressions of a ballerina. Rockliff, 1951. viii, 136 pp. front., 46 pl., illus. 21s.

'My subtitle . . . explains what I have attempted in this book.' The author danced with the Royal Ballet in its early days. 40 of the reproductions of photographs on plates are by Cecil Beaton; the drawings in the text are by the author.

461 MONAHAN, JAMES. 'Margot Fonteyn.' *In: The Adelphi*, v. 29, no. 1, November 1952, pp. 6–11.

462 PERRIN, OLIVIER. 'The art of ballet. [Interview with] Margot Fonteyn.' *In: Opera Ballet Music-Hall in the World 1*, [1952], pp. [34]–8. 5 illus.

463 BEAUMONT, CYRIL WILLIAM. 'Margot Fonteyn.' *In: The Ballet Annual 1954*, 8th issue, pp. 73–7.

464c CLARKE, MARY. Six great dancers: Taglioni, Pavlova, Nijinsky, Karsavina, Ulanova, Fonteyn. Hamilton, 1957. 190 pp. 6 pl., bibliog. (Six Great . . . Series.) 10s. 6d.

Chapter 6, 'Margot Fonteyn'. Factual account of early life, training and work with the Royal Ballet, written for children. The bibliography contains 17 items.

465 Margot Fonteyn in Australia: a souvenir to commemorate the 1957 visit to Australia's Borovansky Ballet . . . and her distinguished colleagues Mr. Michael Somes, Miss Rowena Jackson and Mr. Bryan Ashbridge from the Royal Ballet at Covent Garden. [1957?] [34] pp. illus.

A publicity booklet with 'editorial matter', by Michael Frostick and Cyril Swinson. 54 reproductions of photographs.

466 MONAHAN, JAMES. Fonteyn: a study of the ballerina in her setting. Black, 1957. ix, [116] pp. front., 22 pl.

The author studies his subject under three heads – 'Margot de Arias', a few biographical facts and a study of the personality of the dancer; 'The Dancer', technical issues such as 'line', musicality and acting ability; 'Choreographer, Dancer, Company', Fonteyn's interpretation of the work of various choreographers and her work within the Royal Ballet.

467 'Fonteyn, Margot.' In: Enciclopedia dello Spettacolo, v. 5, 1958, columns 507–11. 1 illus.

Principal interpretations and creations are listed at the end of the article. They cover the period 1934–57. The bibliography contains 14 items and includes periodical articles as well as books.

468 FRANK, ELIZABETH. Margot Fonteyn. Chatto & Windus, 1958. [119] pp. front., 20 pl. 21s.

A popular biography.

469 'Dame Margot at height of her powers.' In: The Times, 5th December, 1963, p. 8.

470 [SWINSON, CYRIL WILLIAM], FISHER, HUGH, pseud. Margot Fonteyn. 3rd rev. ed. Black, 1964. 40 pp. front., illus. (Dancers of To-day Series. No. 1.) 10s. 6d.

First published 1952; this edition revised by Mary Clarke. (See also no. 432.)

471 MONEY, KEITH, photographer. The art of Margot Fonteyn. Joseph, 1965. [272] pp. illus. 84s.

Introduction by Keith Money. Some 356 action photographs of Fonteyn, in 18 ballets, with commentary by Ninette de Valois, Frederick Ashton, Keith Money and Margot Fonteyn herself. '. . . Photographically speaking [Keith Money] has done splendidly'. (Review by Mary Clarke in *The Dancing Times*, December 1965, p. 135.)

472 CRISP, CLEMENT. 'Fonteyn.' *In: About the House*, v. 2, no. 2, June 1966, pp. [2]–15. 18 illus.

Genée

473 CROXTON, ARTHUR. Crowded nights – and days: an unconventional pageant. Sampson Low, Marston, [1934]. 398 pp. front., 12 pl. 10s. 6d.

> Chapter 17, 'Great Farewells and a Return', describes Adeline Genée's retirement and quotes from an article by the dancer in the *Evening News*.

474 GUEST, IVOR. 'Dame Adeline Genée.' *In: The Ballet Annual 1956*, 10th issue, pp. 54–61.

475 GUEST, IVOR. Adeline Genée: a lifetime of ballet under six reigns. . . . Black, 1958. xv, 207 pp. front. (col.), 32 pl., illus., bibliog. 30s.

> 'Based on the personal reminiscences of Dame Adeline Genée-Isitt', the Danish ballerina who danced at the Empire Theatre, London, from 1897–1909. She retired finally in 1917. One of the founders of the Camargo Society and of the Royal Academy of Dancing, she was President of the latter 1920–54. There are 62 illustrations on plates, and drawings in the text; also reproductions of posters and playbills.

Gilpin

476 SWINSON, CYRIL WILLIAM. John Gilpin. Black, 1957. [32] pp. front., illus. (Dancers of To-day Series. No. 12.) 7s. 6d.

> *See also* no. 432.

Grey

477 ANTHONY, GORDON, *photographer*. Beryl Grey. Phoenix House, 1952. 95 pp. front. (col.), 3 pl. (col.), 40 pl. 12s. 6d.

> Introduction by A. L. Haskell.
> Posed photographs, with captions, of the dancer in some of her main roles.

478 CROWLE, PIGEON. Beryl Grey: the progress of a ballerina. Faber,
        1952. 79 pp. front. (col.), 24 pl. 12s. 6d.

> A popular biography. Beryl Grey was a member of the Royal Ballet from
> 1941–57. Appended is a list of leading and soloist roles which she has danced
> with this company.

479 [SWINSON, CYRIL WILLIAM], FISHER, HUGH, *pseud*. Beryl Grey.
        Black, 1955. 32 pp. front., illus. (Dancers of To-day Series.
        No. 8.) 6s.

> *See also* no. 432.

480 GREY, BERYL. Red curtain up. Secker & Warburg, 1958. xi, [84]
        pp. front., 30 pl. 30s.

> Beryl Grey was the first English ballerina to dance in Russia. She spent
> four and a half weeks there, and in this book gives a straightforward account
> of her experiences and impressions during the trip. The majority of the
> 44 original photographs reproduced on plates were taken by her husband,
> S. G. Svenson.

481 GREY, BERYL. Through the bamboo curtain. Collins, 1965. 127 pp.
        32 pl. 30s.

> Beryl Grey's experiences during a month's visit to China. She danced
> with the Peking Ballet Company, and visited Shanghai, Hanchow and
> Canton. 53 original photographs reproduced on plates were taken by S. G.
> Svenson.

Helpmann

BRAHMS, CARYL. Robert Helpmann, choreographer. 1945.

> *See* no. 420.

482 ANTHONY, GORDON, *photographer*. Robert Helpmann: studies. Home
        & van Thal, 1946. [15] pp. front., 31 pl. 21s.

> The Introduction, 'Robert Helpmann: his place in the theatre', is by
> Ninette de Valois. Most of the illustrations portray the expressiveness of
> Helpmann's face rather than his dancing.

483 WALKER, KATHRINE SORLEY. Robert Helpmann . . . Rockliff, 1957.
        126 pp. front., 30 pl. (Theatre World Monographs. No. 9.) 15s.

> A study of Robert Helpmann as actor, choreographer, dancer and pro-

ducer. Appended are 'Career of Robert Helpmann'; 'Films'; 'Choreography'; 'Productions'; arranged chronologically. There are 70 illustrations on plates.

Inglesby

484 HANDLEY-TAYLOR, GEOFFREY. Mona Inglesby: ballerina and choreographer. Vawser & Wiles, 1947. 71 pp. front., illus. 8s. 6d.

A rather uncritical biography of the founder of International Ballet. Appended is a Table of Special Presentations of the International Ballet, giving original cast, choreographer, music and designer etc. Illustrations consist of 36 reproductions of photographs.

Kyasht

485 KYASHT, LYDIA. Romantic recollections. Brentano, 1929. 247 pp. front., 15 pl. 15s.

Edited by Erica Beale.
In Chapters 16–18 the author recounts her life in England, including her experiences as ballerina at the Empire Theatre from 1908.

Markova

486 HASKELL, ARNOLD LIONEL. Penelope Spencer, and other studies. 2nd ed. British Continental Press, 1931. 39 pp. 6 pl. (Artists of the Dance Series. No. 5.) 2s. 6d.

First published 1930.
The third study is 'Alicia Markova and the Classical Tradition' (pp. 26–30). Roles danced during the period 1925–29 inclusive are listed.

487 ANTHONY, GORDON, *photographer*. Markova: a collection of photographic studies. Chatto & Windus, 1935. [9] pp. front., 23 pl. 5s.

Preface by Ninette de Valois.
These studies were taken when Markova was dancing with the Vic-Wells Ballet.

488 BEAUMONT, CYRIL WILLIAM. Alicia Markova. The Author, 1935. 25 pp. front., 11 pl. (Essays on Dancing and Dancers Series. No. 8.) 3s. 6d.

An outline of Markova's early years, with a discussion of her interpretation of roles, including Odette-Odile (*Swan lake*) and Giselle. No Index.

489 ANTHONY, GORDON, *photographer*. Alicia Markova. Phoenix House, 1951. III pp. front. (col.), 2 pl. (col.), 48 pl. 15s.

> An appreciation by Adeline Genée, followed by 50 reproductions of photographs of the dancer in roles performed over the period 1932–50. The captions are by Gordon Anthony.

490 DOLIN, ANTON. Markova: her life and art. W. H. Allen, 1953. 294 pp. front., 28 pl. 17s. 6d.

> Alicia Markova and Anton Dolin worked together for many years (from about 1930) dancing with the Markova-Dolin Ballet, Festival Ballet and as guest artists with other companies. (Markova retired from dancing to become Director of the Ballet at the Metropolitan Opera House, New York, in 1963.)

491 [SWINSON, CYRIL WILLIAM], FISHER, HUGH, *pseud*. Alicia Markova. Black, 1958. 32 pp. front., illus. (Dancers of To-day Series. No. 6.) 7s. 6d.

> First published 1954. *See also* no. 432.

492 BEAUMONT, CYRIL WILLIAM. 'Alicia Markova.' *In: The Ballet Annual 1956*, 10th issue, p. 53.

493 MARKOVA, ALICIA. Giselle and I. Barrie & Rockliff, 1960. 193, [6] pp. front., 62 pl., illus. 25s.

> Tells of the differing circumstances under which Markova has danced this famous role, as guest artist, with several ballet companies and partners; also discusses her interpretation. There are reproductions of 83 photographs and 2 lithographs on plates and 2 illustrations in the text that reproduce early prints of the ballet.

494 NEMENSCHOUSKY, LEON. A day with Alicia Markova. Cassell, 1960. 32 pp. illus. (A Day with . . . Series.) 10s. 6d.

> Attempts to describe the quality of Markova's dancing and her attitude towards ballet. The illustrations are 33 reproductions of photographs.

Nerina

495 SWINSON, CYRIL WILLIAM. Nadia Nerina. Black, 1957. 32 pp. front., illus. (Dancers of To-day Series. No. 11.) 7s. 6d.

> *See also* no. 432.

Nureyev

496 NUREYEV, RUDOLF. Nureyev: an autobiography with pictures. Hodder & Stoughton, 1962. 127, [49] pp. front., 47 pl., illus. 35s.

'A famous literary agency made . . . an offer for his story . . . Nureyev himself was the only source. . . . The talk was, at first, in Russian. This was translated into English.' (Introduction by Alexander Bland, critic of *The Observer*, who also edited the book.) Mainly concerned with the early life and training in Russia and escape to the West, but does give an 'outside' opinion on some aspects of English ballet. There are reproductions of 54 photographs by Richard Avedon, Cecil Beaton, G. B. L. Wilson and others on plates, and 12 in the text.

Shearer

497 TENENT, ROSE. Moira Shearer: a ballet album with a biographical study. Edinburgh, The Albyn Press, [1947]. 45 pp. front., 15 pl. 3s. 6d.

A biographical sketch, followed by posed studies of the dancer in various roles, by photographers Gordon Anthony, 'Baron', Edward Mandinian and Richardby.

498 CROWLE, PIGEON. Moira Shearer: portrait of a dancer. New ed. Faber, 1951. 95 pp. front., 47 pl.

First published 1949.

15 pages have been added to this edition, covering the period from the beginning of the first American tour to the end of the second. Her career is covered to 1951. Two years later Moira Shearer retired as a dancer. Appended is a list of important roles danced, while a member of the International and Sadler's Wells Companies. There are 51 reproductions of photographs on plates.

499 [SWINSON, CYRIL WILLIAM], FISHER, HUGH, *pseud*. Moira Shearer. Black, 1958. 32 pp. front., illus. (Dancers of To-day Series. No. 2.) 6s.

First published 1952. *See also* no. 432.

Somes

500 [SWINSON, CYRIL WILLIAM], FISHER, HUGH, *pseud*. Michael Somes. Black, 1955. 32 pp. front., illus. (Dancers of To-day Series. No. 7.) 6s.

See also no. 432.

IX. TECHNIQUE AND NOTATION

TECHNIQUE

THE technique of ballet has evolved gradually and it seems to be difficult to assign definite names and/or dates to the invention of particular movements. Authorities on ballet seem to agree that much was taken over and adapted from the social dance, both courtly and folk; it seems likely too, that new and more complicated ideas were evolved by trial and error in the classrooms and by individual endeavour until gradually the forms of social dancing and theatrical dancing diverged more widely.

France and Italy were the main contributors. A Frenchman, Pierre Beauchamp (1636–1719?) was credited with having been the first to work out the five positions of the feet which help the dancer to maintain his balance.[1] Beauchamp was dancing master to Louis XIV and one of the members of the Académie Royale de Danse. It was Pierre Rameau[2] who in 1725 claimed this for Beauchamp, although a modern author, G. B. L. Wilson, suggests that Beauchamp merely codified what had already been invented.[3] Another step towards a greater variety in dancing was supplied by a French ballerina Marie Camargo (1710–70), who shortened her skirts slightly and thus was able to move more freely: it also meant that the audience, in theory at least, could see what she was doing with her feet. She has been credited, too, with introducing the *entrechât* into the woman dancer's technique. By the first half of the nineteenth century technique had developed sufficiently to allow Carlo Blasis to write it down in his book *The Code of Terpsichore* (1830). He is said to have been the first teacher[4] to demand a full ninety degrees turnout of the feet and thighs, where before only a forty-five degree turnout had been demanded. This again helped the dancer to achieve a greater freedom of movement. The first use of the '*attitude*' has also been attributed to Blasis.

The early nineteenth century saw the first use of the points by the female

---

[1] Authorities differ as to whether Pierre or Charles Louis Beauchamp (or Beauchamps) formulated the five positions of the feet; they also differ as to which of the two was dancing master to Louis XIV.

[2] *Le Maître a danser*, by P. Rameau. Paris, 1725.

[3] *Dictionary of ballet*, by G. B. L. Wilson. 1961. Under *Beauchamps*.

[4] *Dictionary of ballet*, by G. B. L. Wilson. 1961. Under *Turnout*.

dancer, although it is not known by whom. The names of Fanny Bias, Geneviève Gosselin and Avdotia Istomina, the Russian dancer, have been put forward. It was thought to have been adopted in order to give an impression of lightness and other-worldliness to the fairies, wilis, sylphs, etc. who were so popular in the ballets of the Romantic period.

During the second half of the nineteenth century the Russians emerged as the most brilliant technicians. French and Italian dancers and teachers had been visiting Russia for some time, but the two who were largely responsible for this emergence were Christian Johansson and Marius Petipa. Johansson, a Swedish dancer, travelled to St. Petersburg in 1841 and began to teach in the Imperial School in 1869; Petipa, a Frenchman, arrived there in 1847 and was appointed ballet master in 1862.

As far as is known English ballet has contributed little to the development of technique. This may be due to the lack of a continuous tradition and also to the fact that it was only in 1931 that we possessed the beginnings of a national ballet company backed by a school.

NOTATION

Many experiments have been made to evolve a satisfactory system of notation, in order to reinforce the traditional method of reproducing ballets, that is, the choreographers' and dancers' memory and/or notes. What began as a collection of fairly simple symbols to record dances has now developed into complicated systems which can be used for any form of movement.

As early as 1463 Guglielmo Ebreo of Pesaro used letters and other symbols as an aid to remembering certain basses-danses, and in 1588 Thoinot Arbeau published his *Orchésographie* in which he used alphabetical symbols as a form of notation. The first man to work out a system in any detail was Raoul Feuillet, who in 1700 published *Chorégraphie, ou l'Art de décrire la danse*. Apparently he was not the originator of this system. John Weaver in his translation (1706) of *Chorégraphie* . . . suggests that Feuillet perfected what Pierre Beauchamp had started. Curved lines are used to trace the floor pattern of the dance, and on these are indicated the steps and some of the movements of the arms. Feuillet also published several *Recueil des danses*, in which he notated dances that he and Louis Pécour had composed. His system was used and adapted by Pierre Rameau and Kellom Tomlinson among others. The next innovator of note was Arthur Saint-Léon, who published *Steno-*

chorégraphie in 1852. His system was based on a combination of 'pin-men' with a musical staff. This was followed to a certain extent by Alfred Zorn, who in his *Grammatik der Tanzkunst* (1887) included various methods.

A notation which had a direct bearing on recent English ballet was that devised by Stepanov, a teacher at the Imperial School, St. Petersburg. It was based on a type of music stave using notes of music in conjunction with other signs. Nicholas Sergueeff learned this method and noted down some of the classical ballets as danced by the Russians. When he left Russia he brought his notes with him to western Europe, using them to produce the great classical ballets for the Sadler's Wells Ballet and the International Ballet. Mona Inglesby, former Director of the latter company, possesses them now.

In recent years the two notations used in this country are Labanotation and that worked out by Joan and Rudolf Benesh. Labanotation has been developed by the Dance Notation Bureau of the United States (founded 1940) from a system put forward by Rudolf Laban in *Kinetographie* (published 1928). It is the most international of notations and is used in Germany, Hungary, Brazil and other countries. It can be used to indicate any type of movement. A vertical line indicates the central axis of the body, while a line on either side indicates the right and left side of the body. On these lines are built rectangular shapes, with dots and curved lines as additional symbols. The notation is read from the bottom of the page upwards, and the music for the particular movement can be printed parallel to the notation. The Benesh system (copyrighted 1955) is simpler, and more of a shorthand for the dancer. It is based on a five-line stave printed underneath the musical stave, and uses symbols based on straight and curved lines with additional symbols.

For about the past ten years interest in notation in the United Kingdom seems to have increased. The Benesh notation was taught to all forms in the Royal Ballet School except the first from 1957. In 1956 the British Dance Notation Society was formed and in 1957 a Labanotation Centre was established in London at the Sigurd Leeder School. It was in this year, too, that there was a Dance Notation exhibition at the Royal Festival Hall in which the following took part: The Laban Art of Movement Centre, The Dance Notation Bureau (London Branch), The Sigurd Leeder School of Dance and Benesh Choreographies Ltd. In 1962 the Institute of Choreology was legally constituted and the council met for the first time, although it had been acting as an examining body in dance notation and ballet theory since 1960. The first course in choreology was initiated in September 1965, with half the students coming from Britain and half from foreign countries.[5] The aim of the Institute is 'to maintain a high standard in the use and teaching of notation and ballet theory; to provide a library of choreographic scores of important ballets and classical and folk dances of the world; to carry out research, including analysis and comparative study; to promote systematized study of dance composition'.[6]

BIBLIOGRAPHY

Arrangement. 1. Technique. 2. Notation. Entries under each heading are arranged chronologically by date of publication.

TECHNIQUE

501 WEAVER, JOHN. Anatomical and mechanical lectures upon dancing; wherein rules and institutions for that art are laid down and demonstrated as they were read at the Academy in Chancery Lane. Printed. for J. Brotherton and W. Meadows, . . . J. Graves . . . and W. Chetwood . . . , 1721. xii, 156 pp.

An attempt to explain 'the Laws of Motion, Mechanical and Natural, so far as they relate to the Regular or Irregular Position, Motion, and Gesture of the Body and Parts thereof'. Discussion of the external part of the body, the bones and the muscles is followed by sections on proportion, defects, standing, walking, leaping, and springing. Also 'Rules and Institutions for Dancing' in which Weaver urges the need for a knowledge of other arts in those who intend 'to apply themselves entirely to the stage'. Said to be 'the first time the technique of the dance of the day is treated on scientific lines'. ('Father of English Ballet . . . ', by A. Chatwin and P. J. S. Richardson. *In: Ballet Annual 1961*, p. 51.) There are separate indexes listing the bones and the muscles named in the lectures. The Table of Contents is also appended (Bodleian. 38434. e.28).

502 RAMEAU, PIERRE. The dancing master. Beaumont, 1931. xx, 150 pp. 1 pl., illus., diagrs. 25s.

C. W. Beaumont translated the above from the 1st edition, *Le Maître à danser* . . . , Paris, 1725, with plates by Rameau himself. In 1728 John Essex, an English dancing master, made the first English translation, *The Dancing-*

[5] *The Dancing Times*, January 1966, p. 186.
[6] *The Dancing Times*, December 1962, p. 183.

502a *master: or the art of dancing explained*. . . . (Printed, and sold by him at his
house . . . and J. Brotherton, 1728. xxxii, 160 pp. front. 60 pl.) He
used new plates engraved by G. Alsop. In 1731 a 2nd edition appeared.
There were 2 issues of this; one with the Alsop plates and another with most
of the plates drawn by G. Bickham; nine diagrammatic plates were retained
from the 1728 English edition. The plates by Bickham have been used in the
1931 Beaumont translation. Figures 2 and 16 were re-constructed by
Randolph Schwabe as the translator could not find a complete edition.
(Information from the Introduction to his translation by C. W. Beaumont.)
  The first part explains the positions and attitudes for men and women, with
a description of the minuet, while the second part deals with 'the use and
graceful motion of the arms with the legs'. The introduction by John Essex
in his translation is of some interest for he mentions English dancing masters
and some English dancers who had appeared on the stage. C. W. Beaumont
considers that Rameau's work is 'the standard work on the technique of
eighteenth-century dancing', but gives the warning that modern meanings
should not be read into the terms that Rameau uses.

503 TOMLINSON, KELLOM.   The art of dancing explained by reading and
figures, whereby the manner of performing the steps is made easy . . .
first design'd in the year 1724.   Printed for the author, 1735. [25],
4-[160] pp.   37 pl.
  Written in 1724, but not published until 1735 through lack of subscribers.
  Kellom Tomlinson claims in his preface that he taught both private pupils
and those who danced on the stage. He also arranged dances for the theatre,
including one for Marie Sallé when as a child she visited London with her
brother. Technique for social dancing and ballet dancing had not diverged
widely at this time and Tomlinson could claim for the first part of his book
that it treated of 'all or most of the steps used in genteel dancing, as well as
many of those properly belonging to the stage'; also of the different positions,
and the proper way of standing and walking gracefully. The second part
consists mainly of 30 copper plates showing different positions of the minuet
with movement filled in by notation, based on Feuillet's system and with
the appropriate music for each plate; also country dancing. 4 plates explain
the notation. (Bodleian. Don. d.76.)

504 BLASIS, CARLO.   The code of Terpsichore. The art of dancing: comprising its theory and practice, and a history of its rise and progress,
from the earliest times: intended as well for the instruction of amateurs as the use of professional persons.   Edward Bull, 1830.   vii,
6-548 pp.   22 pp., front., 17 pl.
  The first edition was published by James Bulcock in 1828 as *The Code of
Terpsichore: a practical and historical treatise on the ballet, dancing and pantomime;*

with a complete theory of the art of dancing. . . . The above editions were translated by R. Barton, under the author's supervision. A note after the text of Part 2 states that this part was begun in Paris and completed and published at Milan in April 1820, the original title being *Traité elémentaire théorique et pratique de l'art de la danse*. This work is of great importance for in Part 2, 'Theory of Theatrical Dancing', which includes an appendix of exercises, the technique of the classical ballet was codified for the first time. The plates illustrate Part 2, except the last two which are concerned with social dancing, as is the music printed at the end of the book. Other Parts include 'Rise and Progress of Dancing' which deals with national dances; 'On Pantomime . . .'; 'The Composition of Ballets'; 'Programmes Containing Examples. . . of Ballets'; 'Private Dancing'. (B.M.1042. L.25).

504a   In 1888 *The Theory of theatrical dancing with a chapter on pantomime* was published by Frederick Verinder. This work had been edited by Stewart D. Headlam from Parts 2 and 3 of *The code of Terpsichore*, with the original plates excepting the last two. The editor kept closely to the Barton translation, the occasional changes being in literary style. It is an interesting comment on the lessened importance of the male dancer that in 1830 Barton uses the possessive 'his', while in 1888 Headlam changed it to 'her' in referring to the dancer.

505   [ESPINOSA, EDOUARD], 'ESPINOSA', *pseud*. Technical dictionary of dancing . . . *The Dancing Times*, [1921]. 49 pp. front., 2 diagrs.

About 75 entries deal with the technique of ballet dancing only. The author claims to 'have compiled the various exercises, movements and steps giving . . . the salient points, the qualities to seek, and the dangers to avoid in their execution'.

506   ALBERTIERI, LUIGI. The art of Terpsichore: an elementary, theoretical, physical and practical treatise of dancing. New York, Ricordi, 1923. x, 140 pp. front., illus.

The author produced ballets at the Empire Theatre, which were composed by Katti Lanner, and was ballet master at Covent Garden and the Metropolitan Opera, New York. He writes on first rudiments and composes exercises for each day of the week. There is a glossary and 165 text-figures, 4 anatomical drawings and 8 other illustrations.

507   CRASKE, MARGARET, *and* BEAUMONT, CYRIL WILLIAM. The theory and practice of allegro in classical ballet (Cecchetti method). Beaumont, 1951. 97, [2], [10] pp. of illus., diagr. (12s. 6d., 1935.)

First published 1930, this is the 3rd impression.

A sequel to *A Manual of the theory and practice of classical and theatrical dancing*, by C. W. Beaumont and S. Idzikowsky (below), first published 1922. The authors claim to have simplified the description of exercises and have explained terms. Part 1 deals with 'Basic Steps', Part 2 with 'Enchaînements'. The drawings are by Randolph Schwabe.

508   BEAUMONT, CYRIL WILLIAM, *and* IDZIKOWSKY, STANISLAS.   A manual of the theory and practice of classical theatrical dancing (classical ballet) (Cecchetti method.)   New rev. ed.   Beaumont, 1940.   220, [6] pp.   [22] pp. of illus.

First published 1922, this is a new impression of the revised edition published in 1932.

Cecchetti, one of the great teachers of ballet, was taught by Lepri, who was himself a pupil of Blasis. Cecchetti's method of teaching was codified by Cyril Beaumont and Stanislas Idzikowsky, a former member of the Diaghilev Ballet, with the co-operation of Cecchetti, who wrote the preface (French text). The authors divide the material into Book 1, 'Theory' and Book 2, 'Practice'. The line drawings, which help to clarify the text are by Randolph Schwabe, and are grouped at the end of each book. There is also a folded chart giving a numbered plan of the practice room, for use with the textual descriptions of exercises and steps.

509   BEAUMONT, CYRIL WILLIAM.   A primer of classical ballet (Cecchetti method) for children.   The Author, 1956.   60 pp.   9 pl.   6s.

First published 1933.

510   — — A second primer of classical ballet (Cecchetti method) for children.   The Author, 1956.   [65] pp.   9 pl.   6s.

First published 1935.

511   — — A third primer of classical ballet (Cecchetti method) for children, with ten dances variously arranged by Eleanor Banks, Margaret Craske, Margaret Saul, Peggy van Praagh & Laura Wilson.   The Author, 1954.   61 pp.   6s.

First published 1941.

Intended to cover the theoretical and practical requirements of Grade 1, Grades 2 and 3, and Grade 4 respectively, of the classical ballet examinations of the Imperial Society of Teachers of Dancing. *A Primer* . . . supposes a child of average ability taking one lesson a week, and *A Second Primer* . . . a second year's course, with an additional six months' training. *A Third primer* . . . has 3 sections, A, 'Exercises at the *Barre*' and '*Allegro*', B, 'Unseen *Enchaînements*' and C, 'Dances'. The first two titles have diagrammatic line-drawings by Eileen Mayo; the last, 2 pages of music.

512   BEAUMONT, CYRIL WILLIAM, *comp.*   A French-English dictionary of

technical terms used in classical ballet. Rev. ed. The Author, 1939.
iv, [44] pp. bibliog. 5s.

> First published 1931; 8 pages have been added.
> About 140 terms are arranged alphabetically 'in accordance with their familiar usage'. The bibliography lists 9 un-annotated references and the appendix gives elementary rules of French grammar with references to the terms used in dancing.

513 AMBROSE, KAY. The ballet-lover's pocket-book; technique without tears for the ballet-lover. 2nd ed. Black, 1944. [65] pp. front., illus. 7s.

> First published 1943; 2nd edition sold at 3s. 6d. in 1967.
> About two-thirds of this easily understood book deals with technique. The author provides many sketches, with an explanatory text. There are also sections on costume and theatrical lighting.

514 GABRIEL, JOHN. Ballet school. Faber, 1947. 127 pp. illus. 42s.

> The 5 positions, steps, exercises and *enchaînements* are demonstrated, by experienced dancers, with a minimum of text. Several hundred consecutive reproductions of photographs give a cinematographic effect of movement. '. . . Instructive and provides a useful supplement to the several existing text-books on ballet training' (A.B., *Ballet*, March 1948, p. 51). Acknowledgement is made to Reginald Eyre who invented the camera with which the photographs were taken.

515 NICOLAEVA-LEGAT, NADINE. Ballet education. Bles, 1947. xxiii, 163 pp. front., illus. 18s.

> Nicolas Legat, the Russian ballet dancer, taught in the Imperial Theatre School, St. Petersburg, and in 1929 opened a school in London. His wife, who herself directs a ballet school in England, has expanded his notebooks to produce the present work. The greater part deals with technique – exercises at the *barre* and without the *barre*; *adagio*; *allegro*; *pointe* work; pirouettes. The 3 appendices are by Nicolas Legat, 1, 'What is "*élan*" in Dancing?'; 2, 'An excerpt from the Notebook' and 3, 'Examples of Classes Given'. There are 28 text-figures but no index.

516 AGNEW, ERIC M. Anatomical studies for dancers and teachers of the classical ballet. C. W. Beaumont, for The Imperial Society of Teachers of Dancing, 1949. [29] pp. illus. 10s. 6d.

> Relates anatomy to the movements of the dancer, the text being illustrated by numerous clear line-drawings and supported by a glossary of anatomical terms. No index.

517 DOLIN, ANTON. Pas de deux: the art of partnering. Black, 1950. 61 pp. front., illus. 8s. 6d.

First published by Kamin Dance Publishers, New York, in 1949.
The author is noted for his sympathetic partnering. He discusses general principles in the first two chapters, and follows with practical advice on technique, dealing in some detail with *pas de deux* from *Coppélia*, *Giselle* and *Swan lake*. The introduction is by Arnold Haskell. The 10 drawings are by Phyllis Dolton, and the 18 reproductions of photographs by Fred Fehl are of Alicia Markova and the author in *pas de deux* work. No index.

518 GRANT, GAIL. The technical manual and dictionary of classical ballet. New York, Kamin Dance Publishers, 1950. [8], 87 pp. illus. 32s.

An alphabetical arrangement under technical terms with pronunciation given. Compares and contrasts the French, Italian and Russian schools. The majority of the line drawings by the author are gathered on 6 pages.

519 LIFAR, SERGE. Lifar on classical ballet. Wingate, 1951. [216] pp. 36 pl., illus. 21s.

Translated by D. M. Dinwiddie from the French edition, *Traité de danse académique*.
'Over the foundations of true and immutable principles . . . Serge Lifar builds a structure out of his own experience' (foreword by Tamara Karsavina). He was a leading dancer in the Diaghilev company, a dancer and choreographer at the Paris Opéra from 1930–58 and for much of the time a powerful influence, having been appointed Professor in 1932. 'Portrait of Serge Lifar', by A. L. Haskell, introduces 12 chapters in which Lifar expounds the technique of the positions, *battements*, *ronds-de-jambes*, *ports de bras*, *adage*, jumps, connecting movements, turns and *pointe* work. An appendix gives the text of his inaugural address on 18th December, 1947, when the Choreographic Academy at the Paris Opéra was founded. It should be noted that some terms used have different meanings for the French and English dancer. The plates are reproductions of photographs of scenes from Lifar's ballets; 80 groups of drawings in the text are by Monique Lancelot.

520 SPARGER, CELIA. Beginning ballet. Black, 1955. 40 pp. front., illus. 5s.

First published 1952. This is a second reprint.
'*Placing* depends largely on how the back is held during the early exercises at the *barre*, those exercises which, as we have said every dancer practices every day. This little book . . . show(s) some of the mistakes that occur.' The author juxtaposes 46 reproductions of photographs by G. B. L. Wilson, of a finished dancer and a beginner to illustrate points in her text.

521 AMBROSE, KAY. The ballet-lover's companion: a guide to practical
     aesthetics. Black, 1953. 81 pp. front., illus. 7s.

> Demonstrates to the layman some of the technical and aesthetic problems
> facing the dancer. Steps were posed especially for the author, who also
> sketched dancers at work and discussed her subject with them and with
> teachers and choreographers.

522 AMBROSE, KAY. Beginners please! A concentrated primer for ballet
     students of all ages. Black, 1953. [66] pp. illus. 7s.

> ' . . . The bare bones of elementary ballet', written in collaboration with
> Celia Franca, a former dancer of the Royal Ballet and now Director of the
> National Ballet of Canada. Chapters on exercises at the *barre*, exercises for
> beginners and centre practice, with advice on *pointe* work and character
> dancing, are explained and illustrated with many sketches by the author.

523 NICOLAEVA-LEGAT, NADINE. Preparation for ballet. Duckworth,
     1953. 132 pp. front., 16 pl., illus. 15s.

> The Principal of the Legat Ballet School explains how she has adapted the
> traditional system of ballet training to modern conditions. In Part 1 she deals
> with techniques; also with the school, the teacher and ballet in other countries.
> Part 2, 'Practical approach to Yoga', is followed by a 'Glossary of Terms'
> and an appendix giving the syllabuses of the Association of Russian Ballet
> (British Organization). There are 30 reproductions of photographs on plates
> and drawings in the text to clarify technical points. There is no index.

524 STUART, MURIEL, *and* DYER, CARLUS. The classic ballet: basic tech-
     nique and terminology. Longmans, 1953. xii, 243 pp. illus.
     36s.

> First published by Knopf, New York, 1952.
> 'The Classical Ballet: historical development', by Lincoln Kirstein intro-
> duces the main part of the book which illustrates 'every basic exercise, with
> additional explanation of the muscular control necessary for each one' (Moira
> Shearer's foreword). The many beautiful and extremely clear drawings are
> by Carlus Dyer with explanatory text by Muriel Stuart. 3 pages of illus-
> trations, giving basic principles of anatomy precede the exercises. George
> Balanchine, while making the point that ballet cannot be learnt solely from
> a book, considers that 'Miss Stuart has done more than anyone else to make
> the academic dance clear to students and amateurs' and that 'the drawings of
> Carlus Dyer are superior to any other illustrations to a training-book that I
> have seen, and more accurate as an approximation of ideal perfection,
> because they have been corrected and re-corrected'. (Preface.)

525 VAGANOVA, AGRIPPINA. Basic principles of classical ballet: Russian ballet technique. 2nd ed. Black, 1953. 139 pp. illus., diagrs. 10s. 6d.

> First published as *Fundamentals of the classical ballet*, by Kamin Dance Publishers, New York, 1946. English edition first published in 1948, and edited by Peggy van Praagh. The introduction is by Ninette de Valois.
> The author, a highly respected Russian teacher at the Leningrad School, writes on – Basic Conception of Classical Ballet; *Battements*; Rotary Movements of the Leg; Arms; Poses; Connecting and Auxiliary Movements; Jumps; Beats; Point Work; Turns; Sample Lesson for Advanced Classes. Drawings and diagrams illustrate the text.

526 ELLIS, RICHARD, *and* DU BOULAY, CHRISTINE. Partnering: the fundamentals of pas de deux. Beaumont, 1955. 63 pp. illus., diagrs. 10s. 6d.

> The authors are former members of the Royal Ballet. A short introduction, on the bearing and mental attitudes of the male and female partner, is followed by exercises on the performance of pirouettes, supporting at the waist and by the hand, promenades and lifts. Finally there is a chapter on *enchaînements* which includes exercises from previous chapters and instructions for one of the *pas de deux* from *Coppélia*. The 13 text-figures are by Christine du Boulay. There are also diagrams of floor patterns. No index.

527 FRENCH, RUTH, *and* DEMERY, FELIX. First steps in ballet: a practical and theoretical guide to the five grades of 'children's examinations' and the 'elementary examination' of The Royal Academy of Dancing. [3rd] rev. ed. The Authors, 1955. viii, 76 pp. front., 1 pl., illus. 7s. 6d.

528 — — Intermediate steps in ballet: a practical and theoretical guide to the 'intermediate examination' of the Royal Academy of Dancing. [2nd] rev. ed. The Authors, 1955. 56 pp. front., 1 pl., illus. 7s. 6d.

> First published 1940.

529 — — Advanced steps in ballet: a practical and theoretical guide to the 'advanced' and 'solo seal' examinations of the Royal Academy of Dancing. The Authors, 1950. 46 pp. front., 1 pl.

> Some exercises and steps used by other associations, but not required by the Royal Academy of Dancing have been included, as being useful to

students. Text illustrations have been included in *First Steps* . . . and *Intermediate Steps* . . . , the 3 in the latter are by William Chappell.

530 MARA, THALIA. Ballet: home practice for beginners. Constable, 1955. 64 pp. illus. 8s. 6d.

531 — — Second steps in ballet: basic centre exercises for home practice. Constable, 1957. 64 pp. illus. 8s. 6d.

532 — — Third steps in ballet: basic allegro steps for home practice. Constable, 1958. 63 pp. illus. 10s. 6d.

> The first title was written with the assistance of Lee Wyndham.
> The author, Teacher-Director of the School of Ballet Repertory, New York City, stresses that her 3 books should be used only in collaboration with a capable teacher. Both the instructions and the line drawings are easy to follow.

533 CRASKE, MARGARET, *and* DE MORODA, DERRA. The theory and practice of advanced allegro in classical ballet (Cecchetti method). Beaumont, 1956. 144 pp. 30s.

> Edited by Cyril Beaumont, who writes the preface. Both authors studied under Cecchetti and 'retained extensive notes of the tuition (they) had received from him' (preface). The text consists entirely of exercises for each day, with a note on the time and/or type of music to be used. The appendix explains the following steps – *entrechat six; grand jeté on tournant en arrière; grand jeté en tournant en avant; renversé; tombé.* Unlike the other two connected works (*see* nos. 507, 508) the book contains an index, but no illustrations.

534 KARSAVINA, TAMARA. Ballet technique: a series of practical essays. Black, 1956. 48 pp. front, illus. 10s. 6d.

> Margot Fonteyn wrote the foreword.
> The author, a great ballerina of the Maryinsky and Diaghilev companies, has contributed much to English ballet. She writes here from her wide experience in an interesting and vivid style, giving examples and exercises. Initially for the dancer, but the layman could learn from this book too. These essays were originally written for *The Dancing Times*; they have been revised and rewritten in part. The illustrations consist of 24 reproductions of photographs.

535 LAWSON, JOAN. Mime: the theory and practice of expressive gesture, with a description of its historical development. Pitman, 1957.

xvi, 167 pp. front., illus., bibliog. (Theatre and Stage Series.) 40s.

The book is 'intended for students of mime in its many forms: as an art in itself, as an addition to the words of the actor, and as an integral part of the art of ballet. Part 1 deals with the practice of mime and Part 2 with an historical basis of gesture. . . . The vocabulary of gesture (Chapter 6) is also intended as a form of index, linking the various ways of expressing some feeling, emotion or action. . . . The index proper refers to technical terms, names of ballets and characters' (preface). Claude Newman, reviewing the book in *The Dancing Times* (March 1958, p. 279), considers that the author offers 'some excellent advice' and 'much . . . of interest to the spectator of ballet' but that there is 'over-analysis' and too much detail. The bibliography includes about 71 references not all directly concerned with mime or dancing. The majority of the 99 drawings by Peter Revitt are examples taken from the ballet.

536   Another helpful but more general book on mime is *The Art of mime: its history and technique in education and the theatre*. 4th ed., by Irene Mawer (Methuen, 1946). It was first published in 1932, and is divided into Part 1, 'The History of Mime . . . ', Part 2, 'The Technique of Mime' and Part 3,
537   'Mime in Education'. There is also *Mime*, by Mark Perugini (*The Dancing Times*, [1925]), a brief essay offering certain principles to help the pupil to think for herself on the subject. The French and Italian schools of mime are
538   also touched on. *Practical miming*, 2nd ed., by Gertrude Pickersgill (Pitman, 1957) is 'a record of past experience . . . formulated into a tried and tested system of training [which] may be of practical help' (introduction).

539   SEVERN, GERALD.   Teach your child ballet. Based on Boris Kniaseff's new system.   Heinemann, 1958.   39 pp.   front., illus.   6s.

Boris Kniaseff, Russian dancer, teacher and choreographer opened a school in Switzerland in 1953. His methods are unorthodox in that he requires his pupils to perform exercises without the support of the *barre*. 30 exercises are demonstrated here, with reproductions of photographs by 'Baron' and an explanatory text.

540   SPARGER, CELIA.   Ballet physique, with notes on stresses and injuries. Black, 1958.   64 pp.   front., illus.   12s. 6d.

The author, former Consulting Physiotherapist to the Royal Ballet School, writes very clearly of the physique likely to produce a successful dancer in Part 1, and of the prevention and cure of injuries and strains in Part 2. ' . . . Should be read by all teachers of ballet and by all parents before they allow a child to embark upon the strenuous discipline of the professional ballet school'. (*Dancing Times*, September 1958, p. 546.) The 26 reproductions of photographs and 34 drawings in the text (although the title page states '39 drawings') are by Peter Revitt.

541 [ESPINOSA, EDOUARD], 'ESPINOSA', *pseud*.   Ballet: elementary syllabus
     & technique of operatic dancing.   8th ed.   E. K. Espinosa & Y.
     Espinosa, 1959.   64 pp.   front., illus.   9s. 6d.
     First published 1928.

542 — — Intermediate syllabus & technique of operatic dancing.   2nd ed.
     [E. K. Espinosa & Y. Espinosa], 1952.   108 pp.   2 pl.   9s. 6d.
     First published 1935(?).

543 — — Ballet: advanced syllabus & technique of operatic dancing.
     3rd ed.   E. K. Espinosa and Y. Espinosa, 1956.   90 pp.   front.
     14s. 6d.
     First published 1941.
     The syllabus of the British Ballet Organization of which the author was
     founder-Chairman. He was also a co-founder of the Royal Academy of
     Dancing.

544 FLETCHER, BEALE, *and* FLETCHER, PEGGY.   How to improve your
     ballet dancing: an illustrated guide to allegro, adagio.   Yoseloff,
     1959.   105 pp.   front., illus.   25s.
     First published, Barnes, New York, 1959.
     The text, which deals with the basic positions, limbering and stretching
     exercises, *barre* exercises, poses, *adagio*, *allegro* and *tours sur les pointes*, is
     illustrated with about 60 reproductions of photographs and about 41 series
     of sketches. There is also a section on ballet for children. A list of ballet
     terms is appended, but there is no index.

545 MARA, THALIA.   On your toes! The basic book of the dance on
     pointes.   Constable, 1961.   64 pp.   illus.   10s. 6d.
     First published, Garden City Books, New York, 1959.
     The purpose is 'to set forth, as clearly as possible the correct aspects of the
     technical training in the hope that it will help to clear up some popular
     misconceptions and to correct some evils' (foreword). There are sections on
     'The Care of the Feet' and 'Selecting and Preparing the Slippers'. There are
     about 220 diagrammatic drawings by Louise Holmgren.

546 LAWSON, JOAN.   Classical ballet: its style and technique.   Black, 1960.
     viii, 167 pp.   front., illus., bibliog.   25s.
     ' . . . Inspired by the work of Dame Ninette de Valois during the Annual
     Course for Teachers given at the Royal Ballet School', who allowed the

author 'to quote ... fully from her ... lectures and wise remarks'. In 7 chapters, the book covers, 'An Historical Survey of Ballet'; 'Classical Ballet and the Principles of Line'; 'Principles of Balance'; 'Technique and Conventions'; 'The Qualities of Classical Dance'; 'The Use of Steps'; 'The Dancers' Contribution'.

A controversial review by Andrew Hardie (*The Dancing Times*, December 1960, pp. 167, 169) resulted in a correspondence between the reviewer and the author, which lasted until March 1961, and caused A. L. Haskell to write an article 'Lawson *v*. Hardie with Roslavleva and Haskell intervening', in his series Balletomane's Log Book. (*The Dancing Times*, April 1961, p. 409.) This was answered by the reviewer (*The Dancing Times*, May 1961, p. 489). The 150 drawings by Peter Revitt illustrate movements and poses from ballets, and technical points. The bibliography contains 47 references listed alphabetically by author. There are separate indexes of technical terms and ballets.

547   NERINA, NADIA. 'Some aspects of the classical technique.' *In: The Ballet Annual 1960*, 14th issue, pp. 79–83. 5 illus.

548   BRUHN, ERIK, *and* MOORE, LILLIAN. Bournonville and ballet technique: studies and comments on August Bournonville's 'Études chorégraphiques'. Black, 1963. [70] pp. front., 15 pl.

Reprint of 1961 edition.
The style of the Royal Danish Ballet is based on the teaching and choreography of August Bournonville. His '*Études chorégraphiques* ... consists of various exercises beginning at the *barre*, through centre work and concluding with combinations of steps designed to improve *ballon* and elevation' (Chapter 2, p. 15). Erik Bruhn, himself a Dane and one of the great male dancers of the present age, was trained in this school of dancing; Lillian Moore was an American critic and writer on ballet. There are 31 illustrations on plates, mainly reproductions of photographs, with 5 facsimiles of prints.

549   CATON, EDWARD. Ballet class. Harrap, 1961. [128] pp. illus. 25s.

Written in association with Erik James Martin. Edward Caton was trained at Nelidova's Ballet School, Moscow, and has danced with, and been ballet master of several American companies and the de Cuevas Ballet. This picture book of 'Basic ballet exercises [which] have been dissected into their component parts' has some 550 photographs taken by Robert Christopher and posed by dancers from the Ballet Russe School of Ballet, New York City and the Alexandra Sawicka School of Ballet in Berkeley, California. Exercises are grouped broadly as follows – the *barre*; centre practice; on *pointe*; *pas de deux*. Appended is a list of ballet terms and of suggested music.

Andrew Hardie, reviewing in *The Dancing Times* (May 1961, p. 482), considers that 'many of the photographs show an abysmal lack of any knowledge of the correct execution of the classic steps'.

550 KARSAVINA, TAMARA.   Classical ballet: the flow of movement. Black, 1962. [95] pp. front., illus. 25s.

'When we were first able to persuade Karsavina to write for *The Dancing Times* about technique and interpretation, we soon began to receive highly appreciative comments from students and teachers ... because it is always satisfying to present brilliant teaching on any subject, the same publishers are now offering in book form this further outstanding contribution to the teaching of our time' (introduction, by A. H. Franks). The book is divided into 5 parts – 'At the *Barre*'; 'Centre Practice'; 'Planning the Practice'; 'Elevation'; 'From Class room to Stage'. The illustrations include 112 reproductions of photographs by Houston Rogers and Jack Blake, posed by Antoinette Sibley and Donald Macleary of the Royal Ballet, and 8 groups of line drawings by Rudolf Benesh.

551 KERSLEY, LEO, *and* SINCLAIR, JANET.   A dictionary of ballet terms. 2nd ed. enl. Black, 1964.   112 pp.   illus.   15s.

First published 1952; has been enlarged by 14 pages.

Intended primarily for the layman, but some material for the dancer has been included, owing to the interest shown by professionals in the first edition. Many movements are explained with reference to examples from ballets. There are 127 figures, drawn by Peter Revitt, which are carefully linked with the text. These include 2 pages of illustrations to show variations in arm positions between the different schools.

552 SPARGER, CELIA.   Anatomy and ballet: a handbook for teachers of ballet.   4th ed. rev. and enl.   Black, 1965.   96 pp.   front., illus., diagrs., bibliog.   25s.

First published 1949, the present edition 'has been substantially enlarged principally by the addition of text and illustrations from *Ballet physique* which is now no longer in print' (preface to 4th edition).

The origin 'was a request from the Cecchetti Society for an anatomy syllabus. ... It then became obvious that the prior need was for a text-book' (preface to 1st edition). The human bone structure is explained and related to the movements of the dancer; anatomical faults are discussed too. Chapter 13, 'Stresses and Strains', is new, embodying material from *Ballet physique*. Chapter 14, in which the author answers questions posed by teachers and dancers, has been extended to deal at greater length with some questions. '... Future standard work for the bookshelf of the teacher and the older student' (Ninette de Valois, in the introduction). The bibliography contains

7 items on anatomy. The illustrations consist of 43 reproductions of X-ray and other photographs and 51 drawings to clarify the text.

NOTATION

553 [Two volumes of dances, written in steno-choreography, with music.] 1707–40.

Bodleian Library *Don.d.45,46*. There is no general title-page to either volume so the entry in the Bodleian Library Catalogue has been followed.

Don.d.45, 51 pp. There is a pencilled note on the front end paper stating that 'The British Museum has quite a different collation of dances bound up with "The Union" '. The dances are as follows –

1. *The Union*. The title-page to this dance states that Mr. Isaac composed the dance which was performed on the Queen's birthday in 1707, and that it had been written down in notation by John Weaver.
2. *The Prince's royal*. 1715.
3. *The Shepherdess*, by Mr. Kellom. 1716.
4. *Slow minuet*, by Mr. Caverley. 1729.
5. *Queen Caroline*. 1728.
6. *Pasacaille*, by Mr. Labbee. An incomplete note written in at the top of the page reads: '. . . Stage Dances, and call'd thoro(?) Pasacaille of Armide(a?) by Mrs. Elford and Mrs. Santlow but the figure somewhat differs as being in some part taken from the woman's side where it begins and is in some parts from the man's side.'
7. *The Prince of Orange*. 1733.
8. *The Princess of Hesse*, by Glover. 1740.

Don.d.46. [20] pp.
1. *The Prim rose*, by Mr. Marcelle. 1721.
2. *The Siciliana*, by Mr. Siris. 1714.
3. *The Camilla*. 1709.
4. *The Brawl of Audenarde*, by Mr. Siris. 1709.

The dances in both volumes have been listed in order of binding.

554 FEUILLET, RAOUL.   For the further improvement of dancing, a treatise of chorography or the art of dancing country dances after a new character, in which the figures steps, and manner of performing are describ'd. . . . Sold by J. Walsh & P. Randall . . . J. Hare . . . J. Cullen . . . the Author . . . 1710.   [4], 88 pp.   diagrs.

A translation by John Essex of *Recueil de contredances mises en chorégraphie* . . . Paris, chez l'Auteur . . . 1706. The following dances written in notation, are by the translator – *The Trip to the jubilee, The Great Turk, The Busie body,*

The Tatler and *The To[a]st*. The remainder are French dances, also in notation. (B.M.1042. d.45.)

555   FEUILLET, RAOUL.   Orchesography; or, the art of dancing, by charac- ters and demonstrative figures. Wherein the whole art is explain'd with compleat tables of all steps us'd in dancing, and rules for the motions of the arms. . . . 2nd ed.   Printed for and sold by John Walsh . . .   John Hare, [1710].   [6], 120 pp.   diagrs.

   The first edition of this translation by John Weaver from *Chorégraphie ou l'art de décrire la danse* (Paris, 1700) was published in 1706. (Bodleian. Don.d.5).
   20 dances by Mr. Isaac have been added to this 2nd English edition, written in notation and including the 'rigadoon', 'the louver' and the 'Brittagne'. The arrangement has been altered too. In the first edition the diagrams were gathered together on 44 pages, but in the second they have been interspersed with the text. John Weaver states expressly that he has not made any altera- tion to Feuillet's text. According to Weaver, Feuillet had perfected a system which Beauchamp invented. (Bodleian. Don.d.6.)

556   Another translation by P. Siris, was published also in 1706, under the title *The Art of dancing demonstrated by characters and figures.* . . . Siris writes 'the rules he [Feuillet] has given us for understanding the written-characters of a dance appeared to me so just and intelligible, that I have entirely made use of them in my book, and have added nothing but the seventeenth chapter' which gives 'a short explanation of the steps whose proper names could not be well translated into English'. Siris, like Weaver, considers that Beauchamp had been the originator of this system, asserting that 'he himself [Beauchamp] taught me the grounds of it above eighteen years ago'. (B.M.797. dd.20.)

557   PEMBERTON, E.   An essay for the further improvement of dancing: being a collection of figure dances, of several numbers, compos'd by the most eminent masters; describ'd in characters after the newest manner of Monsieur Feuillet. . . .   Printed, and sold by J. Walsh . . . J. Hare . . . and at the Author's . . . 1711.   [63] pp.   diagrs.

   'Begun at the request of several Masters . . . who express'd their want of such an undertaking . . . I waited a considerable Time for the original of Mr. Feuillet's Treatise of Country Dances translated by Mr. Essex, which Method I have for the most part followed . . . where there is occasion for particular steps I have followed Mr. Weaver . . .' (preface). Three extra dances, a chaconne, a pasacaille and a jig by Isaac, l'Abbé and Louis Pécour respectively have been added. There is a subscription list of 58 masters, of whom 17 lived outside London. (B.M.556. e.16.)

558   TOMLINSON, KELLOM.   Six dances, being a collection of all the yearly

dances, publish'd by him from the year 1715 to the present year. . . .
To be had of the Author at his house . . . [1720 ?].

The dances are listed on the general title-page with a note to the effect that
The Submission was performed at the Lincoln's Inn Field Theatre by Monsieur
and Mademoiselle Sallé, 'the two French children'; there is also a separate
title-page for each dance. Feuillet notation is used, the appropriate phrase of
music for each movement of the dance being printed. The dances are as
follows, being listed in order of binding – *The Gavot* (1720); *The Address a
new rigadoon* (1719); *The Prince Eugene* (1718); *The Submission* (1717); *The
Shepherdess* (1716); *The Passepied round O* (1715). (B.M.K.6.)

559 ZORN, FRIEDRICH ALBERT.   Grammar of the art of dancing, theoretical
and practical: lessons in the arts of dancing and dance writing
(choreography). [Rev. ed.] . . . Boston, Massachusetts, 1905.
xviii, 302 pp.   front., illus., diagrs.

First published in 1887 as *Grammatik der tanzkunst* (Odessa and Leipzig),
this translation has been edited by Alfonso Josephs Sheafe.

'The purpose . . . is to establish a universal method of teaching dancing
and the invention and demonstration of a satisfactory system of dance script'.
The author consulted Arthur Saint-Léon and studied other systems of
notation.

560 MORRIS, MARGARET.   The notation of movement; text, drawings and
diagrams.   Kegan Paul, Trench, Trubner, 1928.   103 pp.   front.,
diagrs. (Psyche Miniatures. Central Series. No. 21.)   2s. 6d.

Margaret Morris, English dancer and teacher of a type of free dance after
the style of Isadora Duncan, began work on her notation in 1913. Its aim is
to plot positions, using arbitrary signs on a stave of lines grouped three and
three with a space between for body movements. There are signs, too, for
contraction and relaxation of muscles and facial movements. Apparently this
system is not in use nowadays. There are many diagrams and some examples
of the notation.

561 HUTCHINSON, ANN.   Labanotation: the system for recording movement.   Phoenix House, 1954.   [14], 274 pp.   diagrs.   25s.

Originally published, New Directions, Norfolk (Conn.), 1954.

George Balanchine considers that the author, co-founder and President of
the Dance Notation Bureau, New York, was 'the ideal person to have
prepared this definitive text book, which will be of inestimable value to all
persons working in the field of the dance' (preface), and the reviewer of *The
Dancing Times*, that the 'book is so clearly written, and so well illustrated . . .
that by application anyone possessed of common intelligence will be able to

master Labanotation' (*The Dancing Times*, August 1954, p.'676). After 'A Brief History of Dance Notation' there follows a detailed explanation with 483 diagrams of a notation which can be used to record any type of movement. Appended is an 'Alphabet of Basic Symbols' and a 'Glossary of Supplementary Symbols'. The illustrations are by D. Anderson, and the Labanotation examples and studies were drawn by Marian van Loen.

Ann Hutchinson, in collaboration with Laura Wilson and Peggy van Praagh is recording, in Labanotation, the theory, *barre*-work, *ports de bras*, *adage* and *allegro* of the grades of the Cecchetti method. These books are known as *The Ballet Reader Series* and supplement the *Primers of Classical Ballet*, by C. W. Beaumont. The volumes for Grades 1–3 have been completed and Grade 4 is in preparation. Complementary to the *Ballet Readers* are the *Ballet ABC Books* 1–4. These give descriptions of correct performances and explanation of the Labanotation symbols.

562 BENESH, RUDOLF, *and* BENESH, JOAN.   An introduction to Benesh dance notation.   Black, 1956.   48 pp.   illus.   10s. 6d.

Sections on – 'How it Works'; 'Writing down Positions'; 'Writing down Movements'; 'First Steps'; 'The Head'; 'Direction'; 'Writing with Music' give the rudiments of this 'accurate 'and 'extremely comprehensive' notation. (A. L. Haskell in the foreword.) Appended is 'Examples of Notation'. The 45 text-figures by Rudolf Benesh are an integral part of the text.

563 LABAN, RUDOLF.   Principles of dance and movement notation.   [New ed.]   Macdonald & Evans, 1956.   56 pp.   diagrs.   17s. 6d.

First published 1954.

Part 1, 'Movement Notation and the Fields of its Application', covers about one-third of the book. It is followed in Part 2, by an explanation of the symbols and the practical application of the notation to movement. There are 114 diagrams giving examples of the notation, with text describing the movements notated.

564 QUIREY, BELINDA.   'Dance and movement notations.'   *In: Journal of the English Folk Dance and Song Society*, v. 8, no. 2, December 1957, pp. 109–11.

Criticizes systems devised by Benesh, Eshkol and Laban.

565 ESHKOL, NOA, *and* WACHMANN, ABRAHAM.   Movement notation.   Weidenfeld & Nicolson, 1958.   ix, 203 pp.   illus., diagrs.   42s.

A detailed explanation of a system based on mathematical principles applied to the upright position of the human body and the limbs moving on an axis, rotary, plane or curved, without consideration of 'the burden of emotional and stylistic notions which may be attached to any movement'. Ann Hutchinson thinks that this notation 'deserves the serious attention of all concerned with the problem of recording human movement through written symbols' and continues, 'These avant garde concepts may well establish a type of choreography which makes use of the body as an instrument to produce moving architecture, a completely contrasting style to those which have grown out of the use of the body as a human, emotional instrument'. (*The Dancing Times*, March 1959, p. 282.) Abraham Wachmann and John Haries provide the illustrations. There are 41 examples of the notation and some 54 diagrams.

566   STEPANOV, VLADIMIR IVANOVITCH.   Alphabet of movements of the human body: a study in recording the movements of the human body by means of musical signs.   Cambridge, The Golden Head Press, 1958.   viii, 47 pp.   diagrs., bibliog.   42s.

Translated by Raymond Lister from the French edition of 1892, *Alphabet des mouvements du corps humain*.

An introduction to the system, the details and application of which were to be published at a later date. (Introduction by the author.) There are chapters on anatomy, notes and signs, and the application of the notation to leg, arm and torso movements, turns, gymnastics and choreography. Appendix 1 is a note on Stepanov, by A. R. Tomsky, Art Director of the Bolshoi Ballet, who also supplies the list of 7 references (Russian) on Stepanov and his work in Appendix 2. 7 pages are devoted to diagrams and examples of notation. No index.

567   HALL, FERNAU.   'Dance notation and choreology.'   *In: The British Journal of Aesthetics*, v. 4, no. 1, January 1964, pp. 58–66.   bibliog.

Benesh dance notation. 6 items in bibliography.

X. DESIGN AND COSTUME

INIGO Jones designed many settings and costumes for the masques produced during the reigns of James I and Charles I. Some of these designs are reproduced from the originals at Chatsworth House, in v. 12 of the Walpole Society publications.[1]

The eighteenth-century scene-painters are not so fortunate, for 'Hardly anything has been put together about the scene painters who have worked here or their conditions of employment'. This quotation is taken from the introduction to *A Checklist of scene painters working in Great Britain and Ireland in the 18th century*, by Sybil Rosenfeld and Edward Croft-Murray.[2] The object of this work is 'to provide a basis for a history of scene painting in England in the 18th century. . . . A good deal of the material has been culled from playbills, London newspaper advertisements and opera libretti. Sources other than these have been given'.[3] The checklist occasionally indicates where the scene painter has designed for a ballet.

In the first half of the nineteenth century William Grieve (1800–44), a scene-painter at Drury Lane and Her Majesty's Theatre, designed the English settings for productions of the Romantic Ballet. In the latter part of the century, with the revival of ballet at the Empire and Alhambra Theatres, the two outstanding designers were Wilhelm and Alias. The former, whose real name was William John Charles Pitcher, designed and supervised the costumes and some settings at the Empire from 1887; also he took a great interest in planning and writing the scenarios. At the Alhambra 'Monsieur Alias' was responsible for the costumes and E. T. Ryan for the scenery.[4]

With the rise and continuous development of English ballet from the nineteen-thirties, stage designers have tended to be employed for a particular

---

[1] *Designs by Inigo Jones for masques & plays at court: a descriptive catalogue of drawings for scenery and costumes mainly in the collection of . . . the Duke of Devonshire . . . introduction and notes* by P. Simpson & C. F. Bell. Printed for the Walpole and Malone Societies at the University Press, 1924. The Walpole Society 1923–4. V. 12.

[2] *Theatre Notebook*, v. 19, no. 1, p. 6. This *Checklist* . . . is published in issues of *Theatre Notebook*. The first part appeared in v. 19, no. 1, autumn 1964, and the last in v. 20, no. 1, autumn 1965. Additions and corrections were made in v. 20, no. 2, Winter 1965–66.

[3] *Ibid.*

[4] *Ballet then and now* . . . , by D. Lynham. 1947, pp. 103–104.

production. They can be divided into those who have made their names primarily as painters, and those who are known almost entirely as designers in the theatre. The following are painters of standing who have designed scenery and/or costume for ballets – Vanessa Bell, Edward Burra, John Piper, Rex Whistler, E. McKnight Kauffer, Gwen Raverat, Michael Ayrton, Sidney Nolan and John Craxton. The 'theatre designers' include Cecil Beaton, Sophie Fedorovitch, Hugh Stevenson, Andrée Howard and William Chappell; the last two were dancers themselves. All the above are or were English by birth or habitation. From time to time, foreign designers have been employed, for example, Lila de Nobili who designed settings and costumes for *Ondine*, Denis Malclès the designer of *Cinderella*, both for the Royal Ballet, and Yuri Piminov and Gennady Epishin, who designed the settings and costumes for Festival Ballet's production of *The Snow maiden*.

There are various factors which influence the design of stage scenery. An elaborate set suitable for the large stage of a London theatre might well have to be adapted for a company which spends most of its time touring. A really small company, which performs in town halls, schools and so on, and which also has to keep expenses to a minimum, will use as little scenery as possible. Such considerations applied equally to Ballet Rambert in its early days, when it was performing 'Chamber ballet' on the small stage of the Mercury Theatre.

The development of ballet costume has been international. The first professional dancers were subjected to heavy costumes in the style of the normal clothing of the day, with embellishments to indicate country, period, trade and so on. This restricted the movement of the dancers and has an influence on the dances evolved. Panniers were worn by the women, and their skirts reached to the ground. The tonnelet, a short skirt stretched over hoops, almost at right-angles to the body, was worn by the male dancer during the eighteenth century, and this, too, must have had a constricting effect on movement. Masks were worn until 1772, when Maximilien Gardel, a pupil of Noverre, made a stand against this convention. First the solo dancers and then the *corps de ballet* abandoned the use of masks.

Noverre had advocated costume reform in his *Lettres sur la danse . . . (see* no. 168). He wished to abolish the tonnelets, panniers, wigs and masks, and to replace the heavy materials of the current costumes with others made of a lighter fabric, and to represent more realistically the circumstances of the characters portrayed. An earlier attempt at reform had been made by Marie Sallé. In 1734 she had danced in a ballet called *Pygmalion*, in London, wearing a simple draped costume made of muslin, but her example was not followed at the time. The shortening of the skirt, said to have been introduced by Marie Camargo, was subsequently adopted by other dancers. Gallini was another who wished to see a change in the dancers' costumes. 'It is not magnificence that is the great point, but their [the costumes] being well assorted to character and circumstances'[5] he wrote, and he pressed, too, for discarding the mask. Some of these changes were brought about after the French Revolution. A light material and straight lines became fashionable, and designers for the ballet followed suit. Tights were worn for the first time during this period.

The Romantic Ballet inaugurated another change in the female dancer's costume. The costume of the Sylph in *La Sylphide* became a type. The tight bodice and full bell-shaped skirt, which to a certain extent followed the shape of the crinoline, was copied, with variations, in many ballets of the period. This trend was continued in the late nineteenth century. The dancer's skirt took on a slight bustle effect. Over the years the ballet skirt has been shortened. In the latter part of the nineteenth century the tutu, the very short skirt, not unlike the tonnelet in shape, was evolved for the female dancer, and is worn in many ballets. From the early twentieth century there has been a tendency to simplify costume, giving greater freedom of movement, and also allowing audiences to appreciate the line and movement of the dancer more fully.

In the eighteenth century, the male dancer's costume approximated to the normal clothing of the period, with the addition of the tonnelet, but by the beginning of the nineteenth century this had changed. In the introduction to *Ballet design past & present* (*see* no. 571) the author states that during the eighteen-twenties there was a standard type of costume for the male dancer in each of the three styles of dancing. For the serious style, the dancer wore 'a Greek chiton of light material, his legs were bare and his feet shod with sandals', for the *demi-caractère* dancer 'doublet, trunks and long hose, . . . and a flat-brimmed cap' and for the *caractère* dancer 'a theatricalised version of the open-necked shirt, short coat, and breeches common to village youths'.[6] Since the Romantic Ballet, the male dancer's costume has remained much the same, i.e. tights and tunic, with adaptations for place and period.

The style of shoe worn by dancers has changed. In the eighteenth century they wore the high-heeled shoes in vogue for everyday wear, and when the

[5] *A Treatise on the art of dancing*, by G.-A. Gallini. 1762, p. 129.
[6] *Ballet design past & present*, by C. W. Beaumont. 1946, p. xxii.

heel-less slipper came in after the French Revolution, the dancers followed
this fashion. It was in the latter part of the nineteenth century that the stiffened
shoe, which assisted the ballerina to rise on her *pointes* was evolved. At first
it was stiffened by darning only. It was 'in the last third of the nineteenth
century [that] ballet-shoes were blocked to give additional support to the
toes'.[7]

BIBLIOGRAPHY

Arrangement. 1. General works on design of scenery or design of scenery and costume,
arranged chronologically by date of publication. 2. General works on costume only,
arranged as above. 3. Works on individual designers arranged alphabetically by the
professional name of the designer. Where there is more than one work under the
name of a designer, the entries have been arranged chronologically by date of publication.

Note: Exhibitions on theatre and ballet designs are included in Appendix C.

GENERAL

568   NASH, PAUL. 'The painter and the stage.' *In: The Listener*, v. 7,
        no. 154, 23rd December, 1931, pp. 1101–2. (Weekly Notes on
        Art.) 1 illus.

     The artist in ballet, particularly the designs of John Armstrong, John
        Banting and Edward Burra for the Camargo Society. Brief.

569   BEAUMONT, CYRIL WILLIAM. 'Ballet settings and costumes in recent
        productions.' *In: The Studio*, v. 117, no. 553, April 1939, pp.
        146–55.   25 illus. (3 col.).

     Décor for *Checkmate* and *Horoscope* is reviewed, also the work of Hugh
        Stevenson, among others.

570   RAFFÉ, WALTER GEORGE. 'Decoration for English ballet.' *In: The
        Studio*, v. 125, no. 600, March 1943, pp. 82–5.   6 illus.

     International Ballet; Ballet de la Jeunesse Anglaise; New Russian Ballet.

571   BEAUMONT, CYRIL WILLIAM. Ballet design past & present. *The
        Studio*, 1946. xxxii, 216 pp.   illus. (46 col.).   30s.

---

[7] *Ballet design past & present*, by C. W. Beaumont. 1946, p. xxiii.

Expanded from the author's *Design for the ballet*, 1937, and *Five centuries of ballet design*, 1939, both published by *The Studio*.

'... An attempt to trace the evolution of design for Ballet from the Italian Renaissance to the present day. Since the process of development is to be seen most clearly in France, the successive innovations effected at the Paris Opéra will provide the main theme ... with occasional consideration of activities in other countries' (introduction). The author outlines the development of ballet design in his introduction, reinforcing it visually with about 580 reproductions of prints and photographs. Designers of English productions represented – Cecil Beaton; Vanessa Bell; Nadia Benois; William Chappell; Phyllis Dolton; Sophie Fedorovitch; Roger Furse; Sylvia Green; Leslie Hurry; E. McKnight Kauffer; Oliver Messel; 'Motley'; John Piper; Gwendolen Raverat; Guy Sheppard; George Sheringham; Hugh Stevenson; C. Wilhelm.

572 AMBERG, GEORGE. Art in modern ballet. Routledge, 1947. 246 pp. 8 pl. (col.), illus. 63s.

The author, Curator of the Department of Theatre Arts in the Museum of Modern Art, New York, in the 1940's, has collected together reproductions of some 200 designs for modern ballets, from c.1917–45. He introduces the indexes and plates with a 16-page historical survey. English designs include – Michael Ayrton (*Le Festin de l'araignée*); Nadia Benois (*Lady into fox*); Edward Burra (*Miracle in the Gorbals*); Sophie Fedorovitch (*Dante sonata*); Roger Furse (*The Prospect before us*); Andrée Howard (*Carnival of animals*); Leslie Hurry (*Hamlet, Le Lac des cygnes*); John Piper (*The Quest*); Rex Whistler (*The Rake's progress*); Ronald Wilson (*Un Songe*). Preceding is 'Ballet Index 1909–45' in which there are '833 titles with data', about 160 being for English productions, giving composer, choreographer, settings and costumes, company, and place of première; also indexes of designers, composers and choreographers.

573 AYRTON, MICHAEL. 'The décor of Sadler's Wells Ballet 1939–46.' *In: The Ballet Annual* [*1947*], 1st issue, pp. 74–[83].

574 MARSHALL, FRANCIS. 'The artist and the ballet.' *In: The Studio*, v. 144, no. 717, December 1952, pp. 161–7. 13 illus. (2 col.).

'Describes the contributions of some well-known artists to the composite effort of creation which is the ballet.'

575 BUCKLE, RICHARD. Modern ballet design; a picture-book with notes. Black, 1955. xv, 128 pp. front. (col.), illus. 30s.

'... Covers ten years since the war, and that in a very desultory way. The designers whose work is illustrated seem to me extraordinarily varied in style' (introduction). The author writes a brief subjective introduction to each designer; most space is allotted to 203 black and white illustrations – reproductions of designers' sketches, and of photographs of designs and costumes taken during performances. English and foreign designers (of productions for English companies) represented are as follows – James Bailey; Cecil Beaton; André Beaurepaire; Christian Bérard; Eugene Berman; Edward Burra; Antoni Clavé; Robert Colquhoun and Robert McBryde; John Craxton; André Derain; Sophie Fedorovitch; Leslie Hurry; Robin Ironside; George Kirsta; Isabel Lambert; Osbert Lancaster; Jean-Denis Malclès; Oliver Messel; John Piper; Kenneth Rowell; Loudon Sainthill. Appended is an 'Index of Ballets Illustrated' giving composer, choreographer, designer, where first performed and date of first performance.

576   BLAND, ALEXANDER.   'Recent ballet design.'   *In: The Ballet Annual 1963*, 17th issue, pp. 58–62.

Persephone, designed by Nico Ghika, *The Rite of spring*, by Sidney Nolan, *Conflicts*, by Ralph Koltai and others.

577   READE, BRIAN.   Ballet designs and illustrations 1581–1940: a catalogue raisonné. H.M.S.O. [for the] Victoria and Albert Museum, 1967. [8],   58 pp.   front. (col.),   178 pl.   (5 col.)   bibliog.

'The designs and illustrations reproduced . . . are all in the Victoria and Albert Museum, and they can be seen either in the Library, or in the Enthoven Theatre Collection, or in the Print Room of the Department of Prints and Drawings.' (introduction).

The notes give details not only on the plates and the artists, but also, where appropriate, on the ballets, dancers and all concerned with the productions. Plate 23 shows plans for an equestrian ballet (1652) and plate 47 shows music and notation for part of a ballet *Dido* (1704).

Records of ballet in England specifically include some reproductions from the Romantic period, costume designs by Wilhelm and others at the end of the nineteenth century, and a number from Diaghilev ballets produced in London.

The bibliography has 36 titles, some in French and German (11 by English authors) giving author, title, place of publication and date.

COSTUME

578   IMAGE, SELWYN.   The art of dancing: on a question of dress.   Church Reformer, 1891.

A defence of the costume of the ballet dancer, in a paper read to the Church and Stage Guild in 1891.

579 MASON, RUPERT. Robes of Thespis: costume designs by modern
     artists. Benn, 1928. xv, 143 pp. 109 pl., illus. £14 14s. od.
     Edited for the author, by George Sheringham and R. Boyd Morrison.
     Section 8, 'Ballet', contains 3 articles as follows – 'Costume for Ballet', by
     Cyril Beaumont; 'The Problem of the Designer', by James Laver; 'Costume
     in Ballet', by Edith Carlyon. These are followed by 24 plates displaying the
     work of 12 designers including Paul Nash, Phyllis Dolton and Laura Knight,
     and 10 drawings in the text, by Randolph Schwabe after designs in the
     Archives of the Paris Opéra. The aim was 'To bring to light unknown
     artists – to enable them to have a chance of success . . . I sought . . . the help
     of eminent men in art and letters, whose names would give a special value
     to the book. . . . With some I placed commissions to produce designs
     specially for this book, and from others I purchased drawings and designs
     hitherto unpublished.' (Author's preface.)

580 LAWSON, JOAN, *and* REVITT, PETER. Dressing for the ballet. Black,
     1958. 96 pp. illus., diagrs., bibliog. 16s.
     'Intended to help both amateur and professional dancers . . . to find suit-
     able costumes for classroom and stage' and 'to make these for themselves'.
     Basic patterns are given on which more elaborate costumes may be built.
     Sections deal with the classroom, the classical and romantic ballet and the
     demi-caractère costume. The bibliography contains 15 items mainly on folk
     costume and published in several European countries. There are 48 diagrams
     and patterns, and 100 drawings of costumes and garments by Peter Revitt.

581 LAVER, JAMES. Costume in the theatre. Harrap, 1964. 223 pp.
     4 pl. (col.), illus., bibliog. 35s.
     The author was formerly Keeper of Prints and Drawings at the Victoria
     and Albert Museum, and first President of the Association of Theatrical
     Designers and Craftsmen. He deals specifically with dance and ballet in –
     'Dressing up to Dance'; 'Pageant and Masque beget Opera and Ballet';
     'Opera and Ballet' (c.1630–1780); 'From Noverre to Diaghilev'. Salient
     points in development and outstanding designers for the later periods are
     discussed in each section, followed by relevant illustrations, 67 in all. These
     reproduce original costume designs and illustrations and photographs. The
     bibliography contains 200 items arranged primarily by sections of the text,
     of which 39 are listed under the above sections.

INDIVIDUAL DESIGNERS

Bailey

582 BAILEY, JAMES. 'Designing the classical ballet.' *In: Souvenirs de
     Ballet, no. 1,* 1949, pp. 90–2. 5 illus.
     The Artist and Ballet Design 2.

Beaton

583   FLEET, SIMON. 'Cecil Beaton as ballet designer.' *In: The Ballet
      Annual 1950*, 4th issue, pp. 79–81.

Chiang

584   CHIANG YEE. 'What can I say about ballet?' *In: The Ballet Annual
      [1948]*, 2nd issue, pp. 113–14.

> Author was designer of the décor for *The Birds*; choreographer Robert
> Helpmann.

Fedorovitch

585   FLEET, SIMON. 'Sophie Federovitch as ballet designer.' *In: The
      Ballet Annual [1948]*, 2nd issue, pp. 73–9.

586   BUCKLE, RICHARD. 'Sophie Fedorovitch.' *In: The Ballet Annual
      1954*, 8th issue, pp. 59–61.

587   FLEET, SIMON, *comp*. Sophie Fedorovitch, tributes and attributes:
      aspects of her art and personality by some of her fellow artists and
      friends. Priv. print., 1955. 69 pp. 12 pl., illus.

> Part 1, 'Paris', Part 2, 'Brancaster', and Part 3, 'London and the Theatre', are
> composed of appreciations of Sophie Fedorovitch as artist and friend. There
> is a prologue, 'Early Days', and an epilogue, 'Summer Holiday', by Simon
> Fleet. Inset as a separate pamphlet is 'Sophie Fedorovitch; a biographical
> sketch', by Simon Fleet. The 29 illustrations on plates are reproductions of
> personal snapshots of the artist and photographs of ballet and opera, with a
> coloured sketch by Peter Brook.

Furse

588   FURSE, ROGER. 'My ambitions in ballet.' *In: Souvenirs de Ballet,
      no. 1*, 1949, pp. 88–9. 1 illus.

> The Artist and Ballet Design 1.

Hurry

589   HURRY, LESLIE. Settings and costumes for Sadler's Wells ballets
      'Hamlet' (1942), 'Le Lac des cygnes' and the Old Vic 'Hamlet'
      (1944). Faber (for Shenval Press), 1946. 72 pp. front. (col.),
      50 pl. (Ariel Books on the Arts.) 5s.

C. W. Beaumont writes the introduction sketching the artist's career and describing and assessing the décor. The editor is Lilian Browse. Plates 1–13 are devoted to the ballet *Hamlet* and 14–36 to *Le Lac des cygnes*. There are 4 vignettes drawn by the artist.

Messel

590   'A scene is born.'   *In: Future Books*, v. 3, *The crowded scene*, [c. 1946], pp. [88]–91.   8 illus.

    Designs for *The Sleeping beauty*, Royal Ballet production.

591   BOYS, ARTHUR. Oliver Messel – stage designer. *In: Souvenirs de Ballet*, no. *1*, 1949, pp. 28–39.   11 illus.

    Mainly on designing for the Royal Ballet's production of *The Sleeping beauty*.

Piper

592   LANCASTER, KAREN. 'John Piper as a designer for the theatre.'   *In: The Adelphi*, v. 29, no. 1, November 1952, pp. 19–25.

    Mostly opera, but his designs for *The Quest, Job, Sea change* and *Harlequin in April* are dealt with briefly.

Whistler

593   WHISTLER, REX. Designs for the theatre.   Batsford, for The Curtain Press, 1950.   8s. 6d.

    Originally published 1946–8 as nos. 2–4 of *The Masque*. In this 1950 publication the 3 parts have been bound together, Parts 2 and 3 retaining separate title-pages and pagination. Details of collation are as follows –
    Part 1. [18] pp. 8 pl. (col.), with an appreciation of Rex Whistler by Cecil Beaton.
    Part 2. [9] pp. 24 pl. (8 col.), with an introduction by James Laver.
    Part 3. 30 pp. 22 pl. (4 col.), with a foreword by Laurence Whistler.
    Appended to Part 3 is a list of 'Designs for the Theatre', by Rex Whistler, in which there is a section for ballet. 8 plates out of the total are devoted to designs for ballet.

Wilhelm

594   WILHELM, C. 'Art in the ballet.'

    Part 1. The author's views on certain aspects of ballet and ballet design. *In: The Magazine of Art*, November 1894, pp. 12–16. 4 illus. [by the author].

Part 2. Description of some of Wilhelm's designs for ballet at the Empire and Crystal Palace and for pantomime at Drury Lane etc. *In: The Magazine of Art*, November 1894, pp. [48]–53. 4 illus. [by the author].
Contribution to a series of articles on 'Art in Theatre'.

595   SPIELMANN, M. M.   'Art in the theatre: the development of spectacle as exemplified in the ballet of "Faust".'   *In: The Magazine of Art*, v. 19, part 1, November 1895, pp. [25]–8.   14 illus. [mainly by C. Wilhelm.]

596   FORSYTH, GERALD.   'Wilhelm: a noted Victorian theatrical designer.' *In: Theatre Notebook*, v. 11, no. 2, January–March 1957, pp. 55–8. 5 pl.

XI. MUSIC

MUSIC and dancing, two of the oldest arts known to man, have always been closely associated, as far as is known. Yet few writers on ballet have considered it worth while to devote a whole book to the history of ballet music.

Edwin Evans pointed out that three elements common to both music and dancing are ritual, lyrical expression and rhythmic energy, and that the choreographer had the task of adjusting the three functions of movement to the corresponding musical elements.[1] There are again three ways in which a choreographer may choose the music for a ballet; he may commission a new work, revive music used for an earlier ballet or use music called from the general repertoire and have it arranged or orchestrated according to his requirements.

While ballet was a court pastime the music was usually specially composed for the occasion. As the art evolved and performances became a matter for professional dancers before public audiences, ballets were presented alone or as part of an opera, but they were still usually performed to the accompaniment of specially composed music until the latter part of the nineteenth century.

In this country, visiting ballet masters and dancers of the Romantic period in London brought their own ballets with the music by foreign composers. Sometimes a ballet was given its first performance in London; in 1834, for instance, the prolific composer Adolphe Adam presented his first ballet, *Faust*, at the King's Theatre.

At the end of the nineteenth century ballet music in London was in the hands of two Germans, Georges Jacobi and Leopold Wentzel. Jacobi was the musical director at the Alhambra Theatre for twenty-six years from 1872–98, 'during which he composed the music for . . . one hundred and three ballets'.[2] Wentzel, the musical director of the Empire Theatre from 1889–1904, composed about twenty scores for the ballets presented there. After Wentzel's retirement in 1904, the Empire drew on the music of several composers, including Delibes, Glinka, Tchaikowsky and Mendelssohn.

Commissioned scores are most certain of success where the collaboration

---

[1] *Music and the dance*, by E. Evans. [1948[, p. 15.
[2] *Ballet then and now*, by D. Lynham. 1947, p. 103.

between composer and choreographer has been close. During the last thirty-five years, as ballet has become part of English culture, many of our finest composers have written scores for ballet. *Job*, by Ralph Vaughan Williams, was originally commissioned by the Camargo Society (1931), and was handed over by that society to the Vic-Wells Ballet when the Camargo Society was wound-up. Arthur Bliss composed *Checkmate* (1937) and *Miracle in the Gorbals* (1944) and William Walton composed *The Quest* (1943) for the Sadler's Wells Ballet. Constant Lambert, Gavin Gordon, Malcolm Arnold and Arthur Oldham have also composed scores for the Ballet Rambert and the Royal Ballet. Benjamin Britten was the first English composer to write a full-length score for an English company; this was *The Prince of the pagodas*, first presented by the Royal Ballet in 1957.

Revivals of music composed for earlier ballets have been particularly noticeable in the last 10–20 years. From the Romantic period, for instance, there have been revivals of *La Sylphide* by Ballet Rambert (using the music of Lovenskjold dating from 1836, not the original by Schneitzhöffer, 1832); *La Fille mal gardée* by the Royal Ballet (using Hérold's music dating from the 1820's, not the original by various composers, 1786) and *Napoli* by Festival Ballet (using the original music by Paulli, Helsted, Gade and Lumbye, 1842). The latter was only a revival from the point of view of this country; it was mounted by Harald Lander of the Royal Danish Ballet, a company which has preserved the Bournonville ballets in its repertoire continuously. The Diaghilev era has been recalled by the Royal Ballet in re-creations of, for example, *The Three cornered hat* (music by de Falla), and *The Firebird*, *Petrushka* and *The Rite of spring* (all with music by Stravinsky). In some cases it has been necessary to arrange old scores and even to interpolate newly composed music. Constant Lambert and later John Lanchbery, two musicians associated with the Royal Ballet, have been notable for carrying out such work. Constant Lambert played a vital part in the development of the national ballet company, for which he was the musical director from its foundation until his death in 1951. John Lanchbery, the principal conductor, arranged the score for the very successful *La Fille mal gardée*.

Music from the general repertoire, carefully selected, can be very effectively adapted for ballet, although in this country, at least, not many have followed the example of Massine in the 1930s in his use of whole symphonies. Some choreographers whose ballets have been matched with excellently chosen music are De Valois, *Gods go a-begging*, 1936 (Handel); Anthony Tudor, *Dark elegies*, 1937 (Mahler's *Kindertotenlieder*); Andrée Howard, *Death and the maiden*, 1937 (Schubert) and *Assembly ball*, 1946 (Bizet's *Symphony in C*); Ashton, *Les Patineurs*, 1937 (from Meyerbeer's opera *Le Prophète*), *Symphonic variations*, 1946 (César Franck's *Symphonic variations for piano and orchestra*) and *The Dream*, 1964 (Mendelssohn's incidental music to *A Midsummer night's dream*); Cranko, *Pineapple Poll*, 1951 (Sullivan) and *The Lady and the fool*, 1954 (Verdi).

CATALOGUES

Scores

A few catalogues contain a form entry under ballet music. *The British Catalogue of Music*. Council of the British National Bibliography, 1957 – has such an entry in Part 1, the alphabetical sequence, which includes entries for composer, title, arranger, instruments, musical forms and so on. Until 1961 there were three supplements, January–March, April–June and July–September, but from 1962 there have been two supplements only covering January–April and May–August. The annual volume is cumulative.

The Central Music Library, Westminster City Libraries, which is housed in the Buckingham Palace Road branch, maintains a card catalogue of its holdings. In the classified section of this catalogue, there are two headings for ballet music. Under 782.79 'Ballet Scores (Full Scores)', 48 items are listed; under 781.4 'Piano Scores' there are the following: Sub-headings 781.47 'Dances', 781.48 'Ballet Exercises' (20 items) and 781.49 'Ballets' (135 items). This library is open to the public.

In 1954, *Liverpool Public Libraries* issued a *Catalogue of the Music Library*, which was printed in dictionary catalogue form. Under 'Ballets' about 100 items are listed, all of which are 'piano scores unless otherwise stated'.

Gramophone Records

Much ballet music has been recorded, but a complete discography would amount to a separate publication. The periodicals *The Dancing Times, Ballet Today, Ballet* (1946–52) and *Dance and Dancers* carry reviews of new gramophone records. *The Gramophone* (monthly) and *The Record Guide*, rev. ed. 1955 and the *Supplement* 1956, published by Collins and compiled by Edward Sackville-West and Desmond Shawe-Taylor arrange entries alphabetically under the name of the composer.

In 1960 Jupiter Recordings issued four records on which dancers talked

about their life and experiences – 'Adeline Genée summarizes her life story.
. . . Tamara Karsavina speaks of her early years of training and of Diaghilev's
great pre-war seasons . . . Marie Rambert describes the high-spots of her life
in ballet and also has a chat with Mme Karsavina about old days when they
worked together . . . Beryl Grey explains about her career and her art.'[1]

BIBLIOGRAPHY

Arrangement. 1. General works, including works on two or more composers, arranged
chronologically by date of publication. 2. Works on individual composers or musicians, arranged alphabetically by their names, and then chronologically by date of
publication.

GENERAL

597   TURNER, WALTER JAMES.   'Music and ballet.   *In: The New Statesman
      and Nation*, v. 12, no. 280, new series, 4th July, 1936, pp. 13–14.

598   WHITE, ERIC WALTER.   'English ballet music.'   *In: Life and Letters
      Today*, v. 27, no. 38, October 1940, pp. [45]–50.

599   HUSSEY, DYNELEY.   'Music – Covent Garden re-opened.'   *In: Britain
      Today*, no. 121, May 1946, pp. [34]–5.   4 pl.
         The Sleeping beauty performed by the Sadler's Wells Ballet. The illustra-
      tions appeared in the following issue – no. 122, June 1946.

600   HUSSEY, DYNELEY.   'Music and ballet.'   *In: Britain Today*, no. 123,
      July 1946, pp. [36]–7.   1 pl.
         Adam Zero and *Symphonic variations.*

601   EVANS, EDWIN.   Music and the dance: for lovers of the ballet. Jenkins,
      [1948].   192 pp.   front.   6s.
         Edwin Evans, music critic, and ballet critic of *The Daily Mail* for 8 years
      was a friend of Diaghilev and Chairman of the Camargo Society. In this
      book, based on material published in *The Dancing Times*, he writes of 'Music
      and the Dance'; 'Guidance in Choice of Music'; 'Some Ballet Music'; 'Some
      Composers of Ballet Music'; 'Some Suggestions' (for music which might be

----

[1] Review in The *Sunday Times* for 5th June, 1960, by R. Buckle.

used); 'History and Form'. There is 'An Appreciation of Edwin Evans', by Ninette de Valois and 'A Memoir', by Dyneley Hussey.

602c CLARK, FLORENCE M.   Ballet tunes to remember.   Nelson, 1949. vii, 79 pp.   illus.   5s.

A brief analysis (with examples) of the music of 15 ballets, all but one of which are or have been performed by English companies; included are *Checkmate* and *Façade*. Appended are notes on composers and choreographers; ballet and musical terms; list of gramophone records. There are 15 drawings in the text.

603 COTON, A. V.   'Music for ballet.'   *In: The Music Review*, v. 12, no. 2, May 1951, pp. [134]–8.

604 HUSSEY, DYNELEY.   'Ballet music since the war.'   *In: The Ballet Annual 1951*, 5th issue, pp. 76–81.

General article, but includes music for *Adam Zero*, by Arthur Bliss, *Les Sirènes*, by Lord Berners and *Don Quixote*, by Roberto Gerhard.

605 FISKE, ROGER.   Ballet music.   Harrap, 1958.   88 pp.   front., illus. 12s. 6d.

Contents – 1, 'Music in the Background'; 2, 'Early Ballet Music'; 3, 'Adam and the Romantic ballet: *Giselle*'; 4, 'Delibes and the French Ballet: *Coppélia* and *Sylvia*'; 5, 'Tchaikowsky and the Classical Ballet: *Swan lake, The Sleeping beauty*, and *Nutcracker*'; 6, 'Stravinsky and the Diaghilev Ballet: *The Firebird* and *Petrushka*'; 7, 'Some Modern Ballets', includes an analysis of *Job* (R. Vaughan Williams) and *The Prince of the pagodas* (Benjamin Britten), both in the repertoire of the Royal Ballet. A short introduction to each work is followed by fairly generous musical quotation interspersed with narrative, Appended is a 'List of Recordings'. The illustrations are 13 reproductions of photographs.

606 SEARLE, HUMPHREY.   Ballet music: an introduction.   Cassell, 1958. ix, [229] pp.   16 pl., bibliog.   21s.

In Chapter 5, 'Ballet Music in the Modern World (1930–57)', the author, a former member of the Sadler's Wells Ballet Advisory Committee, includes musically interesting productions of the Royal Ballet.

The book is 'a general introduction to an enormous subject; it attempts to give an assessment of the most important scores written for ballet' (introduction); occasionally the assessment is overshadowed by the linking of plot and music. For technical details the author recommends *The Decca book of ballet*. The appendix, 'Details of some First Performances', lists date, ballet,

place, choreographer, composer, designer and principal dancers. There is a
bibliography (33 items) arranged alphabetically by author's name and a
discography. 20 illustrations on plates are mainly reproductions of photographs.

607   HYND, RONALD. 'Dancing to music.'   In: The Musical Times, v. 102,
      no. 1,415, January 1961, pp. 28–9.   1 illus.
      The author is a member of the Royal Ballet.

608   LANCHBERY, JOHN, and GUEST, IVOR. 'The scores of "La Fille mal
      gardée".'   In: Theatre Research, v. 3, nos. 1–3, 1961. illus. [in-
      cluding musical quotations and facsimiles].
          1. The Original Music, v. 3, no. 1, 1961, pp. 32–42.
          2. Hérold's Score, v. 3, no. 2, 1961, pp. 121–34.
          3. The Royal Ballet's Score, v. 3, no. 3, 1961, pp. 191–204.

609   MORTON, LAWRENCE. 'Stravinsky and Tchaikowsky: "Le Baiser de la
      fée".'   In: The Musical Quarterly, v. 98, no. 3, July 1962, pp. 313–26.
      1 pl.
      Investigates the sources in Tchaikowsky's music from which Stravinsky
      drew the impetus for his work.

INDIVIDUAL COMPOSERS AND MUSICIANS

Bliss

610   HOPKINS, ANTONY. 'Ballet music of Arthur Bliss.'   In: The Ballet
      Annual [1947], 1st issue, pp. 102–7.

Henze

611   HELM, EVERETT. 'Current chronicle: Germany.'   In: The Musical
      Quarterly, v. 45, no. 2, April 1959, pp. 245–8.   illus.
          Includes a discussion of about 600 words of H. W. Henze's music for the
          Royal Ballet production of Ondine. There are some errors in the 'balletic'
          facts. 1 page of musical quotations.

Irving

612   CRICHTON, ROBERT. 'Robert Irving.'   In: The Ballet Annual 1959,
      13th issue, p. 97.

Lambert

613 FOSS, HUBERT. 'Constant Lambert 23 August, 1905–21 August, 1951.'
In: The Musical Times, v. 92, no. 1,304, October 1951, pp. 449–51.

614 HUSSEY, DYNELEY. 'Constant Lambert.' *In: Britain Today*, no. 188,
December 1951, pp. [20]–3. 2 pl.

> His contribution to the work of the Royal Ballet, and a discussion of
> *Tiresias*, for which he composed the music.

615 GOLDECK, FREDERICK. 'An appreciation of Constant Lambert' *In:
Foyer*, no. 2, winter 1951–2, p. 52. illus.

616 HOWES, FRANK, *and* HASKELL, ARNOLD LIONEL. 'Constant Lambert.'
In: The Ballet Annual 1952, 6th issue, pp. 50–3.

617 AYRTON, MICHAEL. 'A sketch for a portrait of Constant Lambert.'
In: The Ballet Annual 1956, 10th issue, pp. 89–96.

Prokofiev

618 STEVENS, JOHN, *and others*. Shakespeare in music: essays. Macmillan, 1964. ix, 333 pp. 45s.

> Edited by Phyllis Hartnoll; joint authors Charles Cudworth, Winton
> Dean and Roger Fiske.
> Roger Fiske concentrates on Prokofiev's music for *Romeo and Juliet* in
> 'Shakespeare at the Ballet' (pp. 236–41). Appended is 'Catalogue of Musical
> Works based on the Plays and Poetry of Shakespeare', compiled by Winton
> Dean, Dorothy Moore and Phyllis Hartnoll. It is arranged alphabetically by
> title of play; ballet music is indicated.

Seiber

CRISP, CLEMENT. 'The Invitation.' February 1961.

> *See* no. 364.

Stravinsky

619 LEDERMAN, MINNA, *ed*. Stravinsky in the theatre. Owen, 1951.
viii, 228 pp. front., illus., bibliog. 21s.

> First published by Pellegrini and Cudahy, New York, 1949.
> 'Studies of the Music' (pp. 41–113) includes 'Music for the Ballet', by

Arthur Berger; 'The New Orpheus', by Ingolf Dahl; 'The Dance Element in the Music', by George Balanchine. Other sections are 'Reminiscence'; 'Appreciation'; 'Stravinsky's Own Story'; 'Album of Dates and Pictures'. Appended are 'Stage Productions of Stravinsky's Works'; 'Recordings of Music by Igor Stravinsky', compiled in 1949. The bibliography, compiled by Paul Magriel, includes books and periodicals but not newspaper articles. One section of the bibliography refers to specific works. It includes references to the following ballets – *Le Baiser de la fée; L'Oiseau de feu; Persephone; Petrouchka; Le Sacré du printemps*. The many illustrations are mainly reproductions of photographs.

[620] DONINGTON, R., *ed.*   Stravinsky ballet music.   Cassell, in association with the Decca Record Company, 1952.   32 pp.   illus.   (Decca Music Guides. No. 10.)   9d.

> 'The first booklets to appear in a usefully compact little series'. The Guides comprise a brief general note on the composer with an examination of selected ballets, with musical examples. (*The Times Literary Supplement*, 14th November, 1952, p. 750.)

621   NEW YORK PUBLIC LIBRARY.   Dance collection.   Stravinsky and the dance: a survey of ballet productions 1910–62.   New York Public Library, 1962.   [61] pp.   24 pl. (5 illus. col.), illus.

> Compiled in honour of the composer's eightieth birthday, in association with the exhibition 'Stravinsky and the Dance'.
>
> The introduction 'Stravinsky and the Muses' is by Herbert Read and the Survey was compiled by Selma Jeanne Cohen. Initial arrangement is chronological by date of first performance of ballet. There is a short introduction to each ballet and the following information is given under each – place of first performance; company; choreographer; designer of décor and costumes. The 67 illustrations on plates are reproductions of designs for costume and scenery, photographs and drawings, and 14 text illustrations mainly reproductions of sketches of the composer and his collaborators.

Tchaikowsky

[622] BUDDEN, ROY, *ed.*   Tchaikowsky: miscellaneous works.   Cassell, in association with the Decca Record Company, 1952.   32 pp.   illus. (Decca Music Guides. No. 11.)   9d.

> For a note on the series *see* under no. [620].

Vaughan Williams

623   HOWES, FRANK.   The dramatic works of Ralph Vaughan Williams.

Oxford University Press, 1937.   108 pp.   (The Musical Pilgrim
Series.)   1s. 6d.

In '*Job*' (pp. 45–65), the author explains how the ballet was evolved. A
scene-by-scene musical analysis with music examples, and juxtaposition of
scenarios, follows. The scenarios are by Geoffrey Keynes, the originator of
the ballet, and Ralph Vaughan Williams, the composer.

624   DICKINSON, ALAN EDGAR FREDERIC.   'War in Heaven.'   *In: The
      Listener*, v. 39, no. 989, 8th January, 1948, p. 76.

Notes on the music of *Job*, by Ralph Vaughan Williams, prior to a concert
performance.

Walton

625   HOWES, FRANK.   The music of William Walton. Volume 1.   2nd ed.
      Oxford University Press, 1947.   76 pp.   (The Musical Pilgrim
      Series.)   2s.

'*Façade*' (pp. 21–37), lists the individual pieces of the two orchestral suites;
also the pieces used by Frederick Ashton in his ballet of the same title. A
musical analysis with music examples of the two orchestral suites follows

XII. FILM AND TELEVISION

BALLET as an art form in film and television can be a close representation of a stage performance of an established ballet, either complete or in part, or it can be created especially for the medium. Paul Czinner in his *Film of the Royal Ballet* (1960) adopted the first method. The company danced *Ondine*, *The Firebird* and parts of Act 2 of *Swan lake* on the stage of the Royal Opera House in exactly the same way as if they had been dancing to a live audience. Cameras were set up at different angles to the stage and these filmed the performance straight through. The same method was used for the earlier film of the Bolshoi Ballet taken during its 1956 visit; later the Royal Ballet's *Romeo and Juliet* (1966) was filmed under the direction of Dr. Czinner at Pinewood Studios. *The Little ballerina* (1947) a British film, in which Margot Fonteyn danced, included extracts from *Les Sylphides*. *The Red shoes* (1947) a film in which Moira Shearer had the leading role of the young ballet dancer, had a long ballet sequence based on the Hans Andersen fairy story, created especially for the film. *Tales of Hoffmann* (1951) also had balletic interludes for which Frederick Ashton devised the choreography.

Television can deal with ballet in a similar way. Dancers have performed for this medium since 1935 when it was still in an experimental stage, and they continued to do so until the beginning of the Second World War. Television was taken up again in the late nineteen-forties. Choreographers have been commissioned to compose works for the medium; *Turned out proud* (1955), with choreography by Kenneth Macmillan was such a ballet, but the more usual practice appears to be to adapt a ballet already in the repertoire. The majority of the classical and romantic ballets – *La Sylphide; Sleeping beauty; The Nutcracker; Coppélia; Giselle* – have been televised, as well as such widely differing modern works as *Street games* (Western Theatre Ballet); *The Two brothers* (Ballet Rambert); *Graduation ball* (Festival Ballet); *Laudes evangelii* (choreography by Massine). In 1961 a contract was drawn up between the British Broadcasting Company and The Royal Ballet whereby, for three years, the Royal Ballet would be televised in three ballets a year. All the ballets so performed were in the repertoire of the Royal Ballet and included *La Fille mal gardée; Petrushka; Checkmate; Les Rendezvous; The Rake's progress.*

There are occasionally special programmes devoted to one dancer or other person connected with the ballet, e.g. Constant Lambert (1965). Ballet, mainly *pas de deux*, often has a part in such television programmes as *Gala performance* and *Music in camera*, in which artists of high standing in the various arts perform extracts from opera, ballet and the musical repertoire.

Cinema and television have their value as documentary media. In 1948, the Central Office of Information made a film called *Steps of the ballet*. 'Its apparent purpose was to provide lay audiences, particularly children, with a general idea of some of the fundamental poses and figures of classical ballet; and after that to illustrate how a ballet is built up to its final stage of presentation before an audience.'[1] *Ballet for beginners* (1952) a B.B.C. programme, was under the direction of Felicity Gray. An outstanding programme *Ballet class* (1964) was shown on B.B.C. 1. Dancers of the Royal Ballet demonstrated the routine of a daily practice, with spoken commentary to explain the purpose of the exercises.

Many talks and programmes on ballet subjects and ballet music have been presented on B.B.C. radio programmes over the last 35 years; some of these have been printed in *The Listener*.

The library of the B.B.C. is a source of information for television and radio ' . . . The library may be used by special permission of the Director-General . . . It includes radio and television scripts, books. . . . Dates of broadcasts and televised performances and other records are kept, and an index of . . . articles. There is also a music library and the *Radio Times* Hulton Picture Library, which contains many interesting theatrical photographs. The latter is run on commercial lines and prints can be obtained for publication on payment of a fee'.[2]

BIBLIOGRAPHY

Arrangement. 1. General Works on two or more programmes arranged chronologically by date of publication. 2. Individual films and television programmes arranged alphabetically by the title, and then chronologically by date of publication.

626 PERKOFF, H. L. 'The screen and the ballet.' *In: Sight and Sound*, v. 7, no. 27, autumn 1938, pp. 122–3. 2 illus.

[1] *Ballet for film and television*, by A. H. Franks, 1950, p. 37.
[2] *'Centres for theatre research'*, by G. Nash. *In: Who's Who in the Theatre*, 13th ed., 1961, p. 1,543.

627 FRANKS, ARTHUR HENRY. Ballet for film and television. Pitman, 1950. ix, 85 pp. front., 13 pl., bibliog. 12s. 6d.

In Chapters 1–5, the author discusses the pros and cons of filmed ballet, and describes and criticizes specific films including English productions – *The Little ballerina*, *Steps of the ballet* and *The Red shoes;* also gives practical advice on hiring and use of films. In Chapter 6 he discusses ballet on television and in Chapter 7 criticizes the presentation of *Les Sylphides* (presented 21st October, 1942) and *The Dance of Salome* (presented 9th December, 1942). Appended is a briefly annotated reading list (41 items), a list of ballet clubs and a 'short catalogue of dance and ballet films'. There are 17 illustrations on plates.

628 SIMPSON, CHRISTIAN. 'Ballet in television: camera choreography.' *In: The Ballet Annual 1951*, 5th issue, pp. 64–9.

Ballet productions televised November 1949–June 1950 are listed.

629 BRINSON, PETER, *comp.* A catalogue of 120 dance films from sixteen countries, available in Great Britain. *The Dancing Times*, 1954. 25 pp. 2s. 6d.

'Confined to what is available non-theatrically in Britain, listing ballet films, films of national dancing and [some] musicals' (introduction). Information given – title of film; short description; technical detail; library; cost. Primary arrangement is under country. 17 items are listed under England. Amendments to this Catalogue were printed in *The Dancing Times*, May 1961, pp. 509–10.

630 FRANKS, ARTHUR HENRY. 'Television ballet.' *In: The Ballet Annual 1960*, 14th issue, pp. 59–64.

631 MOISEIWITSCH, MAURICE, *and* WARMAN, ERIC, *eds.* The Royal Ballet on stage and screen: the book of the Royal Ballet film. Heinemann, 1960. 56 pp. front. (col.), 27 pl. (3 col.) 18s.

The ballets filmed were *Swan lake*, *The Firebird* and *Ondine*; the plots are given with brief comments on the choreography. Articles include 'Filming the Royal Ballet', by Paul Czinner who produced the film, and 'Staging the Royal Ballet', by Frederick Ashton. The plates are reproductions of photographs by Norman Gryspeerdt, Cornel Lucas and Houston Rogers of scenes from the above ballets.

632 HALL, FERNAU. 'The dance, the dance.' *In: Contrast*, v. 2, no. 1, autumn 1962, pp. 37–49. 8 illus.

All types of television dance, including ballet, especially the B.B.C. programmes *Music in camera*, and the Royal Ballet in *The Rake's progress* and *Les Rendezvous*.

INDIVIDUAL FILMS AND TELEVISION PROGRAMMES

Laudes Evangelii

633 'Laudes evangelii', produced for Independent Television by Associated-Rediffusion London: a miracle play inspired by the Byzantine mosaics, the paintings of Giotto and the canticles of thirteenth and fourteenth century Italy. [1961]. [20] pp. illus. (6 col.).

'This booklet tells something of the background to *Laudes evangelii*, which Massine the choreographer, has described as 'a choreographic religious play'. It was created originally for the Italian Festival, Sagra Musicale Umbra. The 24 illustrations are reproductions of Giotto paintings, sketches of costume, scenery and photographs.

Red Shoes

634 GIBBON, MONK. 'The Red shoes' ballet: a critical study. Saturn Press, 1948. 95 pp. 3 pl. (col.), front., illus. 21s.

A general discussion is followed by the author's estimate of the contribution made by producer, director, artistic director, composer, choreographer and dancers. In spite of the title the approach is rather uncritical. The 43 illustrations include 'stills' from the film, designs of Hein Heckroth (artistic director) and reproductions of informal photographs taken on the set.

635 KELLER, HANS. 'Films and the ballet.' *In: Film Monthly Annual 1948.* pp. [42]–[3]. 2 illus.

Criticism of the film *The Red shoes*, for the most part.

636 CARDIFF, JACK. ' "The Red shoes", and cine-choreography.' *In: The Ballet Annual 1949*, 3rd issue, pp. 56–60.

The Sleeping Beauty

637 BEAUMONT, CYRIL WILLIAM. ' "The Sleeping beauty" on television.' *In: The Ballet Annual 1953*, 7th issue, pp. 94–101.

Tales of Hoffmann

638   GIBBON, MONK.   The tales of Hoffmann: a study of the film.   Saturn
        Press, 1951.   96 pp.   front. (col.), 3 pl. (col.), illus.   21s.

   Includes profiles of Frederick Ashton, Robert Helpmann, Leonide Massine
and Moira Shearer, who danced in the interludes of ballet. Illustrations are
54 reproductions of photographs, mainly by Bert Cann, and 10 sketches of
costumes and designs.

XIII. FICTION

THERE is little adult material in this chapter. Writers who use the ballet as a background for their novels seem to prefer the more spectacular setting of the Romantic ballet period and the Russian ballet to the English scene. The latter period is more popular with the writers of stories for girls, a selection of which are listed below among the few adult titles.

BIBLIOGRAPHY

Arrangement. Chronological by date of publication.

639 MACKENZIE, COMPTON. Carnival. Macdonald, 1951. 384 pp. 10s. 6d.

> First published 1912; then 'in various editions by some eight publishers' and translated into several languages.
> The plot concerns a dancer of the *corps de ballet* at the 'Orient Palace of Varieties' and her marriage to a Cornish farmer. The author worked with the *corps de ballet* of the Alhambra in 1910, and used his experience there to fill in the background of the novel.

640 WILLARD, BARBARA. Ballerina. Nelson, 1936. v, 312 pp. 2s. 6d.

> First published 1932 by Howe.
> The story of an English girl, who begins her career in ballet in England.

641c STREATFEILD, NOEL. Ballet shoes: a story of three children on the stage. Dent, 1962. ix, 234 pp. front., illus. 13s. 6d.

> First published 1936.
> One of the first children's books to use ballet as a background. It has retained its popularity over the years.

642c HASKELL, ARNOLD LIONEL. Felicity dances: a children's tale about the ballet. Nelson, 1938. 167 pp. front. (col.), 8 pl. 3s. 6d.

> First published 1937.
> Imagined experiences of two small girls, at their first dancing lessons, watching performances and so on. Reproductions of photographs on plates are of dancers and ballets of the nineteen-thirties.

643   GODDEN, RUMER.   A candle for St. Jude.   Joseph, 1948.   192 pp.
8s. 6d.

The setting is a school of dancing and the main theme, the events which
take place before the opening performance of a season by the pupils and
ex-pupils.

644c ALLAN, MABEL ESTHER.   The ballet family again.   Methuen, 1964.
183 pp.   front., illus.   13s. 6d.

The life of a family of dancers, during one winter. *The Ballet family* (1963)
was the first title in this series.

645c HILL, LORNA.   The secret.   Evans, 1964.   160 pp.   front., illus.
12s. 6d.

This is the latest title by Lorna Hill. She has written some 18 books in two
series; in one of which she uses the Royal Ballet School as the setting. The
first title in this series was *Dream of Sadler's Wells* (published 1950) and the
latest the above. Her second series is concerned with the life of a student
dancer from school days to the beginning of a career in dancing. The titles
are as follows – *Dancing peel; Dancer's luck; Dancer in the wings; Dancer on
holiday; The Little dancer.*

646c ESTORIL, JEAN.   Drina goes on tour.   Leicester, Brockhampton Press,
1965.   [152] pp.   5s.

Tenth title in a series which began in 1957 with *Ballet for Drina*. The author
adopts the formula of following one dancer through her training and school
days.

XIV. PERIODICALS

THE three main specialist periodicals on the dance today, printed in the United Kingdom, are *The Dancing Times, Ballet Today* and *Dance and Dancers*; each has an individual approach to the subject. The oldest and most substantial is *The Dancing Times*. It provides reasonable and informed comment on all aspects of stage dancing including ballet, and calls on some of the best writers on this subject. *Ballet Today* emphasizes the international nature of the dance and tends to give most space to reports from foreign centres of ballet. *Dance and Dancers* has a fairly wide foreign coverage, too, but reports on actual ballets giving cast lists and reviews. The last two do have general articles as well on dancers, choreographers, history and so on, but these tend to be short.

Two periodicals, no longer published, which made an individual contribution to the dance were *Ballet*, edited by Richard Buckle and *Dance Chronicle*, founded and edited by A. V. Coton. *Ballet* had an imaginative and unusual approach in its choice of subject matter and illustration, and a breadth of interest which none of the other periodicals mentioned above have achieved. *Dance Chronicle* was issued during the war and was the first English periodical to be devoted to ballet.

Guide to Dance Periodicals (see no. 22), an American publication edited by S. Yancey Belknap, indexes articles in all the periodicals mentioned above, with the exception of *Dance Chronicle*. Two American serials, which have published volumes on English ballet are *Dance Index* and *Dance Perspectives*. *Dance Index* (1942–7) was published by Ballet Caravan and sold by subscription. Lincoln Kirstein, Paul Magriel and Baird Hastings were the editors. It was usual for each issue to be a monograph on one subject or writer. In 1958 the first issue of *Dance Perspectives* appeared. It is a quarterly and follows the same policy as *Dance Index*, publishing monographs on critical and historical subjects. An annual index is provided, with a bibliography of current books and selected periodical articles. The bibliography is international in scope.

The leading daily and weekly newspapers provide reviews of performances; *The Times, The Guardian, The Financial Times, The Daily Telegraph, The Sunday Times, The Observer, The Sunday Telegraph* and *The Times Educational Supplement* all carry reviews and most of them the occasional general article on ballet. Information on nineteenth-century ballets can be found in *The Times, Morning Post, Morning Chronicle, Morning Herald* and *The Era*. *The Listener* provides reviews of television ballet shown on B.B.C. 1 and 2, while photographs of new productions and revivals can usually be found in *The Illustrated London News* and occasionally in *The Queen*.

BIBLIOGRAPHY

Arrangement. 1. General. 2. Official publications of organizations. Both sections arranged chronologically by date of first issue of the periodical.

GENERAL

647 The Dancing Times. 1910–. New series, v. 1, no. 1–. Monthly.
     The Dancing Times. 3s.

> Philip J. S. Richardson was founder, and editor until the early nineteen-fifties when A. H. Franks was 'in all practical ways running the magazine',[1] although the founder still took an active interest in it. Since the death of A. H. Franks in 1963, Mary Clarke has been the Editor, with Ivor Guest as Editorial Adviser.
>
> The title was first used in 1894 'as the name of a house journal published in connection with the Cavendish Rooms. The title was acquired by the present proprietors in 1910'.[2] From then until 1956 all types of dancing were covered. In October 1956 the first number of *The Ballroom Dancing Times* was published. All the space in *The Dancing Times* was then given over to stage dancing, most space being allotted to ballet. The proportion in the early days of the magazine had been the reverse, but over the years the interest in ballet has grown. The scope is wide. There are general articles on ballet and dance companies from all over the world; on the history of ballet; on individual dancers and ballets; descriptions of dances for performance. Tamara Karsavina has written series of articles on the technique of the classical ballet and Gillian Lynne on the technique of modern dance. A section is devoted to information on schools of dancing which is supplied by the schools. Activities and performances of ballet clubs are reviewed, as are books, records and films on the dance, and a diary of events and performances is given in each issue. A Book Service to readers was started in March 1960 whereby *The Dancing Times* arranges for the dispatch of books

[1] The Obituary of A. H. Franks. *In: The Dancing Times*, November 1963, p. 77.
[2] '*The Literature of the ballet: a select bibliography, 1830–1948*', by C. W. Beaumont. *In: British Book News*, 1949 (cumulative volume), p. 14.

to its subscribers. Occasionally extracts from books either newly published or about to be published are printed. There are plentiful and clear illustrations in each issue. Regular contributors include Mary Clarke, A. H. Franks, Joan Lawson, P. W. Manchester, James Monahan and Elsa Brunelleschi. A. L. Haskell has contributed a regular feature 'Balletomane's Log Book' since January 1935, and Paul Bedford contributes 'Stage Dance Diary'. An annual index is provided.

648 Ballet. 1939, 1946–52. V. 1, no. 1–v. 12, no. 10. Monthly. Published by The Shenval Press for R. Buckle; from August 1946, Ballet Publications Ltd. 2s. 6d.

Two numbers only July/August and September/October were published in 1939. The third issue was published after the Second World War on 3rd January, 1946, and monthly publication was almost entirely consistent until *Ballet* ceased publication after the October 1952 issue. The founder and Editor was Richard Buckle. Assistant Editors were Peter Wright until October 1949, and Andrew Sykes from January 1950. In the July/August 1950 issue it was announced that subscribers would receive *New York Dance News*, and the following were listed as Associate Editors – Cyril Beaumont; Lincoln Kirstein; Pierre Michaut; Edwin Denby.

In October 1948 the title was changed to *Ballet and Opera*, but the periodical reverted to its original title in January 1950, when the two subjects were divided in two journals. Coverage included all types of dancing as well as 'fringe' subjects such as 'Trooping the Colour', by Iain Moncrieffe; 'The Eglinton Tournament', by Ivor Guest; 'Horse Ballets', by C. W. Beaumont. There were historical articles, reviews of ballets, books and records, and news from abroad. There was a series of articles on stage designers, from May 1948 to 1951, and another on buildings in London connected with the dance. Extracts from Richard Buckle's autobiography *Adventures of a ballet critic* was printed. Regular contributors were C. W. Beaumont; Lionel Bradley; Elsa Brunelleschi; A. V. Coton; Beryl de Zoete; Ivor Guest.

An index to volumes 1–6 was published in 1949. It was compiled by Cecilia Bowman and had 3 sections – author, artist, and title and subject. It did not attempt to be comprehensive. Regular features and photographs were not listed; original drawings, dancers and other personalities, ballets and operas were, when they rated more than one paragraph. From this date the index appeared regularly each year, following the same pattern.

[649] Dance Chronicle. 1940–5. 2s. 6d. per annum.

The co-founders were Peter Alexander and A. V. Coton; the Editor was A. V. Coton. For the first year it was issued as a monthly, but as difficulties in acquiring material and in actual production increased during the war years, the number of issues dropped year by year, i.e. November 1941– October 1942, 10 issues; November 1942–October 1943, 8 issues; November/

December 1943–August/September 1944, 4 issues; November 1944–August 1945, 3 issues. The magazine was typed, stencilled and run-out on borrowed machines, by four of the main contributors, who also dealt with the distribution. The format varied and the number of pages ran from 12 to 30 according to the amount of material available. This was the first magazine to be devoted solely to the ballet in the United Kingdom, and it covered criticism; discussion; advance news of coming events; reviews of books and exhibitions relative to ballet; foreign news when available. Contributors included A. V. Coton; Peter Alexander; Lionel Bradley; Kay Ambrose; Jasper Howlett.[3]

650   The Ballet.   1945–7.   V. 1, no. 1–v. 3, no. 9; as Ballet World 1948–c. 1950.   V. 1–?.   Quarterly.   The Russian Ballet League.   2s. 6d.

The Editor was Nadine Nicolaeva-Legat. The title was changed from *Ballet* to *The Ballet* in March 1946 (v. 1, no. 3) at the request of Richard Buckle, who had established a prior claim to the title, with the publication of two issues of his periodical in 1939. In September 1948 the title was changed again from *The Ballet* to *Ballet World*. Articles on the history and theory of ballet, on the aesthetics of ballet, reviews of performances in the United Kingdom, reports from America and Paris and book reviews were provided. Cartoons by Nicolas Legat were used as illustrations for the cover of the periodical.

651   Ballet Carnaval.   1946–7(?).   V. 1, nos. 1–5.   Bi-monthly (mainly).   Pendulum Publications Ltd.   1s. 6d.

Edited by A. L. Nash. General articles and information on dancers, and reviews of ballets and books were provided. For the most part, the articles were short and lightweight.

652   Ballet Today.   1946–.   V. 1, no. 1–.   Estelle Herf.   2s. 6d.

The founder and first Editor was P. W. Manchester. In 1952 she withdrew her interest from the periodical, and the editorship was taken over by Peter Craig-Raymond until April 1955. Estelle Herf succeeded him as Editor. Frequency of publication varies. The first numbers were issued as a quarterly, then monthly. From 1957 there were 10 issues a year; in 1963 and 1964 there were 9 issues. International coverage is attempted. In the December 1964 issue reports were received from 11 foreign centres of ballet. General articles and reviews of performances by English companies are provided too. Books and record reviews are a regular feature. Contributors over a period include Leo Kersley and Janet Sinclair. Articles tend to be short and non-historical; there are many photographs.

[3] The description of *Dance Chronicle* is based on information supplied by A. V. Coton, the Editor.

653   Ballet Review.   1947.   V. 1, no. 1.   Edinburgh, Albyn Press.   5s.

> The only number issued. Includes 'A Critical Record of New Productions ... of Ballets ... in Britain during 1946 and till June 1947', and 'The Spectator and the Ballet'.

654   Dance and Dancers.   1950–.   V. 1, no. 1–.   Monthly.   Hansom Books.   3s.

> The Editor is Peter Williams. Clive Barnes was the Assistant Editor until April 1962, when he became the Associate Editor. From December 1951 to March 1962, E. C. Mason was an Assistant Editor, then a contributing Editor with M. F. Christout, John Percival and Arthur Todd. Horst Koegler joined the editorial staff in April 1963.
>
> The main feature of the periodical is detailed reviews of new British and foreign ballets and revivals, sometimes giving cast lists. Occasionally one number is devoted almost entirely to an outstanding performer or director, e.g. the number for January 1956 was almost entirely devoted to Anna Pavlova. Clive Barnes wrote a series of articles entitled 'Ballet Perspectives'. Each article was devoted to a well-known ballet. The author dealt with the history and background of the ballet and considered the work of the designer and the leading interpreters; also the most notable productions. 'Ballet Perspective 1' appeared in the September 1957 issue. Number 32 appeared in December 1964. Records, films and books are reviewed and a diary of performances is provided. Regular contributors include Peter Williams, Clive Barnes, Ivor Guest and the contributing editors.

655c The Young Ballet Dancer.   1952.   V. 1, no. 1–v. 1, no. 6.   Monthly. The Young Ballet Dancer Publishing Company.   1s. 6d.

> The Editor was Nadine Nicolaeva-Legat, and the Art Editor Roland Collins. Short articles on the history of ballet, ballets and dancers, with advice on technique, make-up and so on, were provided. Written for children.

OFFICIAL PUBLICATIONS OF ORGANIZATIONS

656   The Dance Journal.   1907–13, 1924–.   V. 1, no. 1.   New series, v. 1, no. 1–.   Members only.

> The official publication of the Imperial Society of Teachers of Dancing, edited by C. W. Beaumont. There was some interruption to the regularity of publication during the Second World War. It is not available to the general public.

657   Royal Academy of Dancing Gazette. 1933–. Quarterly. 10s. 6d.
      per annum (non-members).

      The official publication of the Royal Academy of Dancing. It was pub-
      lished first as *Operatic Dancing of Great Britain Gazette*. The present title was
      adopted in 1935. It was first published four times a year, but from 1958,
      three issues a year were published. Months of issue are February, June and
      September.

658   The British Ballet Organization Bulletin. 1940–. V. 1, no. 1–.
      Monthly. 3s. per annum.

      Edited by E. Kelland-Espinosa. The December 1965 issue contained an
      article on the Australian Ballet, by Oleg Kerensky, apart from British Ballet
      Organization news.

659   The Vic-Wells Association Broadsheet. 1944–.

      Gives news of events organized by the Association and information on
      officers of the Association, subscriptions, dates of performances, and so on.
      Joan Lawson has contributed one or two reviews of ballets, and there has
      been the occasional book review, when the author or publisher has sent a
      complimentary copy.
      Before the Second World War (1931–9) the management of the Sadler's
      Wells Theatre produced the *Old Vic-Sadler's Wells Magazine*, which was
      sold in the theatre. It contained 'snippets written by the artists . . . future
      announcements . . . and dates of first nights etc., and details of any talks
      arranged by the Management or Association'.[4]
      Some ballet clubs produce magazines, e.g. Oxford Ballet Club published
      Arabesque.

      [4] This description is partially based on information supplied by the Honorary Secretary and
      Editor Miss M. L. Rankin.

APPENDIX A
SOME WORKS ON EARLY DANCES

R.A.D. to the right of the entry indicates that the Royal Academy of Dancing possesses a copy of the book.

DOMENICO DA FERRARA.   De arte saltandi et choreas ducendi. MS.

WILLIAM THE JEW.   De pratica seu arte tripudii. MS.[1]

Le manuscrit des basses danses de la bibliotheque de bourgogne. c.1450.

TOULOUZE, MICHEL.   L'art et instruction de bien dancer. c.1486.

ARENA, ANTONIUS.   . . . ad suos compagnones studiantes qui   R.A.D.
sunt de persona friantes, bassas dansas in gallanti stilo
bisognatas. Lyon, Benoist Rigaud, 1572.

BEAUJOYEULX, BALTASAR DE.   Balet comique de la Royne . . .   R.A.D.
Paris, Adrian le Roy, Robert Ballard & Mamert Patisson,
1582.

ARBEAU, THOINOT.   Orchésographie. Langres, 1588.[2]   R.A.D.

CAROSO, FABRITIO. Nobiltà di dame. Venice, 1600. (A revision   R.A.D.
of Il ballarino. Venice, Francesco Ziletti, 1581.)

NEGRI, CESARE.   Nuove inventioni di balli. Milan, Girolamo   R.A.D.
Bordone, 1604.

---

[1] A paperback edition of *A Jewish dancing master of the Renaissance: Guglielmo Ebreo*, by Otto Kinkeldey, has been issued by Dance Horizons, New York, at 10s. 6d.

[2] A paperback edition of this work has recently been issued by Dance Horizons, New York, 1966, at 21s., with drawings and music. The music has been recorded as *Court dances of mediaeval France* by Vox Productions Inc., New York, at 17s. 6d. (Mono TV 4008.)

LUPI, LIVIO. Libro di gagliarda, tordiglione . . . Palermo, Gio.   R.A.D.
Battista Maringo, 1607.

BORDIER, RENÉ. Grand bal de la douairiere de billebahault . . .   R.A.D.
de l'Imprimerie de Louvre, 1626.

[BENSERADE]. Ballet des arts . . . Paris, Robert Ballard, 1663.   R.A.D.

[LA ROCHE GUILHEN], MADAME. Rare et tout comedie meslée de musique
et de balets represantée devant sa majesté sur le Theatre Royal de White-
hall. Jacques Magnes & Richard Bentley, 1677.
   The following modern works are useful for studying the way in which these
dances should be performed.

GUTHRIE, JOHN. Historic dances for the theatre: the pavan and the minuet.
Aldridge . . . for Worthing Art Development Scheme, 1950.

WOOD, MELUSINE. Some historical dances (twelfth to nineteenth century):
their manner of performance and their place in the social life of the time,
described and annotated. C. W. Beaumont for I.S.T.D., 1952.

DOLMETSCH, MABEL. Dances of Spain and Italy from 1400 to 1600. Routledge and Kegan Paul, 1954.

WOOD, MELUSINE. More historical dances. . . . C. W. Beaumont for
I.S.T.D., 1956.

DOLMETSCH, MABEL. Dances of England and France from 1450 to 1600:
with their music and authentic manner of performance. 2nd ed. Routledge and Kegan Paul, 1959.

WOOD, MELUSINE. Advanced historical dances: being a second supplement
to some historical dances. C. W. Beaumont for I.S.T.D., 1960.

CUNNINGHAM, JAMES PATRICK. Dancing in the Inns of Court. Jordan, 1965.

APPENDIX B
GUIDE TO RESOURCES FOR FURTHER STUDY

LIBRARIES

Royal Academy of Dancing

The Royal Academy of Dancing, 15 Holland Park Gardens, London, W.14, owns a library of about 550 books. The greater part of this collection was bequeathed to the Academy by the late P. J. S. Richardson who died in 1963. Other volumes were presented by Dame Adeline Genée, the Founder-President of the Academy, and the late Stewart Headlam. It contains rare and early books on the theory and history of the dance, some of which are listed in Appendix A. Full bibliographical description of all these books, except the last two listed in Appendix A, are given in I. K. Fletcher's *Bibliographical description of forty rare books . . . (see no. 6).*

The collection includes four albums of photographs and the cuttings album of Mark Perugini. One of the photograph albums is devoted to the Empire Theatre and contains photographs of Adeline Genée alone and with the company. There is also a Minute Book of the Camargo Society which covers meetings of the General and Executive Committees for the period January 1930 to October 1931.

There is a Library on various subjects at 6 Addison Road, too, for the use of the students of the Royal Academy of Dancing and the Teachers' Training Course. About 450 are modern works (there are several copies of some works) on all aspects of the dance. There are runs of the following periodicals – *Ballet* (June 1948–December 1951); *The Dancing Times* (a complete run from 1923 onwards, with some of the earlier numbers); *Dance and Dancers* (January 1950–December 1958). The books are arranged by a 'home-made' scheme. There is an author index to the entire library and also a separate index under subject and title for the books on dancing and allied subjects.

The Pavlova Memorial Library

The Pavlova Memorial Library is housed in Westminster Reference Library, St. Martin's Street, London, W.C.2. It was financed from the proceeds of the Gala Performance given on the twenty-fifth anniversary of Pavlova's death, and was opened by Alicia Markova on 22nd January, 1957. Westminster City Library is responsible for 'Theatre' in the Metropolitan Libraries Subject Specialization Scheme. Altogether there are about 450 books on the dance. There are also 5 microfilms of the following works – Heath's *Beauties of the opera and ballet;* Lacanchi's *Bals masques de Paris;* J. B. Martin's *Five engravings of costumes;* Lami's *Quadrille de Marie Stuart.* In addition there are runs of the following periodicals – *Ballet* (almost a complete run); *Ballet Today* (vv. 1–4 incomplete, v. 5 complete c.1952–62); *Dance and dancers* (v. 7 complete, 1956–); *The Dancing Times* (v. 20 complete, 1929–; also many of the earlier numbers). There are incomplete files, in some cases only a few copies, of the following periodicals, from c.1950 to date – *Art de Danse, Balletto; Dance Magazine; Dance News; Dance Observer; Danse et Rhythmes; Toute la Danse; Cahiers de la Danse.* The Library holds a collection of ballet programmes for the Royal Opera House, Covent Garden and for Festival Ballet, which also run from c.1950 to date.

Hendon Central Library

The Hendon Central Library, The Burroughs, London, N.W.4, is responsible for ballet in the South Eastern Region Subject Specialization Scheme. It holds about 300 books on this subject of which about 220 have a bearing on English ballet. There is a subject index which sets out the books on ballet.

Vic-Wells Association Library

The Vic-Wells Association Library is divided into two parts, one housed in the 'Wells' Room at the Sadler's Wells Theatre and the other at the Old Vic which is leased to the National Theatre Company. Mr. R. Mander and Mr. J. Mitchenson are the Archivists to the Sadler's Wells Theatre.

The Library at the Sadler's Wells Theatre is devoted to opera and ballet. In the ballet section there are about 230 books on English and foreign ballet. Of note in this collection are the volumes of press cuttings on the Royal Ballet and the Sadler's Wells Theatre Ballet, the particulars of which are described as follows, although the time limits are not exact in some cases – *End of Season 1934–5* (opera and ballet; larger proportion of ballet. April and May 1935); *Sadler's Wells Theatre Ballet Cuttings* (April 1946–December 1949; 1950; January–September 1951; Tour of Canada and America 1951; 24th April–August 1952 and Edinburgh Festival 1952; Winter Season 1952–3; Tours and London, 9th February, 1953–March 1954; Tours and

London March–May 1956). *Sadler's Wells Theatre Ballet* (28th May, 1956–January 1957 and Royal Ballet II. January–August 1957). *Royal Ballet Press Cuttings* (January–May 1958; June–November 1958; December 1958–February 1959; March–April 1959; 20th April–June 1959; Fonteyn in Panama 20th April ff.). Press cuttings for 1935–45 are housed temporarily at the Old Vic and those for 1959–64 at the house of the Librarian of the Vic-Wells Association. They may be seen by appointment.

These cuttings include extracts from national and local papers and dance and theatre periodicals, but do not appear to have been kept consistently for the earlier years. Cuttings for the later years have been kept with care.

Incomplete runs of the following magazines are also held – *Ballet; Dance and Dancers; The Dancing Times* (3 volumes of odd numbers and extracts relating to Sadler's Wells 1940–January 1951, in 2 volumes).

There is a sheaf catalogue of the Library. The section for ballet is arranged alphabetically, with entries under the author's name and under subject – mainly personal names and companies, although this is not completely consistent. The classification scheme was devised by Miss H. Raven-Hart, who held the Diploma in Librarianship of the University of London. Hours of opening are printed in the Vic-Wells Association Broadsheet. At the time of writing, the Library is open on Tuesday, Thursday and Saturday evenings from 6.30–8.30 p.m., except on first nights and gala nights. Members of the Vic-Wells Association and members of the Companies are allowed to borrow books.

The British Museum and the Bodleian Library

The British Museum Library and the Bodleian Library are copyright libraries, i.e. a copy of every book published in the British Isles, with certain exceptions, must be offered to these libraries, as well as the other three libraries affected by this measure. This privilege is obtained by the Imperial Copyright Acts of 1842 and 1911. The Bodleian Library had a private legal deposit agreement with the Stationer's Company as early as 1610, but had no means of enforcement. Both libraries hold rare books on the dance. The scenarios of the ballets *The Loves of Mars and Venus* and *Perseus and Andromeda*, with choreography by John Weaver, the 1783 English translation of Noverre's *Lettres sur la danse* . . . the first and other editions of Playford's *Dancing master* are in the British Museum Library, while the Bodleian Library has a copy of Kellom Tomlinson's *The Art of dancing*, John Weaver's translation of *Chorégraphie* by Feuillet and Thoinot Arbeau's *Orchésographie*. . . .

British Theatre Museum Library

The ballet library of the late Cyril Swinson, containing about 200 books was donated to the British Theatre Museum, Leighton House, 12 Holland Park Road, London, W.14.[1] The Museum has inadequate premises for housing its possessions, and the Library has had to be stored. It is hoped to make the Cyril Swinson books available to students in the future. The Library of the late Irene Mawer is also in the possession of the Museum. Although the majority of books have little bearing on ballet, there are some albums relating to the Diaghilev ballet, about 20 books on the art of mime, and three letters from Adeline Genée to Mark Perugini concerning *The Flame: a pierrot-drame*, by the latter. The Museum has a collection of programmes including some for ballet performances at Covent Garden. A card catalogue of programmes is being compiled. The entry is under title, with information on casts, designers, producers, and so on. The programmes themselves are arranged primarily by theatre, but most of these also have to be stored away from Leighton House, and are therefore difficult of access; as also are photographs and prints. The Cyril Swinson and Irene Mawer collections are accommodated at Senate House, London University.

The British Drama League Library

The British Drama League Library, 9 and 10 Fitzroy Square, London, W.1, is concerned primarily with the drama, but does preserve some material on ballet. It possesses about 130 books on ballet, and includes references to ballet in its handwritten card indexes to periodical articles and press cuttings.

The Library has three entirely separate indexes. The first is of actual plays and the other books in the Library, the second is the 'comprehensive' index and the third the index to periodicals. The 'comprehensive' index refers mainly to unpublished plays. It gives sources from whence they can be obtained and directs the reader to illustrations and press cuttings, and gives dates of release and so on. Filed in this index are entries under titles of ballets. There are some subject entries and entries under the names of choreographers, dancers and theatres. Under 'ballet' in this index there are about 250 entries, of which about 45 refer to English ballet; there are 18 cards under 'Covent Garden. Royal Ballet'. Press cuttings were collected from the 1930's, although the 'comprehensive' index itself was started in the 1920's.

The index to periodicals contains entries under subject and personal names,

[1] The British Theatre Museum at Leighton House was visited. Information on the Cyril Swinson books was supplied by the Acting Curator, as these were inaccessible.

but not under companies. These are found as sub-headings under the subject entry for ballet. About 45 cards are filed here, about one-third of which refer to English ballet. *Theatre World; Theatre Arts; The Times; World Theatre; Stage Year-Book; Vic-Wells Association Broadsheet* are some of the serials indexed for ballet (in all the Library indexes nearly 100 periodicals, some more fully than others. These include American, French, German and Russian periodicals as well as periodicals from other countries.)

COLLECTIONS OF OTHER MATERIAL

Victoria and Albert Museum. The Gabrielle Enthoven Theatre Collection

The Gabrielle Enthoven Theatre Collection is a renowned source of information on English theatre history. It contains 'over 1,000,000 playbills and programmes and over 6,000 engravings as well as a wealth of newspaper cuttings . . . autographed letters, photographs and souvenirs'.[2] This material is stored in boxes and arranged primarily by the name of the theatre, and then chronologically. The whole collection is succinctly described in Miss Kahn's *Theatre collections*.[3]

The theatres in which ballet is and was performed, are, of course, represented in this collection. For example, there are about 15 boxes covering the years 1730–1852 at the King's Theatre, about 34 covering the years 1931–9 and 1945–59 at the Sadler's Wells Theatre. One box is devoted to items of a personal nature concerning Margot Fonteyn (more records relating to her career are with the programmes for her many performances in the various theatres). Another box is devoted to the 1957 tours of the Sadler's Wells Ballet/Royal Ballet. The Royal Opera House, Covent Garden is covered by about 85 boxes of programmes for the years 1946–63 (these cover opera as well as ballet), and 9 boxes for the tours of the Royal Ballet, with some cuttings from American papers for the United States tours. 3 boxes cover material for the Royal Festival Hall (1951–64), and there is 1 box for the Rudolf Steiner Hall where some ballet performances have taken place, e.g. Ballet Guild programmes for August 1943, material on recitals given by Ruth French and programmes for performances of ballet clubs.

[2] '*Centres for theatre research*', by G. Nash. *In: Who's Who in the Theatre.* 13th ed. 1961, p. 1540.
[3] *Theatre collections . . .* by A. M. C. Kahn. Library Association, Reference and Special Libraries Section (South Eastern Group), 1955. (Library Resources in the Greater London Area, No. 4), pp. 12–13.

The Enthoven Collection has among its indexes, two drawers of cards under the heading 'ballet'. One sequence containing about 90 cards is arranged alphabetically by the name of the dance or ballet company. The greatest number of cards deal with foreign companies visiting the United Kingdom, but there are also entries for English companies. The information given is the theatre where the performance took place and the date. The remainder of the cards are arranged alphabetically by the title of the ballet. Information given varies; in most cases the theatre and the date of performance is supplied and the choreographer, composer, designer, name of performers and company, presumably when known. This index is fairly complete for items for the eighteenth century onwards. It is continually being built up from new information as it is received and records of past performances are added as and when they come to light.

A recent acquisition is a collection of over 5,000 ballet photographs covering the years 1935–58, purchased from the publishing house of A. and C. Black.

The Library of the Victoria and Albert Museum, is open to the general public too. The subject catalogue lists about 150 entries under ballet. About 60 of these items have a direct bearing on English ballet. It also possesses books on subjects closely connected with ballet, particularly design and costume.

The London Archives of the Dance[4]

The London Archives of the Dance was founded under a trust deed in 1945 with a Board of Trustees consisting of Bronson (now Sir Bronson) Albery, Cyril Beaumont, Lionel Bradley, Adeline Genée, Christmas Humphreys and Deryck Lynham. The purpose behind this foundation was to provide the same facilities for research as are available in France and America. One of the first donations was from the Ballet Guild, which handed over a collection containing manuscripts, books, including a 1760 edition of Noverre's *Lettres sur la danse et les ballets* . . . , prints, programmes and personal souvenirs. The London Archives of the Dance also possesses the Jacobi Collection of manuscript scores and the Bolitho Collection of ballet scores. The Jacobi Collection contains a number of original conductor's scores of music arranged or composed by Jacobi when he was Musical Director of the Alhambra Theatre in the latter half of the nineteenth century.

---

[4] This description is based on two articles – '*The London Archives of the Dance and some of its treasures*', by C. W. Beaumont. *In: The Ballet Annual* [1947], pp. 108–113, and an unsigned article in *Ballet Today*, March–April 1946, p. 30.

The Bolitho Collection contains 230 piano scores of ballet music spanning the eighteenth, nineteenth and twentieth centuries. Other possessions of the London Archives of the Dance include a number of photographs; items connected with Marie Taglioni presented by Margaret Rolfe,[5] who was a pupil of the dancer in her old age, when she gave classes in deportment to the aristocracy; the Bradley diaries; 'Balletvaria Miscellanea'. Bequests of books have also been made by the late Lionel Bradley and the late Pigeon Crowle.

This collection is housed at the Headquarters of the Imperial Society of Teachers of Dancing, 70 Gloucester Place, London, W.1. It is in store at the time of writing, but it was hoped to make it available to dance students and to the general public during 1966.

The Raymond Mander and Joe Mitchenson Theatre Collection

The collection includes material on ballet as well as on opera and music hall. There are prints, photographs, a personal file containing press cuttings and pictures, a theatre file containing programmes and pictures of productions and a file of ballet cuttings (London) and reviews for 1937–60. There is also a Library of 5,000 books. The press cuttings are not kept with absolute consistency. In some cases access to the collection is permitted, but not to students.[6]

The Guildhall Library

The Guildhall Library ██████████ghall Street, London, E.C.2, possesses 'a collection of approxi████ 15,000 playbills for London theatres'.[7] These are arranged by the na███ of the theatre, and then chronologically, where there is a good deal of material for any one theatre. Entries in the index are under the name of the theatre, and give information on the number of items, with covering dates. Some of the playbills refer to ballet productions. For example, there are 5 playbills in the box for Her Majesty's Theatre 1705–, which announce performances of ballet; about 50 playbills in the boxes for Drury Lane Theatre covering the periods 1835–7 and 1838. The latter gives a slightly misleading impression however, for several of the playbills repeat the same information, i.e. the same dancers performed in the same ballets and divertissements over a period of two to three weeks.

[5] Extracts from The Diary kept by Margaret Rolfe (owned by C. W. Beaumont) have been published in *Foyer*, no. 1, Autumn 1951, pp. 33–7, and *Foyer*, no. 2, Winter 1951–2, pp. 49–51.

[6] Information supplied from corrections made by the Raymond Mander and Joe Mitchenson Collection; also from '*The Library as a tool of the theatre*', by E. N. Simons. *In: Aslib Proceedings*, November 1949, p. 277, and Nunn, G. W. A., ed. *British sources of photographs and pictures*, 1952.

[7] '*Centres for theatre research*', by G. Nash. *In: Who's Who in the Theatre*. 13th ed. 1961, p. 1541.

British Museum Print Room

The British Museum Print Room is a possible source of supply for prints of individual dancers. For example, it holds two portraits of Hester Santlow and one of Clara Webster. It is essential to know either the name of the artist or the name of the subject of the portrait to be able to trace a print.

Finsbury Central Library

Finsbury Central Library, Skinner Street, London, E.C.1, possesses a collection on the Sadler's Wells Theatre. Most of this material has no bearing on the ballet. There are about 80 items, mainly programmes, which cover intermittently the activities of the ballet companies performing at the theatre.

The Harvard University Theatre Collection[8] was founded in 1901. Among its special collections is the George Chaffee Ballet Collection. Material collected includes playbills, photographs, periodicals, manuscripts, costume studies, posters, clippings, programmes, cartoons and music.

The New York Public Library Dance Collection[9] was founded in 1944. It contains the Cia Fornaroli Toscanini Collection; 26,000 books; 500 bound periodicals; 3,000 manuscripts and letters; 100,000 photographs; 6,000 prints and stage designs; 500,000 clippings; 80,000 programmes; 6,000 librettos. It also maintains a ballet file on cards of 'titles of ballets and concert dances, giving information on composer, choreographer, designer, etc., and including references to critical and historical articles on the ballets and dances in books, periodicals and newspapers'.[10] The collection is housed in the Library-Museum of the Performing Arts at Lincoln Center.

The Institute of Choreology has 'a library containing choreographic, orchestral and piano scores, records, tapes, reference books and H.F. sound equipment'.[11] No attempt has been made to describe fully the resources of The Institute of Choreology Library, as its first course in choreology did not start until September 1965, but it is an important development and should therefore be mentioned.

[8] Information from *Directory of special libraries and information centres*, edited by T. Kruzas. Detroit, Gale Research Company, 1963, p. 205.

[9] This description is based on information in *Directory of special libraries and information centres*, edited by T. Kruzas, Detroit, Gale Research Company, 1963, p. 329 and '*The Dance collection at Lincoln Centre*', by L. Moore. *In: The Dancing Times*, January 1966, pp. 182–4.

[10] Annual Report (Music Division) in the *Bulletin of the New York Public Library*, March 1945, p. 167.

[11] *Choreology course syllabus*, issued by The Institute of Choreology.

APPENDIX C
EXHIBITIONS

BALLET EXHIBITIONS

Exhibition of ballet design. [Catalogue.] Council for the Encouragement of Music and the Arts. 1943–4. 15 pp.

42 designers were represented by 158 items of which about 76 were designs for English ballet productions. The introduction is by A. L. Haskell. The catalogue is not illustrated.

An exhibition of ballet designs from the collection of John Carr-Doughty. [Catalogue.] The Arts Council, 1952. [8] pp.

The 19 designers represented include – Michael Ayrton; Cecil Beaton; Vanessa Bell; Nadia Benois; Sophie Fedorovitch; Roger Furse; Hugh Stevenson.

Ballet: an exhibition of books, MSS., playbills, prints, etc. illustrating the development of the art from its origins until modern times, organized by Ivor Guest. . . . National Book League, 1957. 70 pp. 2s. 6d.

— : supplementary catalogue of pictures, journals, manuscripts, costumes. [4] pp. 1s.

The exhibition was held from 7th November, 1957, to 4th January, 1958, at the National Book League premises in London. It was perhaps the most comprehensive exhibition on ballet in general to be held in this country. The emphasis was on books of which 300 were listed in the catalogue. *See also* no. 7.

Ballet exhibition, 1959.

Held at the Army and Navy Stores, from 30th July–21st August ' . . . no particular theme or pattern but a large number of interesting exhibits were collected together . . . handsome photographs lent by Houston Rogers, Roy Round, "Vivienne", Jas. D. O'Callaghan and others. Among the principal lenders were Phyllis Bedells, Mona Inglesby, Anton Dolin and John Gilpin. There was a large section devoted to *London morning* . . . there was no evidence that the director of the exhibition had special knowledge of his subject. The catalogue was a victim of the printing strike so it would be unfair to list all the mistakes in the booklet (2s. 6d.) which was issued.' (*The Dancing Times*, September 1959, p. 596.)

The Diaghilev exhibition catalogue, edited by Richard Buckle. Edinburgh
Festival Committee, 1954. 60 pp. front., illus., bibliog.

Anna Pavlova 1882–1931. Catalogue of the commemorative exhibition
organized by the London Museum in association with the Anna Pavlova
Commemoration Committee. The London Museum . . . 1956. [28] pp.
12 pl. 3s. 6d.

 Although not entirely relevant, mention should be made of the Pavlova and
Diaghilev exhibitions. The first was brought together by Richard Buckle for the
1954 Edinburgh Festival, and later visited London. A catalogue was produced by
The Observer. The Editor, Richard Buckle, wrote of his experiences while organ-
izing the exhibition in *In search of Diaghilev* (Sidgwick & Jackson, 1955).
 The second was displayed from September to December 1956 at the London
Museum. The catalogue contained an introduction by A. L. Haskell and 'Tributes
to Anna Pavlova's Influence and Inspiration', by Yvette Chauviré, Alexandra
Danilova and Alicia Markova.
 Ballet exhibitions have been put on at the Royal Festival Hall, from time to
time, during the seasons given by Festival Ballet. Catalogues are not available, but
listed below are the titles of the exhibitions and the dates during which they were
on display.
 The Dance (8th July–10th September, 1953).
 Costume designs and décor originals from the ballet 'Esmeralda' (14th July–13th Sep-
  tember, 1954).
 Dance notation (9th July–September 1957).
 The Nutcracker (10th December, 1957–12th January, 1958).
 Ballets and ballerinas (17th December, 1959–17th January, 1960).
 Ballet paintings by Elizabeth Twistington Higgins (22nd December, 1960–15th
  January, 1961).
 Costume designs and décor originals for the ballet 'Peer Gynt' (summer 1963).

EXHIBITIONS ON THEATRE DESIGN

Art in the theatre from XVI to the XX century. Bristol, Royal West of
England Academy, 1955. 24 pp. front.

 Held from 12th May to 1st June, 1955. 'The drawings, paintings, engravings,
books and models which comprise this exhibition are assembled to illustrate the
contribution of the artist and the designer to the theatre from the seventeenth
century to the present day . . . loan of valuable works' by the French Embassy, the
Bibliothèque Nationale, the Bibliothèque de l'Opéra and the Bibliothèque de
l'Arsenal, and 'notable contributions' by the Duke of Devonshire and the Victoria
and Albert Museum (foreword to the catalogue by the President of the Royal
West of England Academy). The preface is written by James Laver. 329 items are
listed. The majority of some 70 items of ballet interest belong to the Diaghilev

period or earlier; about 20 have a direct bearing on English ballet. 14 designs by Inigo Jones, for masques, were displayed.

Sophie Fedorovitch 1893–1953: a memorial exhibition of designs for ballet, opera and stage arranged by The Victoria and Albert Museum. Victoria and Albert Museum, 1955. 16 pp. 8 pl. 2s. 6d.

180 items were shown, including designs for 24 ballets. The exhibition was displayed first at the Victoria and Albert Museum, and was then sent on tour during 1956. The catalogue was prepared by Carol Hogben, Assistant Keeper at the Museum. It included three tributes to Sophie Fedorovitch, by Frederick Ashton, Marie Rambert and Richard Buckle. There were 25 reproductions of photographs on plates, illustrating scenes from ballets for which Fedorovitch designed, and of original designs.

Contemporary English theatre design. The Arts Council, 1957. [15] pp.

This exhibition toured the country from October 1957–August 1958. Of the 80 items displayed, 18 represented ballet, which included designs by Cecil Beaton; Richard Beer; Edward Burra; John Craxton; Sophie Fedorovitch; Nicholas Georgiadis; Isabel Lambert; Robert Medley; John Piper; Kenneth Rowell; Peter Snow.

Stage design in Great Britain since 1945. The Arts Council, 1961. 27 pp.

James Laver organized this exhibition for The Arts Council. The initial impetus was given by The Association of Stage Designers and Craftsmen. There were 172 items and 49 designers were represented; the following displayed designs for English ballet productions – Norman Adams; Michael Ayrton; John Craxton; Sophie Fedorovitch; Nicholas Georgiadis; Andrée Howard; Isabel Lambert; Osbert Lancaster; Lila de Nobili; Leonard Rosoman; Kenneth Rowell; Hugh Stevenson.

3 stage designers: Leslie Hurry; Isabel Lambert: Sophie Fedorovitch. Arts Council, 1963/4.

The catalogue is in the form of a folder. It has notes on the three designers by J. Wood, and gives a checklist of the works displayed.

The Arts Council provides a permanent travelling exhibition of theatre designs. There are 40 items, over half of which are concerned with ballet. Designers for English productions are as follows – Norman Adams; Richard Beer; Robert Colquhoun and Robert MacBryde; John Craxton; Nicholas Georgiadis; Leslie Hurry; Ralph Koltai; Isabel Lambert; Osbert Lancaster; Robert Medley; John Piper; Kenneth Rowell; Yolanda Sonnabend. A duplicated checklist can be obtained from The Arts Council, St. James's Square, London.

ADDENDA

[660] HASKELL, ARNOLD LIONEL. Balletomane's album. Black, 1939. 88 pp. illus. 7s. 6d.

'A book of photographs – studio portraits, action pictures and more intimate snapshots ... honours are divided between the Russian ballet and Sadler's Wells, and there is some explanatory text. There are some exceedingly good pictures of Margot Fonteyn in her *Aurora* variations' ('The Sitter Out' in *The Dancing Times*, August 1939, p. 505). There are 152 illustrations.

661 [ESPINOSA, EDOUARD], 'ESPINOSA', *pseud*. The art of the ballet: technical vade mecum. Eve Kelland, 1948. 136 pp. illus.

Includes – The Encyclopaedia; Notes on Character Dancing; Notes on National Dancing; The Great Dancers of the Past; Technique of Ballet Dancing; Biographies of Old Masters. The Encyclopaedia is a glossary of technical terms. The 49 illustrations reproduce photographs, facsimiles, diagrams, sketches illustrating points of technique.

662 MANCHESTER, PHYLLIS WINIFRED. 'English male dancers: a cautious prophecy'. *In: The Ballet Annual 1950*, pp. 98–9.

663 BRINSON, PETER. Background to European ballet: a notebook from its archives. Leyden, Holland, Sijthoff, 1966. 195 pp. 12 pl., illus. (Council of Europe Series 'European Aspects'; Series A: Culture, no. 7.)

Foreword by Mary Skeaping, Literary Adviser to the Royal Ballet Demonstration Group, and one-time Director of the Royal Swedish Ballet.

The author was awarded a research fellowship by the Council of Europe, and was thus enabled to compile this book. Besides working in the United Kingdom he visited Austria, Denmark, France, Germany, Holland, Italy and Sweden. He describes generally the theatrical history of these countries, how theatrical archives came to be collected and the main holdings of the collections with special reference to ballet and with detailed descriptions of some items. Pp. 155–67 deal with 'Britain and the Development of Theatre Research'. Appendix A gives details of Archives visited where significant ballet material can be found. (Tabulated under Title; Address; Hours; Character and Admission Procedure.) There are 21 illustrations on plates, 5 in the text including plans, theatre interiors, scenes from ballets, sketches for designs, facsimiles of title-pages of early books.

664 "The classicist". *In: The Guardian*, August 30th, 1962, p.6
Frederick Ashton. 1 photograph.

'Ballet for All' is a demonstration group, illustrating lectures on the
ballet prepared by Peter Brinson, its director. Actors, and dancers drawn
from the touring section of the Royal Ballet are employed. 'Ballet for All'
has developed from a couple of dancers and one actor to an enlarged group
whose programmes are aimed at "the small theatre". The latest programme
devised by Peter Brinson is 'Two Coppélias' which deals with the original
and modern versions of this ballet.

INDEX

THE Index includes names, subjects and titles, the latter in the case of anonymous works or where a compilation well known by its title has been entered under a personal name in the main bibliography. The whole work has been indexed except for the Preface, footnotes and titles of the exhibitions in Appendix C.

The names of authors of works included in the Bibliography are indexed in capital letters; other names are indexed in lower case. Hyphenated or well-known double names are entered under the first part of the name.

After each item indexed the abbreviation 'No . . .' indicates the numbered entry in the Bibliography in which the item occurs. The abbreviation 'P.' or 'Pp.' indicates the page or pages of introductory text in which the item occurs.

Where an author or title is represented in the Bibliography and is also mentioned in annotations of other works, numbers for the latter are represented in a separate sequence. E.g. (1) K. Ambrose is the author of items nos. 72, 513 and 521-2 and is mentioned in items nos. 65, 253 and 649. (2) *Ballet Annual* has a main entry as a bibliography, no. 20, and as a yearbook no. 45, but is also mentioned in items nos. 10, 42 and 46-7, and on page 18 of the text.